VISUAL QUICKSTART GUIDE

Photoshop 3

FOR MACINTOSH

Elaine Weinmann
Peter Lourekas

 **Peachpit Press**
a division of Addison-Wesley Publishing Company

Visual QuickStart Guide
Photoshop 3 for Macintosh
Elaine Weinmann and Peter Lourekas

Peachpit Press
2414 Sixth Street
Berkeley, CA 94710
510/548-4393
510/548-5991 (fax)

Find us on the World Wide Web at: http://www.peachpit.com

Peachpit Press is a division of Addison-Wesley Publishing
Company

Cover design: The Visual Group
Interior design & production: Elaine Weinmann and Peter Lourekas

ISBN 1-56609-144-6

9 8 7 6

Printed and bound in the United States of America

TECHNIQUE CHANGES BUT ART REMAINS THE SAME.

— *Claude Monet*

Thank You.

Ted Nace, Peachpit Press publisher, for responding to innovations in computer technology with innovations in computer education.

Paula Baker, Trish Booth, Roslyn Bullas, Gregor Clarke, John Grimes, Keasley Jones, April Netzer, Cary Norsworthy, and the rest of the staff at Peachpit Press, for always being helpful and "on the ball."

John Stuart, New York City-based photographer and friend, for his photographs.

Nadine Markova, Mexico City-based photographer, for her photographs.

Johanna Gillman, New York City-based artist, friend, and desktop publisher, for introducing us to Nadine Markova through her photographs.

Paul Petroff, Great Neck, New York-based motion picture special effects designer, photographer, and traveler, for his photographs.

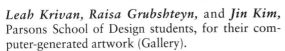

Cara Wood, New York City-based artist and friend, for her photographs, her assistance with the index, and her special tomato sauce.

Leah Krivan, Raisa Grubshteyn, and *Jin Kim,* Parsons School of Design students, for their computer-generated artwork (Gallery).

Phil Allen, New York City-based artist and friend, for exploring another side of Photoshop (Gallery).

Stan Pinkwas, managing editor of Video Magazine and copy editor of this book, for his careful attention to detail.

Bob Schaffel, Executive Director of the Professional Prepress Alliance, for his comments on Chapters 3 and 22.

Howard Greenberg, Vice President of Axiom Design Systems, a New York City prepress service bureau, for his comments on Chapter 22.

Michael Callery, Faculty Coordinator of the New School Computer Instruction Center, for reading our manuscript and offering his comments.

Tad Crawford, attorney, author, and Allworth Press publisher, for contributing *Ten Questions and Answers About Copyright.*

Adobe Systems, Inc. for designing terrific software, and, in particular, Jon Cohan, Matt Brown and the technical support staff who assisted us through the Beta testing and beyond.

And *Teddy and Christ Lourekas,* for introducing their son to art at an early age, and putting up with his art at a later age.

All other pictures originated from photographs taken by or owned by the authors.

Table of Contents

Table of Contents

Chapter 4: **Get Around**

Chapter 5: **Select**

THE BASICS 1

AN ASTOUNDING ARRAY of visual effects can be created using Photoshop, the digital image editing program from Adobe Systems. Photoshop has revolutionized the photography and prepress industries and has provided commercial and fine artists with an exciting new medium.

Using this book, you will learn Photoshop's fundamental techniques. You will learn how to scan pictures and adjust brightness and contrast. How to sharpen, blur, and smudge edges. How to mix, choose, and apply colors. How to paint, draw, work with multiple layers, clone, apply filters, create gradients and textures, create type, adjust color, and print. You will also learn how to modify just a portion of a picture by creating a selection. You can open pictures in many different file formats or create a picture entirely within Photoshop.

In the *Visual QuickStart Guide* tradition, step-by-step instructions are abundantly illustrated with photographs and screen captures. Also included are numerous tips and recommendations. The first six chapters provide a comprehensive orientation for newcomers. The remaining chapters can be sampled in any order. Special terms are defined in a mini-glossary in this chapter and in Appendix A.

You can use Photoshop's wide array of commands to modify many different types of pictures. They can be applied at various intensities and can be combined in different sequences with other commands. The instructions in *Photoshop 3: Visual Quick-Start Guide* will help you learn Photoshop's basic features, but you can also use them as a point of departure for developing your own formulas. Once you learn the basics, you'll be able to explore Photoshop's limitless picture editing possibilities! ∎

PHOTOSHOP FEATURES USED TO PRODUCE "STONE":
ADD NOISE, EMBOSS AND SPHERIZE FILTERS, LEVELS
AND COMPOSITE CONTROLS DIALOG BOXES, AND
SHARPEN/BLUR, DODGE/BURN AND PAINTBRUSH TOOLS.
THE TYPE WAS IMPORTED FROM ADOBE ILLUSTRATOR
USING THE PLACE COMMAND.

Introduction

1

The Photoshop screen.

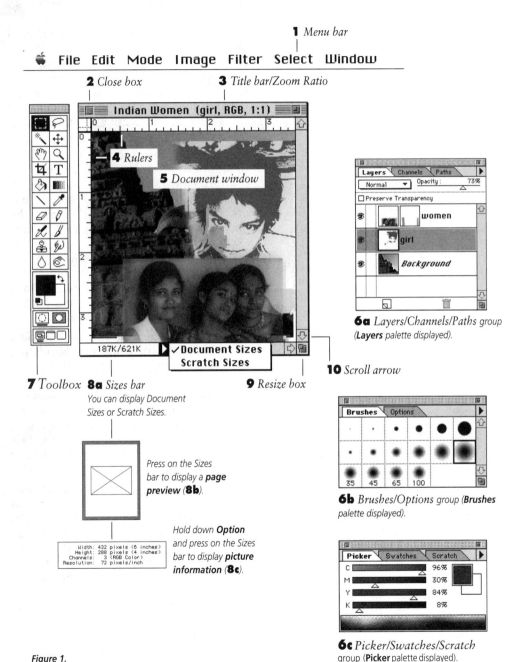

1 *Menu bar*

 File Edit Mode Image Filter Select Window

2 *Close box*   **3** *Title bar/Zoom Ratio*

Indian Women (girl, RGB, 1:1)

4 *Rulers*

5 *Document window*

187K/621K   ✓Document Sizes
             Scratch Sizes

7 *Toolbox*   **8a** *Sizes bar*
You can display Document
Sizes or Scratch Sizes.

Press on the Sizes
bar to display a **page
preview** (**8b**).

Width: 432 pixels (6 inches)
Height: 288 pixels (4 inches)
Channels: 3 (RGB Color)
Resolution: 72 pixels/inch

Hold down **Option**
and press on the Sizes
bar to display **picture
information** (**8c**).

9 *Resize box*

10 *Scroll arrow*

Layers Channels Paths
Normal   Opacity : 73%
☐ Preserve Transparency
    women
    girl
    Background

6a *Layers/Channels/Paths* group
(**Layers** palette displayed).

Brushes Options
35 45 65 100

6b *Brushes/Options* group (**Brushes**
palette displayed).

Picker Swatches Scratch
C 96%
M 30%
Y 84%
K 8%

6c *Picker/Swatches/Scratch*
group (**Picker** palette displayed).

Figure 1.

Key to the Photoshop screen.

1 *Menu bar*
Press any menu heading to access dialog boxes, submenus, and commands.

2 *Close box*
To close a picture or a palette, click its Close box.

3 *Title bar/Zoom ratio*
Displays the picture's title, color mode, and display size ratio.

4 *Rulers*
Choose Show Rulers from the Window menu to display rulers. The position of the cursor is indicated by a mark on each ruler. Choose Ruler Units in the Unit Preferences dialog box *(see page 254)*.

5 *Document window*
The picture display window.

6a, b, c *Palettes*
There are ten moveable palettes. Some palettes are grouped together: Layers/Channels/Paths, Brushes/Options, and Picker/Swatches/Scratch. Click a tab (palette name) in a palette group to bring that palette to the front of its group. The Command and Info palettes are displayed individually. *(More about palettes on page 14)*

7 *Toolbox*
Click once on a tool to select it. Double-click a tool to select it and open its Options palette. The Foreground and Background colors and screen preview modes can also be chosen from the Toolbox. Press Tab to hide the Toolbox

and all open palettes. Press Tab again to display the Toolbox and all previously displayed palettes.

8a, b, c *Sizes bar*
When Document Sizes is selected from the Sizes bar pop-up menu, the Sizes bar displays the file storage size when all layers are flattened (the first amount) and the file storage size when the layers are separate (the second amount). When Scratch Sizes is selected, the bar displays the amount of storage space Photoshop is using for all currently open pictures and the amount of RAM currently available to Photoshop. When the first amount is greater than the second amount, Photoshop is using virtual memory on the scratch disk.

Press and hold on the Sizes bar to display the page preview, which is a thumbnail of the picture relative to the paper size, including custom printing marks, if chosen. Hold down Option and press and hold on the Sizes bar to display information about the picture, including its dimensions, number of channels, mode, and resolution.

9 *Resize box*
To resize a window or a palette, press and drag its resize box diagonally.

10 *Scroll arrow*
Click the down arrow to move the picture upward in the document window. Click the up arrow to move the picture downward.

The Toolbox.

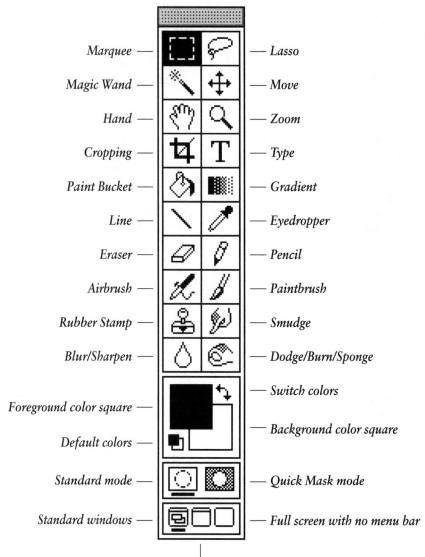

Marquee — — Lasso

Magic Wand — — Move

Hand — — Zoom

Cropping — — Type

Paint Bucket — — Gradient

Line — — Eyedropper

Eraser — — Pencil

Airbrush — — Paintbrush

Rubber Stamp — — Smudge

Blur/Sharpen — — Dodge/Burn/Sponge

— Switch colors

Foreground color square —

— Background color square

Default colors —

Standard mode — — Quick Mask mode

Standard windows — — Full screen with no menu bar

Full screen with menu bar

Figure 2. The **Toolbox**.

The Pen tool is accessed only via the Paths palette (see Chapter 15).

Tool Cursors

The cursor matches the icon on the Toolbox when most tools are used. In addition, you will also see the tool cursors below.

To turn the Eraser, Gradient, Line, Pencil, Airbrush, Paintbrush, Rubber Stamp, Smudge, Blur/Sharpen, and Dodge/Burn/Sponge tools cursors into a **crosshair** for precise editing, choose General from the Preferences submenu under the File menu, then click Painting Tools: **Precise**. Click **Brush Size** to turn those tool cursors into a **circle** whose diameter matches the currently selected brush size.

To turn the Marquee, Lasso, Magic Wand, Cropping, Eyedropper, and Paint Bucket tool cursors into a **crosshair**, click Other Tools: **Precise**.

Or, press **Caps Lock** to turn all Standard cursors into Precise cursors, to turn Painting Tools Precise cursors into Brush Size cursors, and turn Painting Tools Brush Size cursors into Precise cursors.

How to Use the Toolbox

Press Tab to hide or show the Toolbox and all open palettes.

Click once on a tool to select it. Double-click a tool to select it and open its Options palette, from which you can select a mode, opacity, and other settings. You can also customize some tools using the Brushes, Picker, Swatches, and Scratch palettes.

To restore a tool's default settings, click the tool, then choose Reset Tool from the Options palette pop-up menu. Choose Reset All Tools from the Options palette pop-up menu to restore the default settings for all the tools.

Hold down Option and click on a tool to select a Type for that tool (such as Dodge, Burn, or Sponge).

| Arrow | Crosshair | Scissors | Gavel | Cancel |

HOW TO USE THE MOUSE

The mouse is used in three basic ways.

Click 🖰   Press and release the mouse button quickly.

Double-click 🖰🖰   Press and release the mouse button twice in quick succession.

Press and drag ┄🖰   Press and hold down the mouse button, move the mouse on the mousepad, then release the mouse button. Press and drag when you read the instruction "drag" or "move."

INSTRUCTION TERMS

Check/Uncheck
☒ ☐   Click a check box in a dialog box or on a palette to turn an option on or off. An x in a box indicates the option is turned on.

Choose   Highlight a menu, submenu, or pop-up menu command, highlight a layer on the Layers palette, or pick a tool, palette, or dialog box option.

Enter

| 0 | 1.00 | 255 |

A highlighted field.

| 15 | 1.00 | 255 |

A new value entered.

Highlight an entry field (referred to as "field") in a dialog box and replace with a new number. Press Tab to highlight the next field in succession. Press Shift-Tab to highlight the previous field.

Move   Press and drag a triangle slider.

Press   Quickly press and release a key on the keyboard, usually as part of a keyboard shortcut.

Select   Isolate an area of a picture using a selection tool so the area can be modified while the rest of the picture is protected.

MINI-GLOSSARY

Picture The entire contents of a document window, including any border surrounding the image.

Image The picture itself, not including its border.

Target Layer The currently highlighted layer on the Layers palette, and the only layer that can be edited. A picture can have one layer (the Background), or it can be multi-layered. Layers other than the Background can be restacked and moved, and are transparent where there are no pixels.

Selection An area of a picture that is isolated using the Marquee, Lasso, or Magic Wand tool or the Color Range command so it can be modified while the rest of the picture is protected. A moving marquee marks the boundary of a selection.

Floating Selection A selection that floats above, and can be altered without affecting, the underlying pixels in the target layer. A floating selection is created when the Type tool is used, a selection is Option-dragged or the Float or Paste command is executed. "Floating Selection" will be listed just above the target layer on the Layers palette.

Pixels (Picture Elements) The dots used to display a bitmapped picture on a rectangular grid on a computer screen.

Underlying Pixels The pixels comprising the unmodified target layer, on top of which a selection, path, pasted image or placed image can float. When a floating selection is deselected, it replaces or merges with pixels on the target layer.

Size The file storage size of a picture or the amount of scratch space, measured in bytes, kilobytes, or megabytes.

Dimensions The width and height of a picture.

Brightness The lightness (luminance) of a color.

Hue The wavelength of light that gives a color its name — such as red or blue — irrespective of its brightness and saturation.

Saturation The purity of a color. The more gray a color contains, the lower its saturation.

See "Appendix A: Glossary" for other definitions.

MENUS

Each menu heading provides access to related commands for modifying pictures. The seven Photoshop menus are illustrated on the following pages.

To choose from a menu, press and drag downward through the menu or to the right and downward through the submenu, then release the mouse when a desired entry is highlighted.

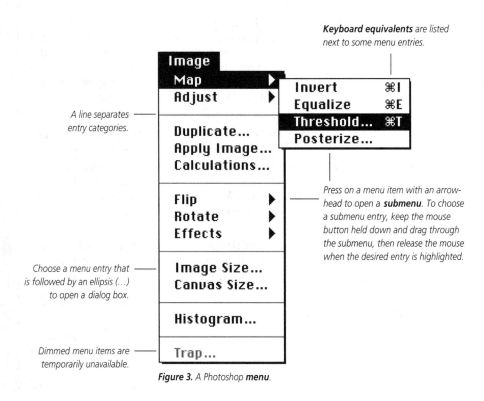

Keyboard equivalents are listed next to some menu entries.

A line separates entry categories.

*Press on a menu item with an arrowhead to open a **submenu**. To choose a submenu entry, keep the mouse button held down and drag through the submenu, then release the mouse when the desired entry is highlighted.*

Choose a menu entry that is followed by an ellipsis (...) to open a dialog box.

Dimmed menu items are temporarily unavailable.

Figure 3. *A Photoshop **menu**.*

Menus

The File menu.

File menu commands are used to create, open, place, close, save, scan, export or print a picture, set defaults, and quit Photoshop.

The Edit menu.

Edit menu commands include Undo, which undoes the last modification made, the Clipboard commands Cut and Copy, and the Paste commands. The Fill and Stroke commands are also executed via the Edit menu.

File	
New...	⌘N
Open...	⌘O
Place...	
Close	⌘W
Save	⌘S
Save As...	
Save a Copy...	
Revert	
Acquire	▶
Export	▶
File Info...	
Page Setup...	
Print...	⌘P
Preferences	▶
Quit	⌘Q

Figure 4. The **File** menu.

Edit	
Undo Marquee	⌘Z
Cut	⌘X
Copy	⌘C
Paste	⌘V
Paste Into	
Paste Layer...	
Clear	
Fill...	
Stroke...	
Crop	
Create Publisher...	
Publisher Options...	
Define Pattern	
Take Snapshot	

Figure 5. The **Edit** menu.

File and Edit Menus

The Mode menu.

A picture can be converted to any of eight black-and-white or color modes using the Mode menu. Choose CMYK Preview to see how your picture looks in CMYK color without actually changing its mode. The Gamut Warning marks colors that won't print on a four-color press.

Mode

Bitmap
Grayscale
Duotone
Indexed Color...
✓RGB Color
CMYK Color
Lab Color
Multichannel

Color Table...

CMYK Preview
Gamut Warning

*Figure 6. The **Mode** menu.*

The Image menu.

Commands under the Image menu are used to modify a picture's color, brightness, contrast, orientation, size, dimensions, and resolution. The Canvas Size dialog box is used to add a border to a picture.

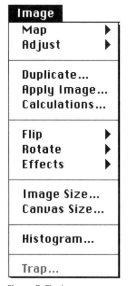

Image

Map ▶
Adjust ▶

Duplicate...
Apply Image...
Calculations...

Flip ▶
Rotate ▶
Effects ▶

Image Size...
Canvas Size...

Histogram...

Trap...

*Figure 7. The **Image** menu.*

The Filter menu.

Filters are organized in pop-up menu groups. Some filters are applied in one step by choosing the filter name. Other filters are applied via a dialog box.

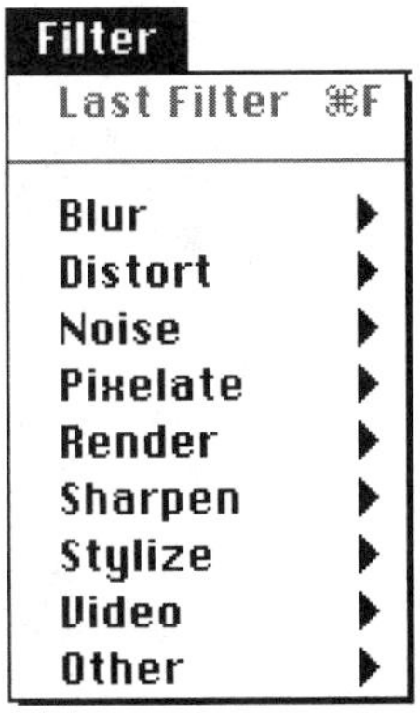

```
┌─────────────────────────┐
│ Filter                  │
├─────────────────────────┤
│ Last Filter    ⌘F       │
├─────────────────────────┤
│ Blur              ▶     │
│ Distort           ▶     │
│ Noise             ▶     │
│ Pixelate          ▶     │
│ Render            ▶     │
│ Sharpen           ▶     │
│ Stylize           ▶     │
│ Video             ▶     │
│ Other             ▶     │
└─────────────────────────┘
```

Figure 8. *The **Filter** menu.*

The Select menu.

The "All" Select menu command selects an entire picture. The None command deselects all selections. Other Select menu commands float, enlarge, reduce, load, and modify the edges of selections, and save selections to and from channels. The Color Range command creates selections based on color.

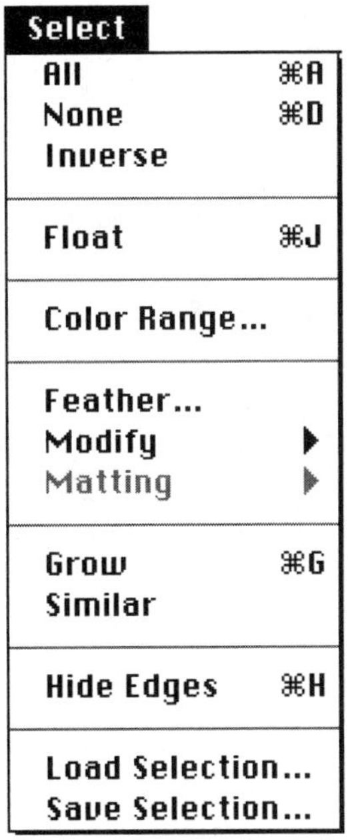

```
┌─────────────────────────┐
│ Select                  │
├─────────────────────────┤
│ All             ⌘A      │
│ None            ⌘D      │
│ Inverse                 │
├─────────────────────────┤
│ Float           ⌘J      │
├─────────────────────────┤
│ Color Range...          │
├─────────────────────────┤
│ Feather...              │
│ Modify            ▶     │
│ Matting           ▶     │
├─────────────────────────┤
│ Grow            ⌘G      │
│ Similar                 │
├─────────────────────────┤
│ Hide Edges      ⌘H      │
├─────────────────────────┤
│ Load Selection...       │
│ Save Selection...       │
└─────────────────────────┘
```

Figure 9. *The **Select** menu.*

Filter and Select Menus

The Window menu.

Window menu commands control new window creation, display sizes, and the display of rulers and palettes. Open pictures are listed and can be activated using the Window menu.

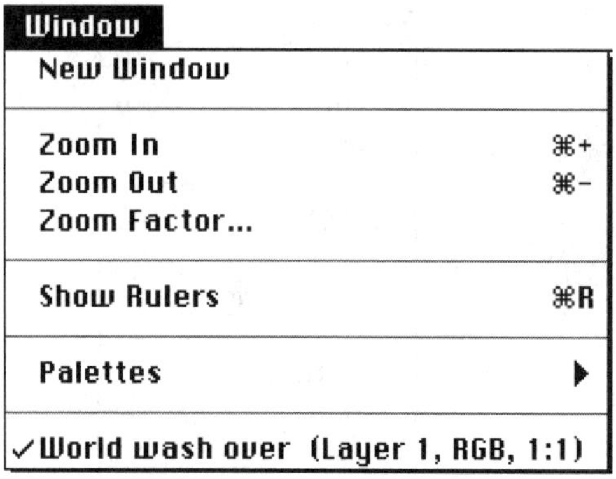

Figure 10. *The* **Window** *menu.*

DIALOG BOXES

Dialog boxes are like fill-in forms with multiple choices. The various ways to indicate choices are shown in **Figure 11**.

To open a dialog box, use a keyboard shortcut, or select any menu item followed by an ellipsis (...).

Some modifications are made by entering numbers in entry fields. Press Tab to highlight the next field in a dialog box. Hold down Shift and press Tab to highlight the previous field.

Other modifications are made by moving sliders to the left or to the right. Slider modifications preview in the picture while the dialog box is open.

Click OK or press Return to accept modifications and exit a dialog box.

Dialog Boxes

*To move a dialog box, press and drag its **title bar**.*

*Press a down-pointing arrow to open a **pop-up menu**.*

*Click **OK** or press **Return** to exit a dialog box and accept the new settings.*

*Click **Cancel** to exit a box with no modifications taking effect. Hold down **Option** and click **Reset** to undo changes made in a dialog box. (The word **Reset** will appear in place of **Cancel**.)*

Click a button with an ellipsis (...) to open a related dialog box.

Histograms *graph the distribution of pixels.*

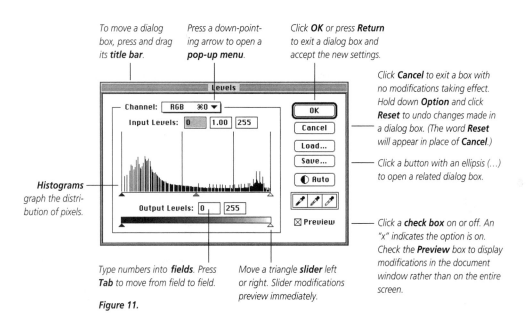

*Click a **check box** on or off. An "x" indicates the option is on. Check the **Preview** box to display modifications in the document window rather than on the entire screen.*

*Type numbers into **fields**. Press **Tab** to move from field to field.*

*Move a triangle **slider** left or right. Slider modifications preview immediately.*

Figure 11.

About the Palettes

PALETTES

There are ten moveable palettes that are used for picture editing. To save screen space, some of the palettes are joined into groups: **Picker/Swatches/Scratch, Layers/Channels/Paths,** and **Brushes/Options.** The other palettes are **Commands** and **Info.**

You can separate a palette from its group by dragging its tab (palette name) **(Figures 12a-b)**. You can add a palette to any group by dragging the tab over the group (a black or colored frame will appear as the palette is dragged over the window). When you release the mouse it will be the frontmost palette in the group. The Layers/Channels/Paths group window can be widened, so you might want to add other palettes to this group so the tabs (palette names) will be readable across the top.

To open a palette, choose Show [palette name] from the Palette submenu under the Windows menu. That palette will appear in front in its group. You can also open a palette by clicking Show [palette name] on the Commands palette or by executing the corresponding shortcut listed on the Commands palette.

To move a palette to the front in its group, click a tab (palette name) or use the keystroke assigned to that palette.

Resize a palette by dragging its size box (lower right corner).

Press Tab to hide or display all open palettes and the Toolbox.

To shrink a palette, double-click a tab or click the palette zoom box (upper right corner). If the palette is not at its default size, click the zoom box once to restore its default size, then click a second time to shrink the palette.

If the Restore Dialog Positions box is checked in the More Preferences dialog box (choose General from the Preferences submenu under the File menu, then click More), palettes that are open when you quit Photoshop will appear in their same location the next time you launch Photoshop. Uncheck this box to restore the palettes' default groupings.

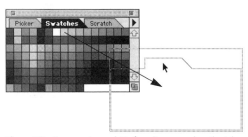

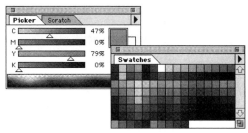

Figure 12a. *To separate a palette from its group, drag the tab (palette name) away from the palette group.*

Figure 12b. *The Swatches palette is on its own.*

Picker palette

The Picker palette is used for mixing and selecting colors to apply with the painting, editing, and fill tools. Choose a color models for the palette from the palette command menu. You can quick-select a color from the Color Bar on the bottom of the palette.

Foreground color square. The currently chosen square has a white border.

Background color square.

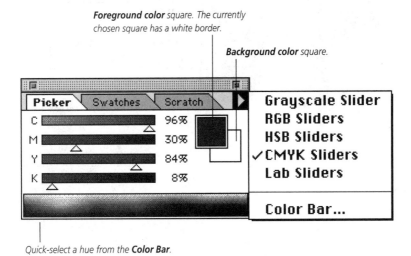

*Quick-select a hue from the **Color Bar**.*

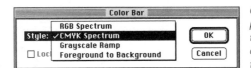

Choose **Color Bar** from the Picker palette command menu to open the **Color Bar** dialog box, then choose a **Spectrum** (display style) from the **Style** pop-up menu.

The Picker palette resized by clicking once on its Zoom box. You can resize any palette this way.

The Picker palette resized by double-clicking the palette name or by holding down **Option** and clicking the Zoom box.

Figure 13. The **Picker** palette.

Swatches palette

The Swatches palette is used for selecting already mixed colors to be applied with the painting, editing, and fill tools. Individual swatches can be added to and deleted from the palette. Custom Swatch palettes can also be loaded, appended, and saved using Swatches palette commands.

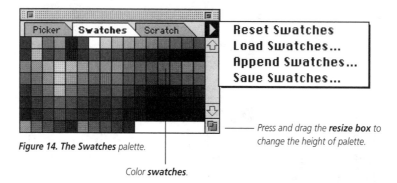

Figure 14. The Swatches *palette.*

*Press and drag the **resize box** to change the height of palette.*

*Color **swatches**.*

Scratch palette

The Scratch palette is used for mixing and selecting colors to apply with the painting, editing, and fill tools. The paint and smudge tools can be used to draw and mix colors on the Scratch pad. Scratch pads can also be locked, loaded, and saved. You can use the Eyedropper tool to sample from the Scratch pad.

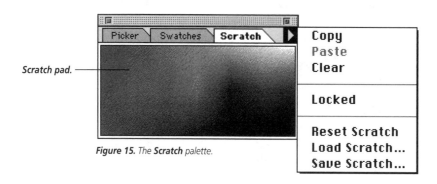

Scratch pad.

Figure 15. *The **Scratch** palette.*

Brushes palette

The Brushes palette is used for defining tool tip size, edge, and angle. You can choose from preset brushes or you can create your own brushes. You can also load, append, and save brushes using the Brushes palette command menu.

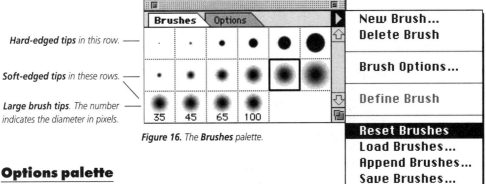

Hard-edged tips in this row. ——

Soft-edged tips in these rows. ——

Large brush tips. The number indicates the diameter in pixels. ——

Figure 16. The **Brushes** palette.

Options palette

The Options palette is used for defining painting and editing tool attributes, such as Opacity/Pressure, Fade distance, and mode. Options are set for each tool individually. You can reset the currently selected tool or all tools using Options palette commands.

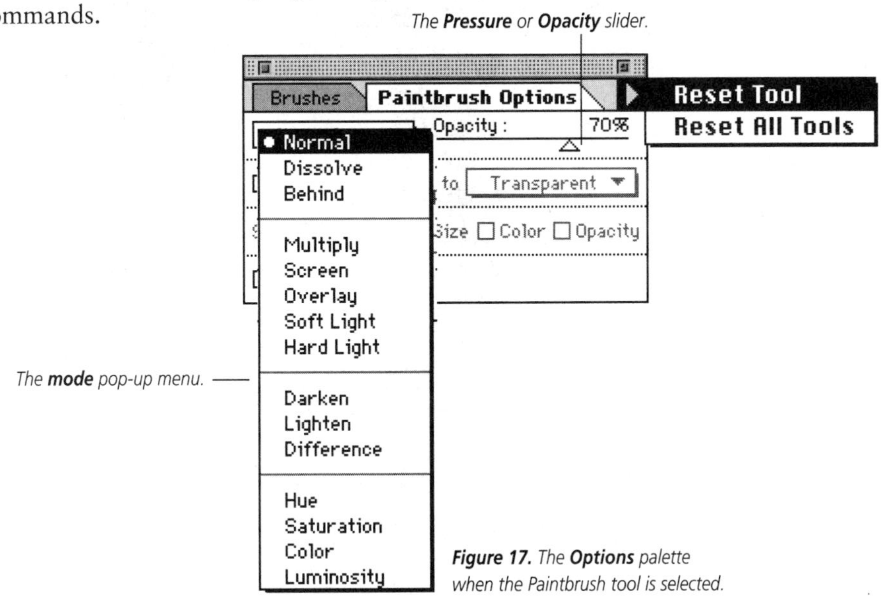

The **Pressure** or **Opacity** slider.

The **mode** pop-up menu. ——

Figure 17. The **Options** palette when the Paintbrush tool is selected.

one.

Layers palette

Every picture automatically has a Background layer. Using the Layers palette, you can add, delete, hide/display, and rearrange additional layers. Each layer can be assigned its own mode and opacity and can be edited separately without changing the other layers. You can also attach a mask to a layer.

Only the currently highlighted layer, called the **target layer**, can be edited. Click on a layer name on the Layers palette to highlight it. The name of the target layer will be listed on the document window title bar.

Layers take up storage space, so when you're done with your multi-layer picture, you can merge or flatten the layers into one.

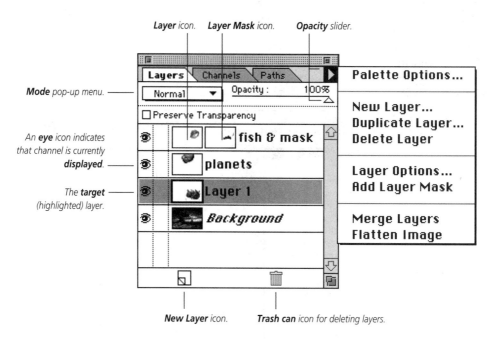

Layer icon.   *Layer Mask* icon.   *Opacity* slider.

Mode pop-up menu.

An **eye** *icon indicates that channel is currently* **displayed**.

The **target** *(highlighted) layer.*

Palette Options...

New Layer...
Duplicate Layer...
Delete Layer

Layer Options...
Add Layer Mask

Merge Layers
Flatten Image

New Layer *icon.*   **Trash can** *icon for deleting layers.*

Figure 18. The **Layers** palette.

Layers Palette

Channels palette

The Channels palette is used to display one or more of the channels that make up a picture and any specially created alpha channels, which are used for saving selections. The Channels palette is also used for displaying Layer Masks.

*An **eye** icon indicates that channel is currently **displayed**. To display a channel, click its name or use the keystroke listed on the palette.*

*A selected **alpha channel**.*

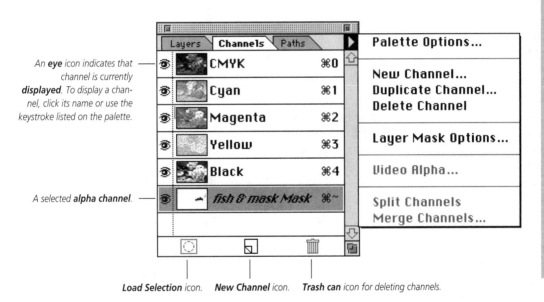

Load Selection *icon.*   New Channel *icon.*   Trash can *icon for deleting channels.*

Figure 19. *The **Channels** palette.*

Paths palette

The Pen tool creates curved and straight line segments connected by anchor points. Together they form a path. The Pen tool and its variations for modifying a path are selected from the Paths palette. A path can be saved and used as a selection, and it can be stroked or filled.

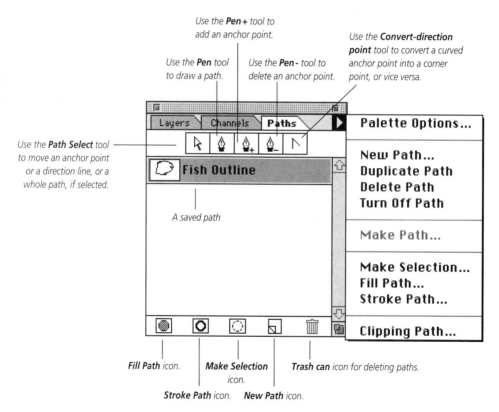

Use the **Pen+** tool to add an anchor point.

Use the **Pen** tool to draw a path.

Use the **Pen-** tool to delete an anchor point.

Use the **Convert-direction point** tool to convert a curved anchor point into a corner point, or vice versa.

Use the **Path Select** tool to move an anchor point or a direction line, or a whole path, if selected.

A saved path

Fill Path icon.

Stroke Path icon.

Make Selection icon.

New Path icon.

Trash can icon for deleting paths.

Figure 20. The Paths palette.

Info palette

The Info palette displays a breakdown of the color of the pixel under the cursor.

The Info palette also shows the position of the cursor on the picture, as in Figure 21, and may show the dimensions and the angle of rotation of a selection, depending on which tool is highlighted. To make these options available, choose Palette Options from the palette command menu, and check the Show Mouse Coordinates box. You can choose a different unit of measure for the palette from the same dialog box.

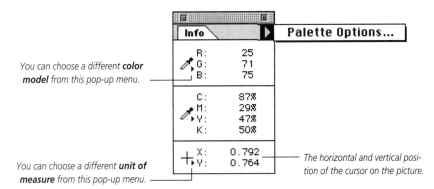

*You can choose a different **color model** from this pop-up menu.*

*You can choose a different **unit of measure** from this pop-up menu.*

The horizontal and vertical position of the cursor on the picture.

Figure 21. *The **Info** palette.*

Commands palette

The Commands palette is used for choosing F-key shortcuts to activate frequently used commands. You can use the default shortcuts or you can assign your own shortcuts in the New Command dialog box (**Figure 23**) (choose **New Command** from the palette command menu).

To execute a command, click any command name listed on the palette or use the assigned shortcut listed on the palette.

To change a command, choose **Edit Commands** from the palette command menu (**Figure 24**). Choose **Reset Commands** to restore the default F-keys.

Command lists can also be appended, loaded, and saved using the Commands palette. Five predefined command sets are supplied with Photoshop. They are located in the Command Sets folder, which is in the Goodies folder in the application folder.

To reshape the Commands palette, change the number in the Display/Columns field in the Edit Commands dialog box. The palette in Figure 22 has one column; the palette in Figure 25 has two columns.

Shortcuts

Hold down Shift and click a command name on the palette to open the Change Command dialog box.

Hold down Command (⌘) and click a command name on the palette to delete it.

Figure 22. The default Commands palette.

Figure 23. With the New Command dialog box open, choose a command from any Photoshop menu, submenu, or palette pop-up menu. The command you choose will be automatically entered into the Name field. Then choose any available F-Key from the Function Key pop-up menu. (Check the Shift box to include the Shift key in the shortcut.) You can also choose a color from the Color pop-up menu for the command name so you can spot it quickly on the palette.

Figure 24. In the Edit Commands dialog box, click a command name on the scroll list, then click New, Delete, or Change. The Change Command dialog box functions just like the New Command dialog box, which is shown in Figure 23.

Figure 25. This is our customized Commands palette. It lists commands that we use frequently.

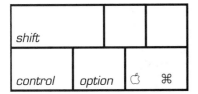

Figure 26. The Shift, Command (⌘), and Option keys are situated on the left and right side of the keyboard, and are used in keyboard shortcuts.

Keyboard shortcuts:

Some commands have keyboard equivalents. To perform a keyboard shortcut, hold down one or more keys, such as Command (⌘) and Shift, press and release a second key, then release the first key or combination of keys (**Figure 26**). *(See Appendix B for a list of shortcuts)*

To perform the Save command:

1. Hold down Command (⌘).

2. Press and release the "S" key.

3. Release Command (⌘).

HARDWARE

Photoshop will run on a Macintosh with a 68020 or higher processor, System 7 or later, a hard disk with at least 20 megabytes of available space, and at least 8 megabytes of RAM (random access memory) allocated to the application. (Photoshop will run on 5 megs of RAM, but you will not be able to access some of the filters and commands.) Photoshop will run faster on a Quadra with 8 to 16 megabytes of RAM allocated to the application and a large hard disk with at least 50 megabytes of available space. For optimal speed, we recommend a Power Mac with 16 megabytes or more of RAM allocated to the application and a large, fast-access hard drive (500 megabytes to 1 gigabyte/9-11 ms).

Photoshop requires a lot of RAM because it works with three copies of a picture: a copy to work on directly, a copy for the Undo command, and a copy for the Revert and From Saved commands. Added layers also use RAM and occupy storage space. To improve Photoshop's performance speed, the first step is to increase your RAM. In addition, you can purchase a Power Mac upgrade card for a Mac II from a third-party vendor or an upgrade card for a Quadra from Apple. The Power Mac processor will make your computer's performance more like that of a PowerPC. Filter applications, color mode changes, and image size changes will be faster if you install an accelerator card bearing the "Adobe Charged" logo.

Color monitors display 8-bit, 16-bit, or 24-bit color, depending on the video card. With an 8-bit card, 256 colors are available for on-screen color mixing. With a 24-bit card, 16.7 million colors are available. A 24-bit card provides optimal display, because every color can be represented exactly. All Photoshop pictures are saved as 24-bit, regardless of the resolution of the monitor.

You may also want to purchase a removable storage device — such as a SyQuest or an optical drive — to save files and to transport files to and from a service bureau.

DISK STORAGE

Disk Type	Capacity
High density (HD) floppy	1.4MB
SyQuest removable	44MB, 88MB *or* 200MB
Hard drive	170MB to 2GB...

FILE SIZE UNITS

Byte = 8 bits of digital information *(approx. one black or white pixel, or one character*

Kilobyte (KB) = 1,024 bytes

Megabyte (MB) = 1,024 kilobytes

Gigabyte (GB) = 1,024 megabytes

HOW PHOTOSHOP WORKS

THE FOLLOWING summarizes basic Photoshop operations. You may want to refer back to this chapter occasionally, particularly the section on image modes. Special terms are defined in the Mini-Glossary on page 7 and in the full Glossary in Appendix A.

Pixels

The screen image in Photoshop is a **bitmap**, which is a geometric arrangement (mapping) of a layer of dots of different shades or colors on a rectangular grid. Each dot, called a pixel, represents a color or shade. By magnifying an area of a picture, you can edit pixels individually (**Figure 1**). Every Photoshop picture is bitmapped, whether it originates from a scan, from another application, or entirely within the application using painting and editing tools. (Don't confuse Bitmap image mode with the term "bitmapped.")

If you drag with a painting tool across an area of a layer, new pixels will replace the **underlying pixels**. Once modified, the exact attributes of the underlying pixels can be restored only by choosing Undo or Revert or by using the Rubber Stamp tool with its From Saved option.

Selections

Pictures are modified using tools, menu commands, palettes, and dialog boxes. You can make picture-wide changes, or you can restrict modifications to an area by selecting it before you apply a filter or any other editing command. The rest of the picture will be protected from

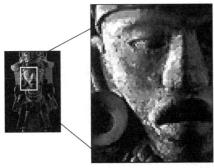

Figure 1. Close-up of a picture, showing individual **pixels**.

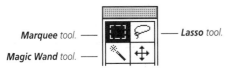

Marquee tool. —— —— **Lasso** tool.

Magic Wand tool. ——

Figure 2. Photoshop's *selection tools.*

changes. The **selection tools** (Marquee, Lasso, and Magic Wand) are used to create differently shaped selections, from rectangular to irregular (**Figures 2-3**). Some menu commands are only available when an area is selected.

When the Paste or Float command is chosen, type is created, or a selection is Option-dragged, a **floating selection** is created — it floats above the underlying pixels. A floating selection can be edited without affecting the underlying pixels. Once deselected, it replaces the underlying pixels.

A selection can be duplicated, moved within a picture, superimposed over another image to create a double exposure effect, or moved to another picture to create an electronic collage.

Layers

Every picture automatically contains a background layer. Additional layers can be created, accessed, and restacked using the **Layers palette** (**Figures 4-5**). The currently highlighted layer on the Layers palette is called the **target layer**. Only the target layer is editable.

Areas on a layer that contain imagery contain pixels, and they are opaque. Areas on a layer that are blank contain no pixels, and are transparent. You can actually see through a whole stack of layers. The advantage of working with multiple layers is that you can assign picture components to separate layers and edit them individually without changing the other layers.

Only the Photoshop 3.0 file format supports multiple layers. If you save a multi-layer picture in another file format, all its layers will be merged into one.

Figure 3. *A selected area of a picture.*

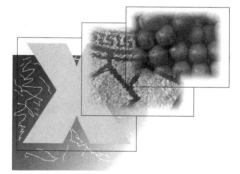

Figure 4. *Layers are like clear acetate sheets: opaque where there is imagery and transparent where there is no imagery.*

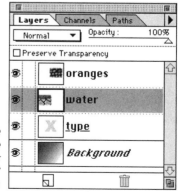

Figure 5. *The* **Layers palette** *for a four-layer picture. "water" is the target layer.*

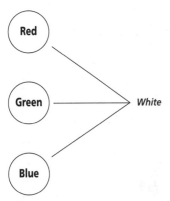

*Figure 6. The **additive primaries** on a computer monitor.*

Figure 7. Subtractive primaries — printing inks.

RGB vs. CMYK Color

Red, Green, and Blue light are used to display a color picture on a monitor. When Red, Green and Blue (RGB) light (the additive primaries) in their purest form are combined, they produce white light (**Figure 6**).

The three subtractive primary inks used in process printing are Cyan (C), Magenta (M), and Yellow (Y). When combined, they produce a dark, muddy color. To produce a rich black, printers usually mix Black (K) ink with Cyan, Magenta, and/or Yellow (**Figure 7**).

The display of color on a computer screen is highly variable and subject to ambient lighting and monitor and room temperature conditions. Only a carefully calibrated monitor can display color accurately, but even very carefully calibrated screens can only simulate CMYK ink colors. Many colors seen in nature cannot be printed, some colors that can be displayed on a screen cannot be printed, and some colors that can be printed can't be displayed on a screen.

A warning indicator will appear on the the **Picker** palette or the **Color Picker** dialog box if you choose a non-printable color. Using Photoshop's **Gamut Alarm** command, you can display non-printable colors in your picture in gray. Then, using the **Sponge** tool, you can desaturate them to bring them into gamut.

(Of course you don't need to convert to CMYK Color mode if you're doing multimedia work or are going to output your file to a film recorder.)

Channels

Every Photoshop picture is a composite of one or more semi-transparent color "overlays" called channels. For example, a picture in RGB Color mode is composed of Red, Green and Blue channels. To illustrate, open a color picture, choose

Color, Channels

Show Channels from the Window menu, then click Red, Green, or Blue on the Channels palette to display only that channel (**Figure 8**). Click RGB to restore the full channel display. *(For this exercise, choose General from the Preferences submenu under the File menu, then check the Color Channels in Color box)*

Modifications can be made to an individual channel, but normally modifications are made and displayed in the multichannel, composite image (The topmost channel name on the Channels palette), and affect all of a picture's channels at once.

The more channels a picture contains, the larger its file storage size. The storage size of a picture in RGB Color mode, composed of three channels (Red, Green, and Blue), will be three times larger than the same picture in Grayscale mode, which is composed of one channel. The same picture in CMYK Color mode will be composed of four channels (Cyan, Magenta, Yellow, and Black), and will be four times larger.

Image Modes

A picture can be converted to, displayed in, and edited in eight image modes: Bitmap, Grayscale, Duotone, Indexed Color, RGB Color, CMYK Color, Lab Color and Multichannel. Modes are selected from the Mode menu (**Figure 9**).

If a picture is converted to a different image mode, its colors may change. Some mode conversions cause noticeable changes; others cause subtle changes. Very dramatic changes may occur if a picture is converted from RGB Color mode to CMYK Color mode, because printable colors are substituted for rich, glowing RGB colors. Color accuracy may diminish if a picture is converted back and forth between RGB and CMYK modes too many times. You can use the **CMYK Preview** command to preview an

Highlighted channels can be edited.

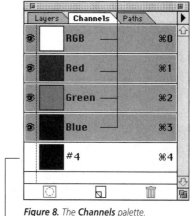

Figure 8. *The Channels palette.*

An Alpha channel.

Mode
- **Bitmap...**
- ✓ **Grayscale**
- **Duotone...**
- **Indexed Color**
- **RGB Color**
- **CMYK Color**
- **Lab Color**
- **Multichannel**

- **Color Table...**

- **CMYK Preview**
- **Gamut Warning**

Figure 9. *The Mode menu.*

RGB picture in CMYK without actually changing its mode. This way, the picture's multiple layers and color information will be preserved.

Some output devices require that a picture be saved in a particular image mode. For example, a picture must be in CMYK Color mode to color separate it on an imagesetter. Commands and tool options in Photoshop also vary depending on the currently selected image mode.

Here are brief descriptions of some commonly used **image modes**:

In **Bitmap** mode, pixels are 100% black or 100% white only, and no editing tools, filters, or Adjust commands are available. The Invert command is available. A picture must be in Grayscale mode before it can be converted to Bitmap mode.

In **Grayscale** mode, pixels are black, white, or up to 255 shades of gray. A Grayscale picture can be colorized by first converting it to a color mode. If a picture is converted from a color mode to Grayscale mode and then saved, its color information is deleted and it cannot be restored. Its luminosity (light and dark) values remain intact.

A picture in **Indexed Color** mode has one channel and a color table containing a maximum of 256 colors or shades. To open a Photoshop picture in some painting or animation programs, it must first be converted to Indexed Color mode. You can also convert a picture to Indexed Color mode to create "arty" color effects.

RGB Color mode is the most versatile because it is the only mode in which all the tool options and filters are accessible. Some video and multimedia applications can import a Photoshop picture in RGB Color mode.

Photoshop is one of the few Macintosh programs in which pictures can be displayed and edited in **CMYK Color** mode. Convert a picture to CMYK Color mode

Image Modes

to output it on a color printer or to color separate it (unless the output device is a PostScript Level 2 printer).

Lab Color is a three-channel mode. The channels represent lightness, the colors green-to-magenta, and the colors blue-to-yellow. Photo CD pictures can be converted to Lab Color mode or RGB Color mode in Photoshop. Save a picture in Lab Color mode to print it on a PostScript Level 2 printer or to export it to another operating system.

(Duotone mode is discussed on page 250)

File formats

A picture can be created, opened, edited, and saved in 17 different file formats (**Figure 10**). Of these, you may use only a few, such as TIFF, PICT, EPS, and the native Photoshop file format. Because Photoshop accepts so many formats, images can be gathered from a wide variety of sources, such as scans, drawing applications, CDs, video captures, and other operating systems — and output from Photoshop on many types of printers. Using the Save As or Save a Copy dialog box, you can generate a new version of a file and save it in a different format.

Resolution

In most applications, a picture's resolution cannot exceed the monitor's 72-dots-per-inch resolution. In Photoshop, however, a picture's resolution is independent of the monitor's resolution, and can be customized for a particular output device, with or without modifying its file storage size (**Figure 11**). It is best, though, to scan your picture at the resolution required for your final output device.

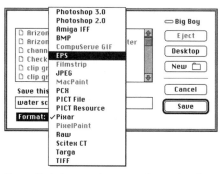

Figure 10. *A picture can be converted to another File Format using the Save As command.*

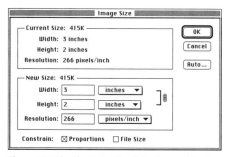

Figure 11. *Using the Image Size dialog box, a picture's dimensions, resolution, and file storage size can be modified.*

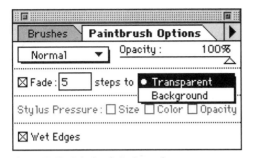

*Figure 12. The **Paintbrush Options** palette.*

Figure 13. An alpha channel. The selected area is white, the protected area is black.

A Few Production Tips

Customize each tool.

For each painting and editing tool, you can choose from 15 modes on the tool's **Options palette (Figure 12)**. A tool's mode affects how its strokes modify pixels. For example, if you stroke with a painting tool with Normal mode chosen, pixels of any color under the stroke will be replaced with the stroke color. With Luminosity mode chosen, only luminosity values are modified. Try using a tool with different modes to see how its effects vary. With practice, you will learn which modes produce which effects. *(More about modes on page 135)*

Other tool attributes — like opacity, hardness, and pressure — can also be specified using the Options palette. From the Brushes palette, you can choose a predefined brush tip or you can create your own brush tip. For example, you can make an Airbrush tool tip soft and transparent, or a Paintbrush stroke round and opaque. An illusion of semi-transparency can be created using a tool or the Fill command with a light opacity.

Mask it.

A selection can be saved to a special gray-scale channel called an alpha channel. An alpha channel selection can be loaded onto a picture at any time and used like a stencil (**Figure 13**). Alpha channels are accessed via the Channels palette.

Photoshop's Quick Mask mode can be used to turn a selection into a translucent mask. Usually, the Quick Mask covers the protected areas of the picture with transparent color, leaving the unprotected area as a cutout. Painting tools can be used to modify the contours of the mask. When Quick Mask mode is turned off, the cutout area turns into a selection.

Using a layer mask, you can temporarily hide pixels on an individual layer so you can experiment with different compositions. When you are finished using a layer mask, you can discard the effects or permanently apply them to the layer.

Stay flexible.

Some modifications require only one step, but many involve multiple steps. In this book, the same command or feature may be used in different sequences to produce different results.

You can choose the Undo command from the Edit menu to undo the last modification, or you can choose the Revert command from the File menu to restore the last saved version of a picture. You can restore part of the last saved version of a picture by dragging across it using the Rubber Stamp tool with its From Saved option.

You can also save different versions of a picture as you work on it using the Save As or Save a Copy command. When you're satisfied with one of the versions, just discard the copies.

For maximum flexibility, divide or build your picture into layers, so you can work on one element in a picture without affecting the non-target layers.

Shorten your production time.

Interrupt screen redraw after executing a command or applying a filter by choosing a different tool or command.

Use the Commands palette to execute commands quickly (**Figure 14**). *(See page 22)*

Take advantage of the preview box in most filter dialog boxes. You'll be able to see the effect of a filter with its various options and at a variety of intensities before you actually apply it (**Figure 15**).

Now you're ready for Chapter 3, Startup!

Figure 14. *Execute commands quickly using the* **Commands** *palette.*

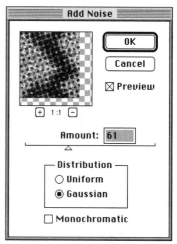

Figure 15. *Take advantage of the* **preview** *box in most filter dialog boxes.*

I N THIS CHAPTER you will learn how to launch Photoshop, scan a picture, create a new document, open an existing document, change a picture's dimensions, resolution, and file storage size, crop, flip, rotate, or add a border to a picture, save a picture in a variety of file formats, copy a picture, close a picture, and quit Photoshop.

To launch Photoshop:

Double-click the Adobe Photoshop folder on the desktop (**Figure 1**), then double-click the square Photoshop application icon (**Figure 2**).

or

Double-click a Photoshop file icon (**Figure 3**).

✔ Tip

■ If you are using System 7 or later, you can create an alias of the application icon so Photoshop can be launched from the Apple menu. Click the Photoshop application icon, choose Make Alias from the File menu, then move the alias to the Apple Menu Items folder in the System Folder.

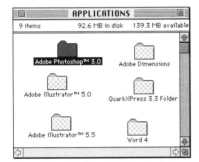

Figure 1. Double-click the **Adobe Photoshop folder**.

Figure 2. Double-click the **Adobe Photoshop application icon**.

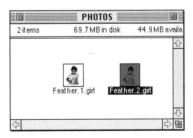

Figure 3. Or double-click a **Photoshop file icon**.

Launch Photoshop

Where pictures come from.

Scans, video captures, and computer-generated artwork in most file formats can be opened and edited in Photoshop. Pictures can also be created entirely within the application.

Kodak Photo CD files can also be opened in Photoshop. If your Macintosh doesn't have a built-in CD-ROM drive, you can purchase one separately. Be sure it's compatible with the Photo CD format. Each Photo CD disk can hold a hundred or more digitized photographs. You can purchase stock photographs on a CD, a service bureau can scan transparencies onto a CD, or film can be developed onto a CD.

Scanning

Using a scanning device and scanning software, a slide, flat artwork, or a photograph can be translated into numbers (digitized) so it can be read, displayed, edited, and printed by a computer. You can scan directly into Photoshop or use other scanning software and save the scan in a file format that Photoshop imports.

Scanners

The quality of a scan will partially depend on the type of scanner you use. If your print shop is going to use the original photograph for printing and the scan will only be used to indicate the picture's position or you are planning to dramatically transform the picture in Photoshop, you can use an inexpensive flat-bed scanner. If color accuracy is critical, scan a transparency on a slide scanner. Scan a picture that is going to be printed electronically on a high-resolution CCD scanner, such as a Scitex Smart-Scanner, or on a drum scanner. A high-quality scan can be obtained from a service bureau. Unfortunately, high-resolution scans usually have very large file sizes.

SCANNING TIP

To produce a high-quality scan, start with a high-quality original. Some scanners compress gray values and increase contrast, so use a photograph with good tonal balance. Set the scanning parameters carefully, weighing such factors as your final output device and storage capacity. The most sophisticated retouching or correction techniques cannot make a lousy scan look good.

Service providers (also known as *service bureaus*), perform essential prepress operations, such as high-resolution scanning, imagesetting and color proof printing. They provide the link between your digital files and the printing press. Some print shops perform these services in-house.

Scanner software

Scanning software usually offers most of the following options, although terms may vary. The quality and file storage size of a scan are partially defined by the mode, resolution, and scale you specify, and whether you crop the picture.

Preview: Place the art in the scanner, then click Preview or PreScan.

Scan mode: Select Black-and-White Line Art (no grays), Grayscale or Color. A picture scanned in Color will be approximately three times larger in file size than the same picture scanned Grayscale.

Resolution: Scan resolution is measured in pixels per inch (ppi). The higher the resolution, the better the scan, and the larger its file size. Choose the minimum resolution necessary to obtain the best possible printout from your final output device. Don't choose a higher resolution than required, because the picture will be larger in storage size than necessary. It will take longer to render on screen and print, and there will be no improvement in output quality *(see Chapter 22: Printing").*

Before selecting a resolution, determine the resolution of the printer or imagesetter and the halftone screen frequency your offset printer intends to use. (The scan resolution is not the same as the resolution of the output device.)

As a rule, choose a resolution that is 1½ times the halftone screen frequency (lines per inch) of your final output device for a grayscale picture, and twice the halftone screen frequency for a color picture. Use a high scanning resolution (600 ppi or higher) for line art.

For example, if your offset printer intends to use a 133-line screen frequency for black-and-white printing, choose a scanning resolution of 200. *(See "Tip" on page 45)*

Scanning

Cropping: If you intend to use only part of a picture, reposition the handles of the box in the preview area to reduce the scan area. Cropping will reduce the storage size of a scan.

Scale: To enlarge a picture's dimensions, choose a scale percentage larger than 100%. Enlarging a picture in Photoshop or any other software program may cause it to blur, because the program uses mathematical "guesswork" to fill in additional information. A picture's original information is recorded only at the time of scanning.

Scan: Click Scan and choose a location in which to save the file.

Note: To scan into Photoshop, the plug-in module for the scanner must be in the Photoshop Plug-ins folder. The first time you choose a scanning module from the Acquire submenu, choose TWAIN Select Source and choose a TWAIN device (the scanner), then choose TWAIN Acquire. Thereafter, to access the scanning software, just choose TWAIN Acquire. *(See the Photoshop documentation for information about scanning modules)*

To scan into Photoshop:

1. Choose a scanning module or choose TWAIN Acquire from the Acquire pop-up menu under the File menu (**Figure 4**).

2. Click Prescan.

3. Following the guidelines outlined above, choose a Mode (**Figure 6**). *and* Choose a Resolution.

4. *Optional:* Choose a different Scale percentage.

5. *Optional:* Crop the picture.

6. Click Scan. The scanned picture will appear in a new, untitled window.

7. Save the picture *(see pages 52-53)*.

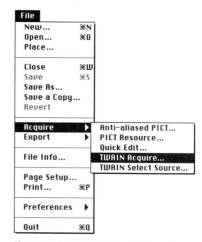

Figure 4. *Choose* **TWAIN Acquire** *from the* **Acquire** *submenu under the* **File** *menu.*

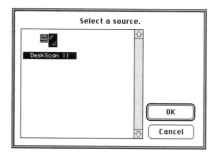

Figure 5. *The* **TWAIN Select Source** *dialog box.*

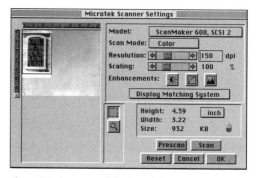

Figure 6. *In the scanner dialog box, click* **Prescan***, choose a* **Scan Mode**, **Resolution***, and* **Scaling** *percentage, crop the picture, if desired, then click* **Scan***.*

Scan Into Photoshop

File storage sizes of scanned images.

Size (In inches)	PPI (Resolution)	Black/White 1-Bit	Grayscale 8-Bit	CMYK Color 24-Bit
2 x 3	150	17 K	132 K	528 K
	300	67 K	528 K	2.06 MB
4 x 5	150	56 K	440 K	1.72 MB
	300	221 K	1.72 MB	6.87 MB
8 x 10	150	220 K	1.72 MB	6.87 MB
	300	879 K	6.87 MB	27.50 MB

Potential gray levels at various output resolutions and screen frequencies.

Output Resolution (DPI)	Screen Frequency (LPI)				
	60	**85**	**100**	**133**	**150**
300	26	13			
600	101	51	37	21	
1270	256*	224	162	92	72
2540		256*	256*	256*	256*

Note: *Ask your print shop what screen frequency (lpi) you will need to specify when imagesetting your file. Also ask your print shop or prepress provider what resolution (dpi) to use for imagesetting. Some imagesetters can achieve resolutions above 2540 dpi.*

At the present time, PostScript Level 1 and Level 2 printers produce a maximum of 256 gray levels.

To create a new document:

1. Choose New from the File menu (**Figure 7**).

2. Enter a name in the Name field (**Figure 8**).

3. Choose a unit of measure from the pop-up menus next to the Width and Height fields.

4. Enter numbers in the Width and Height fields.

5. Enter the resolution required for your final output device in the Resolution field *(see "Resolution" on page 35).*

6. Choose a mode from the Mode pop-up menu. The picture can be converted to a different mode later *(see "Image Modes" on page 28).*

7. Click Contents: White or Background Color for the Background layer.

8. Click OK or press Return. A document window will appear (**Figure 9**).

✔ Tips

■ If there is a document open and you want the new document to be the same size as the open document, with the New dialog box open, choose the name of the picture that has the desired dimensions from the Windows menu. Fields in the New dialog box will conform to the dimensions of the open document you choose.

■ If there is an image on the Clipboard, the New dialog box will automatically display the dimensions of that image. To prevent those dimensions from displaying, hold down Option when you choose New from the File menu.

Figure 7. Choose **New** from the **File** menu.

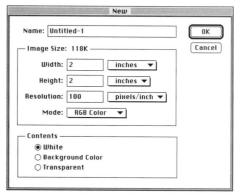

Figure 8. In the **New** dialog box, enter a **Name** and enter numbers in the **Width, Height,** and **Resolution** fields. Also choose a **Mode** and click a **Contents** type for the Background.

Figure 9. A new document window will appear.

Create a New Document

Figure 10. Choose **Open** from the *File* menu.

Note: To open an Adobe Illustrator file, follow the instructions on page 42 or 43.

To open a picture from within Photoshop:

1. Choose Open from the File menu (**Figure 10**).

2. *Optional:* For a PICT file, click the Create button to create a thumbnail of the picture for display on the scroll list.

3. Locate the file you wish to open (**Figure 11**).

Note: If the document name does not appear on the scroll list, you must convert the file to a format that Photoshop supports. To do this, check the Show All Files box, then choose a format from the File Format pop-up menu. Once opened, a picture can be saved in any format Photoshop supports. Don't leave the Format as Raw.

4. Highlight the file name, then click Open.
or
Double-click the file name.

✔ Tips

■ To create a thumbnail icon of any newly saved picture for display in the Open dialog box, choose General from the Preferences submenu under the File menu. Click More, click Always Save, then click Thumbnail. Also, make sure the Apple QuickTime extension is in the System Folder. To create pictures icons for the Finder, click Icon. To choose icons for individual files as you save them, click Ask When Saving. Saving a picture with a preview slows the Save command and increases the picture's storage size.

■ If you open an EPS file or an Illustrator file that has not already

(Continued on the following page)

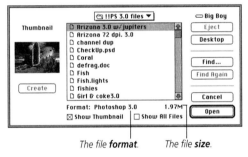

*The file **format**.   The file **size**.*

Figure 11. *Double-click a file name in the **Open** dialog box. If your document does not appear on the scroll list, check the **Show All Files** box, then choose a format from the **Format** pop-up menu.*

Open a Picture

been rasterized (converted from object-oriented to bitmap), the EPS Rasterizer dialog box will open. Follow steps 3-8 on page 42.

■ To open a QuarkXPress page in Photoshop, save it in QuarkXPress using the Save Page as EPS command, then choose EPS Pict Preview from the Format pop-up menu.

To open a Photoshop picture from the Finder:

Double-click a Photoshop picture file icon in the Finder (**Figure 12**). Photoshop will be launched if is not already open.

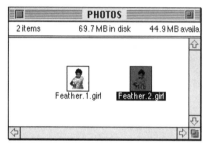

*Figure 12. Or double-click a **Photoshop file icon**.*

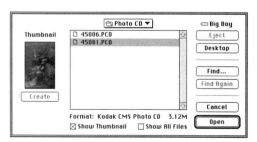

*Figure 13. Double-click a Photo CD file name in the **Open** dialog box. The **Format** will be listed as **Kodak CMS Photo CD**.*

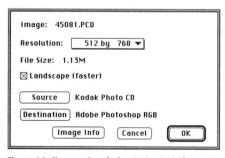

*Figure 14. Choose a **Resolution** in the **CMS Photo CD Plug in** dialog box. Leave the **Landscape** box checked (Use one of Photoshop's Rotate commands if you need to change the orientation of the picture.) Click **Image Info** to read about the original film medium.*

*Figure 15. Note the **Medium of Original** and **Product Type** of Original in the **Image Info** dialog box.*

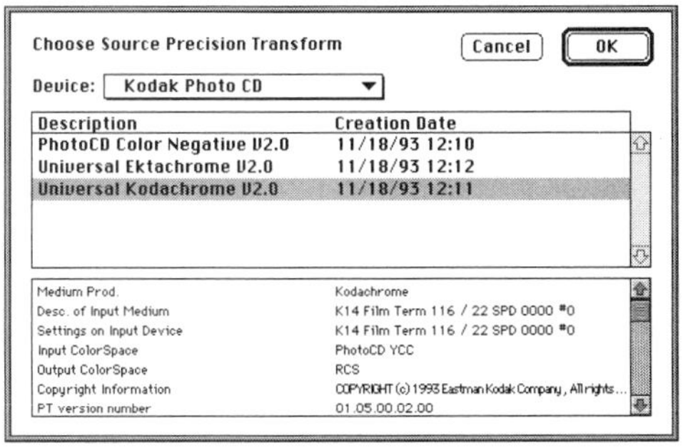

*Figure 16. Click on a **Description** that is the closest match to the film medium of the original photo listed in the Image Info dialog box. The image info dialog box for this picture listed Color Reversal as the Medium of Original and the Product Type as 116/-9, so we chose Universal Kodachrome V2.0 as the profile. Kodak recommends choosing **Universal Kodachrome** when the Product Type is unknown.*

*Figure 17. Choose **Adobe Photoshop RGB** or **Adobe Photoshop CIELAB** (Lab) as the color mode for the Photoshop picture from the **Device** pop-up menu.*

The Kodak CMS Photo CD plug-in for Photoshop opens Photo CD images from the File menu. It uses Kodak's Color Management System to produce accurate image translation from the Kodak file format into Photoshop's RGB Color or Lab Color mode.

To open a Photo CD file:

1. Choose Open from the File menu.

2. Locate and double-click the Photo CD file name.
   or
   Highlight the Photo CD file name and click Open (**Figure 13**).

3. Choose a Resolution (**Figure 14**). The Base resolution is 512 by 768 pixels, which will produce an image about 7 by 10.5 inches at 72 pixels/inch. A higher resolution will produce a larger image at 72 pixels/inch.

4. Click Image Info.

5. Make a note of the Medium of the Original and Product Type info (the type of film used to create the picture) (**Figure 15**). Color Reversal is the term for a color slide. 55/xx is Ektachrome slide. 116/xx is Kodachrome slide. Click OK.

6. Click Source.

7. Click on the closest available match to the Image Info description (**Figure 16**). Click OK.

8. Click Destination.

9. Choose Adobe Photoshop RGB or Adobe Photoshop CIELAB (Lab) as the color mode for the picture in Photoshop (**Figure 17**). Click OK.

10. Click OK in the Photo CD Plug in dialog box.

Open a Photo CD File

When an EPS file is opened or placed in Photoshop, it is rasterized. That is, it is converted from its native object-oriented format into Photoshop's pixel-based format. Follow these instructions to open an EPS file, such as an Adobe Illustrator graphic, as a new document. Follow the instructions on the next page to place an EPS file in an existing Photoshop file.

Note: Patterns, a stroke color on text, text used as a mask, or placed artwork in your Adobe Illustrator file will disappear if you open the file in Photoshop. To preserve those elements, save the file as an EPS in Illustrator, then choose the EPS Pict Preview format in the Open dialog box in Photoshop.

Figure 18. *Choose* **Open** *from the* **File** *menu.*

To open an EPS file as a new document:

1. Choose Open from the File menu (**Figure 18**).

2. Locate and highlight an EPS picture to be opened, then click Open.
   or
   Double-click a file name.

3. *Optional:* In the EPS Rasterizer dialog box, check the Constrain Proportions box to preserve the file's height and width ratio (**Figure 19**).

4. *Optional:* Choose a unit of measure from the pop-up menus next to the Height and Width fields, and enter new dimensions.

5. Enter the resolution required for your final output device in the Resolution field.

6. Choose an image mode from the Mode pop-up menu. *(See "Image Modes" on page 28)*

7. Check the Anti-aliased box for optimal rendering of the picture.

8. Click OK or press Return.

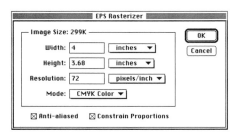

Figure 19. *In the* **EPS Rasterizer** *dialog box, enter the required* **Resolution,** *choose a* **Mode,** *and check the* **Anti-aliased** *box.*

Open an EPS File

*Figure 20. Choose **Place** from the **File** menu.*

*Figure 21. Highlight an EPS file, then click **Open**.*

Figure 22. The word "Delphi" was created in Adobe Illustrator, then placed in a Photoshop file.

(See the "Note" on the previous page)

To place an Adobe Illustrator picture into an existing Photoshop file:

1. Open a Photoshop picture.

2. Choose Place from the File menu (**Figure 20**).

3. Locate and highlight the Illustrator file to be opened, then click Open (**Figure 21**). A box will appear on top of your picture. Pause to allow the image to draw inside it (**Figure 22**).

Steps 4 and 5 are optional.

4. Drag a handle to resize the image.

5. To reposition the image, place the cursor over the "x" in the middle of the box and drag with the arrow cursor.

6. To accept the placed image, position the cursor over it and click with the gavel icon. The image will become a floating selection.

✔ Tips

■ For optimal rendering of a placed image, before choosing the Place command, choose General from the Preferences submenu under the File menu, click More, then check the Anti-alias PostScript box. This setting will be the default for future placed images.

■ To remove the placed image, click outside it with the cancel icon. If you already clicked with the gavel icon, press Delete to remove the floating selection.

Place an Adobe Illustrator File

To modify a picture's dimensions:

1. Choose Image Size from the Image menu (**Figure 23**).

2. To preserve the picture's width-to-height ratio, check the Proportions box. To modify the picture's width independently of its height, uncheck the Proportions box (**Figure 24**).

3. *Optional:* To preserve the picture's resolution, uncheck the File Size box.

4. Choose a unit of measure from the pop-up menu next to the Width and Height fields.

5. Enter new numbers in the Width and/or Height fields. The Resolution will change if the File Size box is checked.

6. Click OK or press Return.

✔ Tips

■ If you modify a picture's dimensions and/or resolution with the File Size box unchecked, you will not be able to use the Rubber stamp tool with the From Saved option to restore a portion of it. Save a picture immediately after modifying its dimensions and/or resolution to establish a new From Saved reference *(see page 207)*.

■ Changing a picture's dimensions in Photoshop may cause it to blur, so it is best to scan it at the desired size. If you must change a picture's dimensions in Photoshop, apply the Unsharp Mask filter afterward to resharpen *(see page 46)*.

Figure 23. Choose *Image Size* from the *Image* menu.

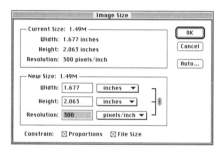

Figure 24. Enter numbers in the *Width* and/or *Height* fields in the *Image Size* dialog box.

Modify a Picture's Dimensions

Figure 25. *Choose* **Image Size** *from the* **Image** *menu.*

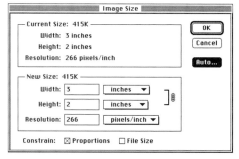

Figure 26. *Enter a number in the* **Resolution** *field in the* **Image Size** *dialog box. Click* **Auto** *to have Photoshop calculate the resolution.*

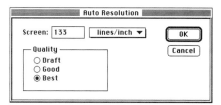

Figure 27. *Click* **Draft, Good,** *or* **Best** *Quality in the* **Auto Resolution** *dialog box.*

Note: When you increase a picture's resolution (resample up), pixels are added and the picture's file storage size increases, but sharpness diminishes. When you decrease resolution, information is deleted and cannot be retrieved once the picture is saved. Blurriness caused by resampling may only be evident when the picture is printed; it may not be discernible on screen. It is best to scan a picture at the proper resolution. Follow the instructions on the next page to resharpen a resampled picture. *(See "Resolution" on page 35)*

To modify a picture's resolution:

1. Choose Image Size from the Image menu (**Figure 25**).

2. *Optional:* To preserve the picture's dimensions (Width and Height), uncheck the File Size box (**Figure 26**).

3. Enter a number in the Resolution field.

4. Click OK or press Return.

✔ Tip

■ To calculate the proper resolution and file size for a scan or for an existing picture, create a new RGB document and choose 72 ppi. Then open the Image Size dialog box, click Auto, and enter the resolution of your final output device (the lpi that your printer will use), click Draft (1x Screen frequency), Good (1½x Screen frequency), or Best (2 x Screen frequency), and click OK (**Figures 26-27**). Note the resolution and file size, and use those values when you scan your picture.

Modify a Picture's Resolution

If you modify a picture's dimensions or resolution or convert it to CMYK Color mode, it may blur as a result of a process called interpolation. Despite its name, the Unsharp Mask filter has a sharpening effect.

You can choose from three interpolation methods in the General Preferences dialog box *(see page 250)*.

To apply the Unsharp Mask filter:

1. Choose Unsharp Mask from the Sharpen submenu under the Filter menu (**Figure 28**).

2. Enter a number in the Amount field (the amount of sharpening) or move the Amount slider (**Figure 29**). Use a low setting (below 25) for figures or natural objects and a higher setting if the picture contains sharp-edged objects.

3. Enter a number between 0.1 and 100 in the Radius field or move the Radius slider to specify the number of pixels surrounding high contrast edges that will be modified.

4. Enter a number between 0 and 255 in the Threshold field or move the Threshold slider. The Threshold is the minimum amount of contrast an area must have before it will be modified. At a Threshold of 0, the filter will be applied to the entire picture. At a high Threshold, the filter will be applied only to high contrast areas.

5. Click OK or press Return.

✔ Tip

■ To soften a grainy scan, apply the Gaussian Blur filter (Blur submenu) at a low setting (below 1) and then apply the Sharpen Edges filter (Sharpen submenu) once or twice afterward to resharpen.

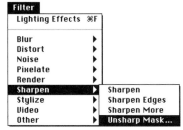

Figure 28. *Choose* **Unsharp Mask** *from the* **Sharpen** *pop-up menu under the* **Filter** *menu.*

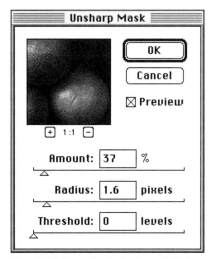

Figure 29. *Enter numbers in the* **Amount, Radius,** *and* **Threshold** *fields in the* **Unsharp Mask** *dialog box.*

Figure 30. *Choose* **Canvas Size** *from the* **Image** *menu.*

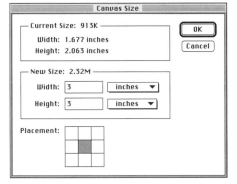

Figure 31. *In the* **Canvas Size** *dialog box, enter numbers in the* **Width** *and/or* **Height** *fields.*

To add a border to a picture:

1. Choose a Background color. *(See pages 111-114)*

2. Choose Canvas Size from the Image menu (**Figure 30**).

3. *Optional:* Choose a different unit of measure from the pop-up menus.

4. Enter higher numbers in the Width and/or Height fields (**Figure 31**). Changing the Width will not change the Height, and vice versa.

5. *Optional:* To reposition the image, click a white Placement square. The gray square represents the image relative to the new border.

6. Click OK or press Return. The border will automatically fill with the Background color (**Figures 32-33**).

Figure 32. *The original picture.*

Figure 33. *The same picture with a border.*

Add a Border to a Picture

To crop a picture:

1. Click the Cropping tool (**Figure 34**).

2. Drag a marquee over the portion of the picture you wish to keep (**Figure 35**).

3. *Optional:* To resize the marquee, drag any handle with the arrow cursor (**Figure 37**).

4. *Optional:* To reposition the marquee, hold down Command (⌘) and drag a handle (**Figure 38**).

5. *Optional:* To rotate the marquee, hold down Option and drag a handle in a circular direction (**Figure 39**).

6. Click inside the marquee (the cursor will turn into a scissors icon) (**Figure 36**). If you rotated the marquee, the rotated image will be squared off in the document window.

✔ Tips

■ To stop the cropping process before clicking with the scissors, click outside the marquee.

■ To specify a height-to-width ratio and/or a resolution for a cropped picture, double-click the Cropping tool, check the Fixed Target Size box on the Cropping Tool Options palette, enter values in the Width, Height, and/or Resolution fields, then follow steps 2-6 above.

■ To resharpen a picture after cropping, apply the Unsharp Mask filter. *(See page 46)*

The **Cropping** tool. ——

Figure 34.

Figure 35. *Drag a marquee over the portion of the picture you wish to keep, then click inside it.*

Figure 36. *The cropped picture.*

Crop a Picture

Figure 37. *To resize a crop marquee, drag any corner handle.*

Figure 38. *To reposition a crop marquee, hold down Command (⌘) and drag a corner handle.*

Figure 39. *To rotate a crop marquee, hold down Option and drag a corner handle in a circular direction.*

Crop a Picture

To flip a picture:

From the Flip submenu under the Image menu, choose Horizontal to flip the picture left to right (**Figures 40-42**).
or
Choose Vertical to flip the picture upside-down to produce a mirror image (**Figure 43**).

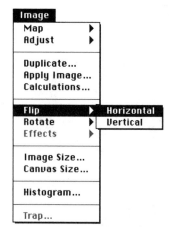

*Figure 40. Choose **Horizontal** or **Vertical** from the **Flip** submenu under the **Image** menu.*

Figure 41. The original picture.

Figure 42. The picture flipped horizontally.

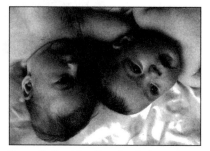

Figure 43. The picture flipped vertically.

Flip a Picture

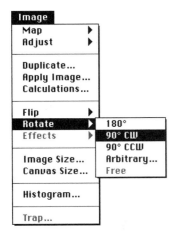

Figure 44. *Choose **180°**, **90°CW**, **90°CCW**, or **Arbitrary** from the **Rotate** submenu under the **Image** menu.*

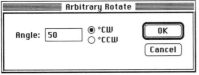

Figure 45. *In the **Arbitrary Rotate** dialog box, enter a number in the **Angle** field, and click **°CW** or **°CCW**.*

To rotate a picture a preset amount:

Choose 180°, 90° CW (clockwise), or 90° CCW (counterclockwise) from the Rotate submenu under the Image Menu (**Figure 44**).

To rotate a picture by specifying a number:

1. Choose Arbitrary from the Rotate submenu under the Image Menu (**Figure 45**).

2. Enter a number between -359.9° and 359.9° in the Angle field.

3. Click °CW (clockwise) or °CCW (counterclockwise)

4. Click OK or press Return (**Figure 46**).

Figure 46. *After rotating a picture 180°. Compare with Figure 43 on the previous page.*

Rotate a Picture

Special instructions for saving in the EPS, PICT, and TIFF file formats appear after the general instructions below. Other file formats are covered in the Photoshop User Guide.

To save a new document:

1. Choose Save from the File menu (**Figure 47**).

2. Enter a name in the "Save this document as" field (**Figure 48**).

3. Click Desktop.

4. Highlight a drive, then click Open.

5. *Optional:* Highlight a folder in which to save the file, then click Open.

6. Choose a file format from the Format pop-up menu.

7. Click Save.

✔ Tip

■ Most programs will not import a picture in the Photoshop file format, but multiple layers are only preserved in the native Photoshop 3.0 format.

An EPS file can be imported into many drawing and page layout programs, such as **Adobe Illustrator** and **QuarkXPress**.

To save a picture as an EPS:

1. Follow steps 1-5 above.

2. Choose EPS from the Format pop-up menu.

3. Click Save.

4. From the Preview pop-up menu, choose 1-bit Macintosh for a gray-scale preview; choose 8-bit Macintosh for a color preview (**Figure 49**).

5. Choose Encoding: Binary.

6. Click OK or press Return.

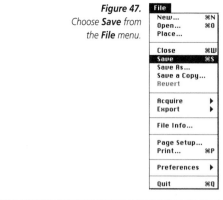

Figure 47. Choose **Save** from the **File** menu.

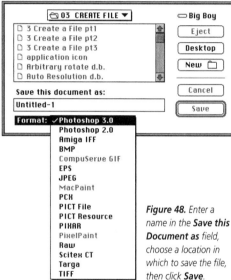

Figure 48. Enter a name in the **Save this Document as** field, choose a location in which to save the file, then click **Save**.

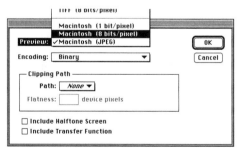

Figure 49. Click **1-bit Macintosh** or **8-bit Macintosh** in the *EPS Format* dialog box. **Binary Encoded** files are smaller and process more quickly than **ASCII** files. However, some applications and some PostScript "clone" printers cannot handle Binary files.

Save a New Document, Save as an EPS

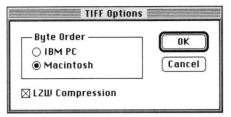

*Figure 50. Click **Macintosh** in the **TIFF Options** dialog box.*

A TIFF file can be imported by **Quark-XPress.** A CMYK TIFF can be color separated from QuarkXPress.

To save a picture as a TIFF:

1. Follow the first five steps on the previous page.

2. Choose TIFF from the File Formats pop-up menu.

3. Click Save.

4. Click Macintosh (**Figure 50**).

5. *Optional:* Check the LZW Compression box to reduce the file size. No picture data will be lost.
(File compression is discussed on page 242)

6. Click OK or press Return.

A PICT file can be opened as a template in **Adobe Illustrator.** A PICT file can also be opened in most **multimedia animation** applications.

Note: PICT compression options are available only if the QuickTime extension is installed in the System Folder.

To save a picture as a PICT:

1. Follow the first five steps on the previous page.

2. Choose PICT File from the File Formats pop-up menu.

3. Click Save.

4. Click 16 bits/pixel or 32 bits/pixel (**Figure 51**). For a picture in Grayscale mode, check 2, 4, or 8 bits/pixel.

5. Read page 240 before choosing any Compression setting other than None.

6. Click OK or press Return.

✔ Tip

■ A picture in CMYK Color mode cannot be saved in the PICT file format.

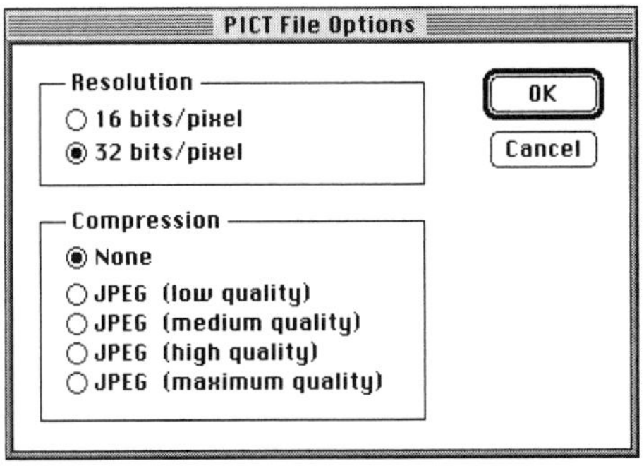

*Figure 51. Click a **Resolution** in the **PICT File Options** dialog box.*

Save as a TIFF or PICT

The prior version of a file is overwritten when the Save command is chosen.

To save an existing file:

Choose Save from the File menu (**Figure 52**).

or

Hold down Command (⌘) and press "S".

*Figure 52. Choose **Save** from the **File** menu.*

To revert to the last saved version:

1. Choose Revert from the File menu (**Figure 53**).

2. Click Revert when the prompt appears (**Figure 54**).

✔ Tip

■ To revert only a portion of a picture, use the Rubber stamp tool with its From Saved option. *(See page 207)*

*Figure 53. Choose **Revert** from the **File** menu.*

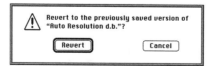

*Figure 54. Click **Revert** when this warning prompt appears.*

After using the **Save As** command to copy a file, you can then save the copy in a different image mode or use the copy as a design variation. For example, you can save a version of a picture in CMYK Color mode and keep the original version in RGB Color mode. You can also use the Save As dialog box to save a picture in a different file format.

Note: Use the Save a Copy command to copy a file and continue working on the original *(instructions on the next page).*

To save a new version of a file:

1. Open a file.

2. Choose Save As from the File menu (**Figure 55**).

3. Enter a new name in the "Save this document as" field (**Figure 56**).
or
Modify the existing name.

4. Choose a location in which to save the new version.

5. Choose a different file Format.

6. Click Save. For an EPS file, follow instructions on page 52. For a TIFF or PICT file, follow instructions on page 53. Consult the Photoshop manual for other formats. The new version will remain open; the original file will close automatically.

✔ Tips

■ If you don't change the name of the file and you click Save, a warning prompt will appear. Click Replace to save over the original file or click Cancel to return to the Save As dialog box.

■ Your picture may need to be in a particular mode for some Formats to be available. *(See "Image Modes" on page 28)*

■ If your document is multi-layered, you must flatten it to make other file formats available on the Format pop-up menu.

*Figure 55. Choose **Save As** from the **File** menu.*

*Figure 56. In the **Save As** dialog box, modify the name in the **Save this document as** field, choose a file **Format**, and choose a location in which to save the new version.*

Save a New Version of a File

You can use the **Save a Copy** command to save a flattened version of a multi-layer file in the Photoshop 3.0 format or in any other available file format. The multi-layer version of the picture will stay open so you can continue to work on it. The flattened version of a picture will be smaller in file size than the multi-layer version.

Note: Choose Duplicate from the Image menu to save a copy of the picture in the same location as the original. The original picture will remain open and the duplicate will appear in a new window.

To copy a file and continue to work on the original:

1. Open a file.

2. Choose Save a Copy from the File menu (**Figure 57**).

3. Enter a new name in the "Save a copy in" field (**Figure 58**).
   or
   Modify the existing name. By default, the word "copy" will be appended to the file name.

4. Choose a location in which to save the copy.

5. *Optional:* For a picture in the Photoshop 3.0 format, check the Flatten Image box to flatten all layers.

6. *Optional:* Choose a different file Format. If you choose any format other than Photoshop 3.0, the Flatten Image box will be checked automatically and layers will be flattened.

7. Click Save. For an EPS file, follow the instructions on page 52. For a TIFF or PICT file, follow the instructions on page 53. Consult the Photoshop manual for other formats. The original file will remain open.

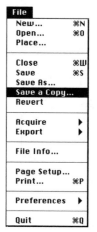

Figure 57. *Choose* **Save a Copy** *from the* **File** *menu.*

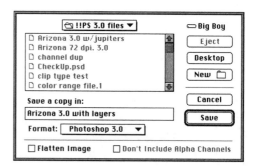

Figure 58. *In the* **Save a Copy** *dialog box, check the* **Flatten Image** *box for a Photoshop 3.0 file to flatten layers in the copy. If you choose any file format other than Photoshop 3.0, the Flatten Image box will be checked automatically.*

Save a Copy of a File

To close a picture:

Click the Close box in the upper left corner of the document window (**Figure 59**).

or

Choose Close from the File menu (**Figure 60**).

✔ Tip

■ If you attempt to close a picture and it was modified since it was last saved, a warning prompt will appear. Click Don't Save to close the file without saving, click Save to save the file before closing, or click Cancel to cancel the Close operation (**Figure 61**).

Click the **Close** *box.*

Figure 59.

Figure 60. Choose **Close** *from the* **File** *menu.*

Figure 61. If you chose **Close** *and the file has been modified since it was last saved, this prompt will appear.*

To quit Photoshop:

Choose Quit from the File menu (**Figure 62**).
or
Hold down Command (⌘) and press "Q".

✔ Tip

■ If you Quit Photoshop, all open Photoshop files will close. If changes have been made to an open file since it was saved, a prompt will appear. Click Don't Save to close the file without saving, click Save to save the file before quitting, or click Cancel to cancel the Quit operation (**Figure 63**).

Figure 62. *Choose* **Quit** *from the* **File** *menu.*

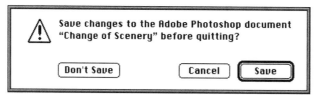

Figure 63. *If you chose* **Quit** *and changes have been made to an open file since it was saved, this prompt will appear.*

The display ratio.

Figure 1.

Figure 2. Choose **Zoom In** or **Zoom Out** from the **Window** menu.

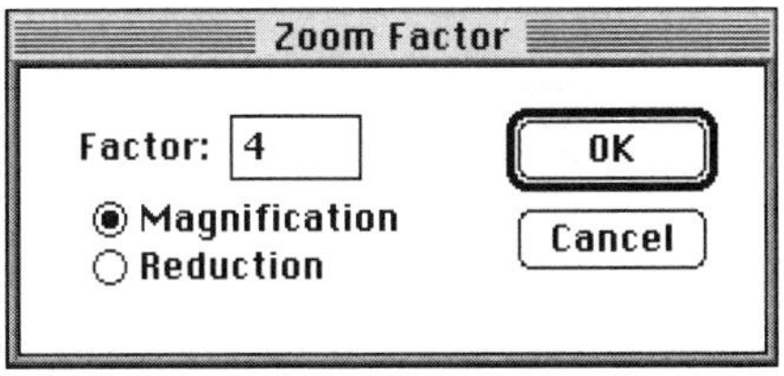

Figure 3. In the **Zoom Factor** dialog box, enter a **Factor** between 1 and 16 and click **Magnification** or **Reduction**.

THIS CHAPTER covers how to change display sizes, how to display a picture in two windows simultaneously, how to switch screen display modes, and how to move a picture in its window.

You can display an entire picture within its window, or magnify a detail of a picture to modify individual pixels. The display size is indicated as a ratio in the title bar (**Figure 1**). The display size can range from a minimum of 1:16 (reduced 16 times) to a maximum of 16:1 (enlarged 16 times). The display size of a picture does not affect its printout size.

To modify the display size via the Window menu:

Choose Zoom In from the Window menu (or hold down Command (⌘) and press "**+**") to magnify the picture (**Figure 2**).

or

Choose Zoom Out from the Window menu (or hold down Command (⌘) and press "**–**") to reduce the display size.

or

Choose Zoom Factor from the Window menu, enter a number between 1 and 16, click Magnification or Reduction, then click OK (**Figure 3**).

To modify the display size via the Zoom tool:

1. Click the Zoom tool (**Figure 4**).

2. Click on the picture or drag a marquee across an area to magnify that area (**Figure 5**).

or

Hold down Option and click to reduce the display size (**Figure 6**).

or

Click Zoom 1:1 on the Zoom Tool Options palette to display the picture in 1:1 view (**Figure 7**).

or

Click Zoom to Screen to display the entire picture in the largest possible size that will fit on your screen.

✔ Tips

■ Click Never Resize Windows on the Zoom Tool Options palette to prevent the document window from resizing when you use the Window menu commands.

■ A picture's display size equals its actual size only when the display ratio is 1:1 and the picture resolution and monitor resolution are 72 ppi.

■ To magnify the display size when another tool is selected or a dialog box with a Preview option is open, hold down Command (⌘) and Space bar and click. To reduce the display size, hold down Option and Space bar and click.

*The **Zoom** tool.*

Figure 4.

Figure 5. *Click on the picture with the Zoom tool to enlarge the display size. Note the plus sign in the magnifying glass pointer.*

Figure 6. *Hold down* **Option** *and click on the picture with the Zoom tool to reduce the display size. Note the minus sign in the magnifying glass pointer.*

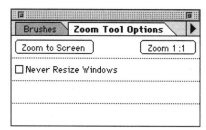

Figure 7. *The **Zoom Tool Options** palette.*

The number of pictures that can be open at the same time depends on available RAM and Scratch disk space. You can open the same picture in two windows simultaneously: one in a large display size, such as 4:1, to edit a detail and the other in a smaller display size, such as 1:1, to view the whole image.

To display a picture in two windows:

1. Open a picture.

2. Choose New Window from the Window menu (**Figures 8-9**). The same picture will appear in a second window.

3. *Optional:* Reposition either window by dragging its title bar, and/or resize either window by dragging its resize box.

✔ Tip

■ Leave the picture in RGB Color mode in one document window and choose CMYK Preview from the Mode menu for the same picture in a second document window.

Figure 8. Choose *New Window* from the *Window* menu.

Figure 9. A picture displayed in two windows simultaneously: one in a large display size for editing, the other in a smaller display size for previewing.

Display a Picture in Two Windows

To change the screen display mode:

Click the left display mode icon on the Toolbox to display the picture, menu bar, scroll bars on the document window, and Finder (Desktop). This is the Standard mode (**Figure 10**).

or

Click the center icon to display the picture and menu bar, but no scroll bars or Finder. The area around the picture will be gray (**Figure 11**).

or

Click the right icon to display the picture, but no menu bar, scroll bars, or Finder. The area around the picture will be black.

✔ Tips

■ Press Tab to hide the Toolbox and any open palettes; press Tab again to display the Toolbox and previously open palettes.

■ Use the Hand tool to move the picture in its window when the scroll bars are hidden and the picture is magnified (**Figure 11**). Hold down the Space bar to use the Hand tool while another tool is selected.

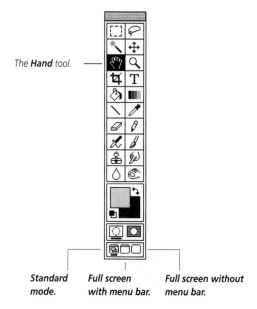

*The **Hand** tool.*

Standard mode.   Full screen with menu bar.   Full screen without menu bar.

Figure 10. Display modes.

Figure 11. Full screen with menu bar mode.

Note: If the scroll bars are not active, the entire picture is displayed, and there is no need to move it.

To move a picture in its window:

Click the up or down scroll arrow (**Figure 12**).

or

Move a scroll box to move the picture more quickly.

or

Click the Hand tool, then drag the picture.

✔ Tips

■ Double-click the Hand tool to fit the picture in the largest document window your monitor accommodates.

■ Hold down Space bar to to use the Hand tool while another tool is selected.

Move the picture in the window with the **Hand** tool.

— Click a *Scroll arrow*.

— Move a *Scroll box*.

Figure 12.

YOU CAN USE any Photoshop selection tool — Marquee, Lasso, or Magic Wand — to isolate an area of a picture (**Figure 1**). When a command, such as a filter, is applied to a selection, only the selection is affected — the rest of the picture is protected. A selection is defined by a moving marquee. Some Image menu commands are available only when an area is selected.

The creation of selections is covered in this chapter, including using the Marquee tool to create rectangular or elliptical selections, the Lasso tool to create irregular or polygonal selections, and the Magic Wand tool and Color Range command to select areas by color. Other topics include creating a frame selection and deselecting a selection.

The selections covered in this chapter are non-floating — they contain a layer's underlying pixels. If a non-floating selection is moved on the background layer, the exposed area is covered with the Background color. If a non-floating selection is moved on any other layer, the exposed area will be transparent.

Note: Make all your modifications to a selection before deselecting it, because it is very difficult to precisely reselect an area.

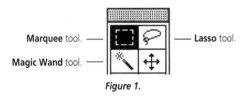

Marquee tool. — — Lasso tool.

Magic Wand tool. —

Figure 1.

*Figure 2. Choose **All** from the **Select** menu.*

To select an entire picture:

Choose All from the Select Menu
or
Hold down Command (⌘) and press "A" (**Figure 2**). A marquee will surround the picture.

To create a rectangular or elliptical selection:

1. For a multi-layer picture, choose a target layer. *(See page 91)*

2. Double-click the Marquee tool (**Figure 3**).

The **Marquee** tool. —

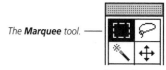

Figure 3.

3. Choose Rectangular or Elliptical from the Shape pop-up menu on the Marquee Options palette (**Figure 4**).

4. *Optional:* To specify the dimensions of the selection, choose Fixed Size from the Style pop-up menu on the Marquee Options palette, then enter values in the Width and Height fields.

To specify the width-to-height ratio of the selection, choose Constrained Aspect Ratio from the Style pop-up menu, then enter values in the Width and Height fields. Enter the same number in both fields to create a circle or a square.

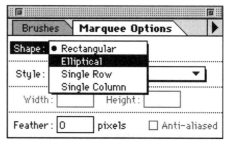

*Figure 4. Choose **Rectangular** or **Elliptical** from the **Shape** pop-up menu on the **Marquee Options** palette.*

5. *Optional:* To soften the edges of the selection, enter a number in the Feather field.

6. If you entered Fixed Size values, just click on the picture. For any other Style, drag diagonally. A marquee will appear (**Figures 5-6**).

✔ Tips

■ As you drag the mouse, the dimensions of the selection will be indicated in the W and H fields on the Info palette. (If the W and H fields are not displayed, choose Palette Options from the Info palette command menu and check the Show Mouse Coordinates box.)

■ To drag from the center of a selection, hold down Option and drag. Release the mouse, then release Option.

■ Hold down Shift while dragging to create a square or a circular selection. Release the mouse, then release Shift.

Figure 5. Drag diagonally to create a rectangular selection.

(Detail)

Figure 6. Drag diagonally to create an elliptical selection.

——— The **Lasso** tool.

Figure 7.

To create an irregular selection:

1. For a multi-layer picture, choose a target layer. *(See page 91)*

2. Double-click the Lasso tool (**Figure 7**).

3. *Optional:* To soften the edges of the selection, enter a number in the Feather field.

4. Drag around an area of the layer. When you release the mouse, the open ends of the selection will join automatically (**Figure 8**).

Figure 8. Drag around the area to be selected.

To create a polygonal selection:

1. For a multi-layer picture, choose a target layer. *(See page 91)*

2. Click the Lasso tool (**Figure 7**).

3. To create straight sides, hold down Option and click to create points. The open ends of the selection will join automatically when you release Option (**Figure 9**).

✔ Tip

■ To create a curved segment while drawing a polygonal selection, press and drag while continuing to hold down Option. Release the mouse before clicking again to create the next straight side.

*Figure 9. Hold down **Option** and click to create points.*

Irregular or Polygonal Selection

When you click on a layer pixel with the Magic Wand tool, a selection is created that includes adjacent pixels of a similar shade or color. After clicking once with the Magic Wand, you can then add non-adjacent pixels to the selection using the Similar command.

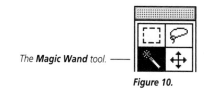

*The **Magic Wand** tool.* ——

Figure 10.

To select by color (Magic Wand):

1. For a multi-layer picture, choose a target layer. *(See page 91)*

2. Double-click the Magic Wand tool (**Figure 10**).

3. Check the Sample Merged box on the Magic Wand Options palette to include all currently displayed layers in the selection.
or
Uncheck the Sample Merged box to select only pixels on the target layer. (Only pixels on the target layer can be edited, but you can apply changes to the same selection through successive target layers.)

4. Click on a shade or color on the target layer (**Figure 13-14**).

5. *Optional:* To enlarge the selection, choose Grow from the Select menu one or more times (**Figure 11**) or hold down Command (⌘) and press "G."

6. *Optional:* To select other, non-contiguous, areas of similar color or shade on the layer, choose Similar from the Select menu.

7. *Optional:* To specify a different Tolerance range, modify the number in the Tolerance field on the Magic Wand Options palette, then click on the picture again (**Figures 12-14**).
(See "Tolerance" on the following page)

✔ Tips

■ Choose Undo from the Edit menu to undo the last command or selection.

■ To quickly select all the pixels on a target layer, use the Command (⌘)-

Figure 11. *Choose **Grow** or **Similar** from the **Select** menu.*

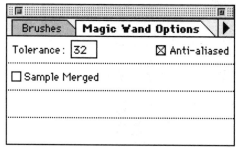

Figure 12. *Enter a number between 0 and 255 in the **Tolerance** field on the **Magic Wand Options** palette.*

Select by Color

Option-T shortcut. (Or choose Load Selection from the Select menu, choose "[layer name] Transparency" from the Channel pop-up menu, then click OK.)
or

If you move selected objects on a layer, you may leave leftover pixels behind from the edge of the object. To prevent this, use the following method to create your selection. Choose the Magic Wand tool, uncheck the Anti-aliased box on the Magic Wand tool Options palette, click on a transparent area in the document window, then choose Inverse from the Select menu.

■ To add to a selection with the Magic Wand tool, hold down Shift and click outside the selection. To subtract from a selection, hold down Command (⌘) and click inside the selection. You can also use another selection tool, such as the Lasso, to add to or subtract from a selection. *(See page 77)*

■ To Expand or Contract the selection, choose either command from the Modify submenu under the Select menu.

Tolerance

To increase or decrease the range of shades or colors the Magic Wand tool selects, enter a number between 0 and 255 in the Tolerance field on the Magic Wand tool Options palette (**Figures 12-14**).

For example, with a Tolerance of 32, the Magic Wand will select within a range of 16 shades below and 16 shades above the shade on which it is clicked. Enter 1 to select one color or shade.

To gradually narrow the range of shades or colors selected with the Magic Wand tool, modify the Tolerance value between clicks.

Figure 13. *A Magic Wand selection using a Tolerance of 16.*

Figure 14. *A Magic Wand selection using a Tolerance of 40.*

The **Color Range** command selects from all the layers, but only the target layer will be available for editing.

To select by color (Color Range):

1. For a multi-layer picture, choose a target layer. *(See page 91)*

2. Choose Color Range from the Select menu (**Figure 15**).

3. Choose from the Select pop-up menu in the Color Range dialog box. You can limit the selection to a color range (Reds, Yellows, etc.), to a luminosity range (Highlights, Midtones, or Shadows), or to Sampled Colors (shades or colors you'll click on with the Color Range eyedropper) (**Figure 16**).

4. Choose a preview option for the document window from the Selection Preview pop-up menu. Choose Quick Mask to preview in the original picture colors.

5. If you chose Sampled Colors in step 3, click in the preview window or on the picture with the eyedropper cursor to sample colors in the picture.

6. *Optional:* Move the Fuzziness slider to the right to increase the range of colors or shades selected, or move it to the left to decrease the range.

7. *Optional:* If you chose Sampled Colors in step 3, hold down Shift and click with the eyedropper cursor on the picture or in the preview box to add more colors or shades to the selection. Hold down Command (⌘) to remove colors or shades from the selection. Or, click the "+" or "-" eyedropper icon button in the Color Range dialog box and click on the picture or in the preview box without holding down Shift or Command.

8. Click OK or press Return.

(Tips on the following page)

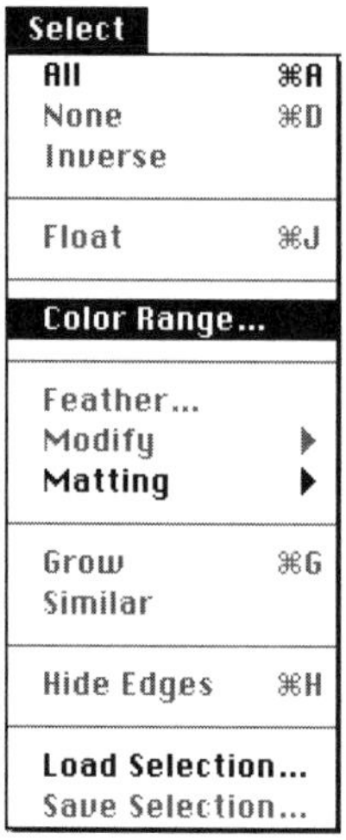

*Figure 15. Choose **Color Range** from the **Select** menu.*

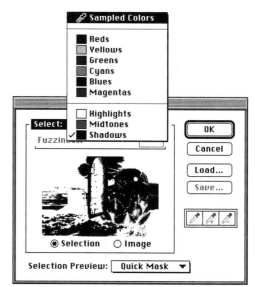

*Figure 16. In the **Color Range** dialog box, choose a color or luminosity range from the **Select** pop-up menu, or choose **Sampled Colors** to sample colors from the picture using the Color Range eyedropper, and choose a **Selection Preview** method. Move the **Fuzziness** slider to the left or to the right to reduce or expand the range of colors selected.*

Select by Color

✔ Tips

- Click the Selection button to preview the selection. Click the Image button to display the picture in the preview box. Use this option if the picture extends beyond the edges of your monitor — the entire picture will be displayed in the preview box to facilitate sampling.

- If you select an area of your picture first using the Marquee tool or Lasso tool, the Color Range command will select only from within that selection.

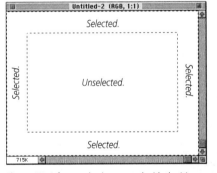

Figure 17. *A frame selection created with the Marquee tool.*

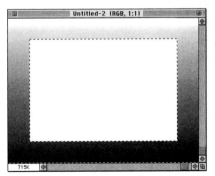

Figure 18. *A gradient was applied to a frame selection to produce this illustration.*

To create a frame selection:

1. For a multi-layer picture, choose a target layer. *(See page 92)*

2. Double-click the Marquee tool.

3. Choose Rectangular or Elliptical from the Shape pop-up menu on the Marquee Options palette.

4. Press and drag to create a selection (**Figure 17**).

5. Hold down Command (⌘) and drag to create a smaller selection inside the first selection (**Figure 18**).

Create a Frame Selection

To deselect a selection:

With any tool selected, choose None from the Select Menu, or hold down Command (⌘) and press "D" (**Figure 19**).

or

Click anywhere on the layer with the Marquee or Lasso tool (**Figure 20**).

or

Click **inside** the selection with the Magic Wand tool. If you click outside the selection with the Magic Wand, you will create an additional selection.

✔ Tip

■ Deselect only when you have finished modifying a selection, because it will be difficult to reselect the same area of pixels. If you unintentionally deselect, choose Undo from the Edit Menu immediately.

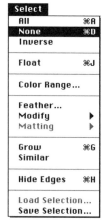

Figure 19. *Choose* **None** *from the* **Select** *menu.*

Figure 20. *Click* **outside** *a selection to deselect it with the* **Marquee** *tool or* **Lasso** *tool. Click* **inside** *a selection to deselect it with the* **Magic Wand** *tool.*

Deselect a Selection

RESHAPE SELECTIONS

I N THIS CHAPTER you will learn how to move and how to hide a selection marquee. You will also learn how to flip, rotate, resize, add to, subtract from, feather, defringe, and smooth a selection, and how to create a vignette.

Note: Read Chapter 5 first if you are not familiar with how the selection tools work.

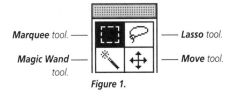

Marquee *tool.* — *Lasso* tool.

Magic Wand — *Move* tool.
tool.

Figure 1.

To move a selection marquee:

1. Click any selection tool (Marquee, Lasso, or Magic Wand) or the Move tool (**Figure 1**).

2. Hold down Command (⌘) and Option and press and drag from inside the selection (**Figure 2**).

✔ Tip

■ To determine the exact position of a marquee, position the cursor directly over it and note the X and Y coordinates on the Info palette. (If the X/Y coordinates are not displayed on the palette, choose Palette Options from the Info palette command menu and check the Show Mouse Coordinates box.)

Figure 2. *A marquee being moved.*

To hide a selection marquee:

Choose Hide Edges from the Select menu (**Figure 3**). The selection will remain active.

✔ Tips

- ■ To display the selection marquee again, choose Show Edges from the Select menu.

- ■ To verify that a selection is still active, press on the Select menu. Most commands will be available if a selection is active.

- ■ You can choose the Hide Edges command while many of the Image menu and Filter menu dialog boxes are open.

Figure 3. *Choose* **Hide Edges** *from the* **Select** *menu.*

To flip a selection:

Choose Horizontal from the Flip sub-menu under the Image menu to flip a selection left to right (**Figures 4-6**).
or
Choose Vertical to flip a selection upside-down, creating a mirror image.

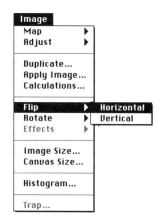

Figure 4. *Choose* **Horizontal** *or* **Vertical** *from the* **Flip** *submenu under the* **Image** *menu.*

Figure 5. *The original picture with an area selected.*

Figure 6. *The selection flipped horizontally.*

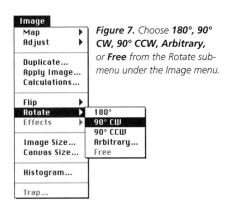

*Figure 7. Choose **180°, 90° CW, 90° CCW, Arbitrary,** or **Free** from the Rotate sub-menu under the Image menu.*

To rotate a selection a preset amount:

Choose (180°, 90° CW (clockwise), or 90° CCW (counterclockwise) from the Rotate submenu under the Image Menu (**Figure 7**).

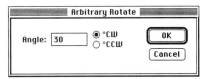

*Figure 8. Enter a number in the **Angle** field and click °**CW** or °**CCW** in the **Arbitrary Rotate** dialog box.*

To rotate a selection by specifying a number:

1. Choose Arbitrary from the Rotate submenu under the Image Menu (**Figure 7**).

2. Enter a number between -359.9° and 359.9° in the Angle field (**Figure 8**).

3. Click °CW (clockwise) or °CCW (counterclockwise).

4. Click OK or press Return (**Figure 9**).

Figure 9. A floating selection rotated 30°.

To free rotate a selection:

1. Choose Free from the Rotate submenu under the Image Menu (**Figure 7**). Corner handles will appear.

2. Drag a handle in a circular direction with the arrow cursor (**Figure 10**).

3. To accept the new rotation angle, click on the selection with the gavel cursor.

✔ Tip

■ To restore the original angle, click outside the selection with the cancel cursor. The selection will remain active.

Figure 10. Drag a corner box, then click on the selection to accept the new angle.

Rotate a Selection

To resize a selection manually:

1. Choose Scale from the Effects sub-menu under the Image Menu. Corner handles will appear (**Figure 11**).

2. Drag a corner handle (**Figure 12**).

3. Position the cursor over the selection and click with the gavel cursor (**Figure 13**).

✔ Tips

■ Hold down Shift while dragging a corner handle to preserve the height-to-width ratio of the selection.

■ To restore the selection's original size, position the cursor outside it and click with the cancel cursor. The selection will remain active.

■ Choose a Background color from the picture before scaling a selection, so any exposed area will be filled with a matching color. *(See pages 112-114)*

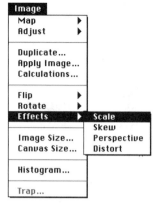

Figure 11. *Choose* **Scale** *from the* **Effects** *submenu under the* **Image** *menu.*

Figure 12. *Drag a corner handle.*

Gavel cursor.

Figure 13. *Click inside the selection with the gavel cursor.*

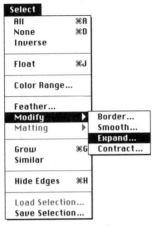

Select		
All	⌘A	
None	⌘D	
Inverse		
Float	⌘J	
Color Range...		
Feather...		
Modify ▶	Border...	
Matting ▶	Smooth...	
	Expand...	
Grow ⌘G	Contract...	
Similar		
Hide Edges ⌘H		
Load Selection...		
Save Selection...		

Figure 14. *Choose* **Expand** *or* **Contract** *from the* **Modify** *submenu under the* **Select** *menu.*

Figure 15. *Hold down Shift and drag with the Marquee tool to define an additional selection area.*

Figure 16. *Hold down Command (⌘) and drag with the Lasso tool around an area to be subtracted.*

To resize a selection using a command:

1. Choose Expand or Contract from the Modify submenu under the Select menu (**Figure 14**).

2. Enter a number of pixels in the Expand By or Contract By field.

3. Click OK or press Return.

To add to a selection:

Double-click the Marquee tool, choose Rectangular or Elliptical from the Shape pop-up menu on the Options palette, then hold down Shift and drag to define an additional selection area (**Figure 15**).
or
Click the Lasso tool. Position the cursor over the selection, then hold down Shift and drag to define an additional selection area.
or
Click the Magic Wand tool, then hold down Shift and click on any unselected area.

✔ Tip

■ If the additional selection overlaps the original selection, it will become part of the new, larger selection. If the addition does not overlap the original selection, a second, separate selection will be created.

To subtract from a selection:

Double-click the Marquee tool, choose Rectangular or Elliptical from the Shape pop-up menu on the Options palette, then hold down Command (⌘) and drag over the area to be subtracted.
or
Click the Lasso tool, then hold down Command (⌘) and drag around the area to be subtracted (**Figure 16**).
or
Click the Magic Wand tool, then hold down Command (⌘) and click on the area of shade or color to be subtracted.

Resize/Add To/Subtract from a Selection

Apply the **Feather** command to fade the edge of a selection a specified number of pixels inward and outward from the marquee. For example, a Feather Radius of 5 will create a feather area 10 pixels wide.

Note: The feather will not appear until the selection is modified with a painting tool, copied, pasted, moved, or filled, or a filter or Image menu command is applied to it.

To feather a selection:

1. Choose Feather from the Select menu (**Figure 17**).

2. Enter a number between 1 and 250 in the Feather Radius field (**Figure 18**).

3. Click OK or press Return (**Figures 19-20**).

✔ Tip

■ To specify a Feather Radius for a selection before it is created, double-click the Marquee or Lasso tool and enter a number in the Feather field on the Options palette.

Figure 17. *Choose* **Feather** *from the* **Select** *menu.*

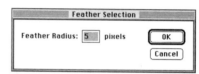

Figure 18. *Enter a number between 1 and 250 in the* **Feather Radius** *field in the* **Feather Selection** *dialog box.*

Figure 19. *A selection copy with a Feather Radius of 0.*

Figure 20. *The same selection copy with a Feather Radius of 5 pixels.*

Figure 21. *An elliptical area of this picture was selected.*

To vignette a picture:

1. Choose white as the Background color. *(See pages 112-114)*

2. Click the Marquee tool.

3. On the Marquee Tool Options palette, choose Rectangular or Elliptical from the Shape pop-up menu. *and* Enter 15 or 20 in the Feather field.

4. Select an area of a picture (**Figure 21**).

5. Choose Inverse from the Select menu.

6. Press Delete (**Figures 22-23**).

✔ Tip

■ If you create a vignette on one layer in a multi-layer picture, the vignette will appear to fade into the layer or layers below it. Uncheck the Preserve Transparency box on the Layers palette before creating the vignette (**Figure 24**).

Figure 22. *Auntie Alias, Uncle Fill and other relatives.*

Figure 23. *Another vignette.*

Figure 24. *A vignette layer on top of a pattern layer.*

Vignette a Picture

Use the **Defringe** command to blend pixels on the edge of a moved or pasted selection with pixel colors from just inside the edge to eliminate a noticeable "seam." You can specify a width in pixels for the Defringe area.

To defringe a selection:

1. With the selection still floating, choose Defringe from the Matting submenu under the Select menu (**Figure 25**).

2. Enter a number in the Width field. Try 1, 2 or 3 first (**Figure 26**). The edge of the selection may lose definition if you specify too high a Width.

3. *Optional:* Move the selection.
   and/or
   Apply any Image or Filter menu command.

4. Choose None from the Select menu (**Figures 27-28**).

✔ Tip

■ You can also Defringe any layer other than the Background without creating a selection.

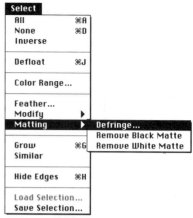

*Figure 25. Choose **Defringe** from the **Matting** submenu under the **Select** menu.*

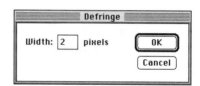

*Figure 26. Enter 1, 2, or 3 in the **Width** field in the **Defringe** dialog box.*

Figure 27. A pasted image before choosing the Defringe command. Note the white edge around the hat and around the boy's head.

Figure 28. After applying the Defringe command.

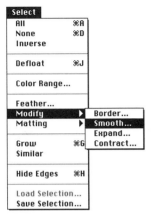

Figure 29. *Choose* **Smooth** *from the* **Modify** *submenu under the* **Select** *menu.*

The **Smooth** command adds pixels to a selection from within a Sample Radius that you specify. Use this command to add pixels on a layer that are within or on the border of a selection but were not originally included in that selection.

To smooth a selection:

1. Choose Smooth from the Modify submenu under the Select menu (**Figure 29**).

2. Enter a number between 1 and 16 in the Sample Radius field (**Figure 30**). The larger the Sample Radius, the more unselected pixels will be added to the selection.

3. Click OK or press Return (**Figures 31a-b**).

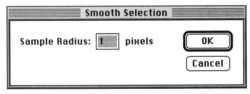

Figure 30. *Enter a number in the* **Sample Radius** *field in the* **Smooth Selection** *dialog box.*

Figure 31a. *The original Background selection made with the Magic Wand tool.*

Figure 31b. *The selection after applying the Smooth command with a Sample Radius of 3.*

To switch the selected and unselected areas:

Choose Inverse from the Select menu (**Figures 32-34**).

✔ Tips

■ Choose Inverse again to switch back.

■ If a shape has a flat color background behind it, you'll be able to select it easily. Choose the Magic Wand tool, enter 5 in the Tolerance field on the Magic Wand Options palette, click on the flat color background to select it entirely, then choose Inverse from the Select menu to select the shape.

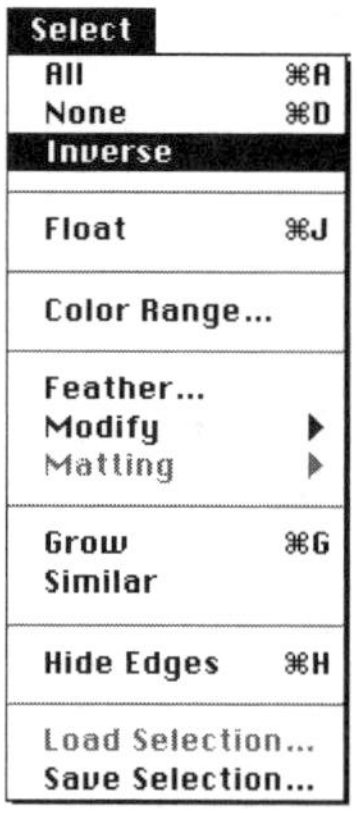

Figure 32. *Choose* **Inverse** *from the* **Select** *menu.*

Figure 33. *The background selected with the* **Magic Wand** *tool.*

Figure 34. *After choosing the* **Inverse** *command, the girl is selected.*

Switch Selected/Unselected Areas

MOVE SELECTIONS

THIS CHAPTER covers how to move selections using the Move tool and using the Clipboard commands — Cut, Copy and Paste and Paste Into.

There are two types of selections: non-floating and floating. A **non-floating selection** is created when the Marquee, Lasso, or Magic Wand tool or the Color Range command is used to select underlying pixels on one or more layers. If you Delete or Cut selected non-floating pixels from the Background layer, the area left behind will automatically fill with the currently selected Background color. If you remove pixels from any other layer, the area left behind will be transparent if the Preserve Transparency box on the Layers palette is unchecked, or will be filled with the Background color if the Preserve Transparency box is checked.

A **floating selection** is created when Type is created, the Float command or a Paste command is executed, or when a selection is dragged with the Option key held down. Pixels in a floating selection are suspended above the former target layer or above a new target layer. A floating selection will be listed on the Layers palette as a new temporary layer called "Floating Selection."

You can modify a floating selection without changing pixels in the underlying layer. Once you are satisfied with the way the floating selection looks, you can merge the floating pixels into the underlying layer or you can make the floating selection into its own layer and leave pixels on the underlying layer unchanged. (Or, of course, you can press Delete to remove the floating selection altogether.)

(Instructions for moving a selected area of a layer or a whole selected layer to another document are on page 96)

Floating and Non-Floating Selections

To move a selection:

1. Choose any selection tool (Marquee, Lasso, or Magic Wand) or the Move tool (**Figure 1**).

2. *Optional:* If the selection is on a layer other than the Background and the Preserve Transparency box is checked on the Layers palette, choose a Background color for the area that will be exposed. *(See pages 112-114)* You'll also need to choose a Background color if the selection is on the Background layer (unless your picture was created with a Transparent Background).

3. Position the cursor over the selection, then drag. The selection marquee and its contents will move together (**Figures 2-3**).

✔ Tips

- ■ Press any arrow key to move the selection in 1-pixel increments.

- ■ Hold down Command (⌘) to temporarily use the Move tool while any tool other than a selection tool is highlighted.

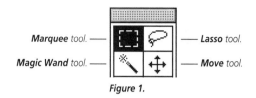

Marquee tool. —— | —— **Lasso** tool.
Magic Wand tool. —— | —— **Move** tool.

Figure 1.

Figure 2. *Drag a selection.*

Figure 3. *The selection in a new position.*

Move a Selection

*Figure 4. Hold down **Option** and drag a selection.*

Figure 5. A copy of the selection is moved.

```
Select
  All            ⌘A
  None           ⌘D
  Inverse
─────────────────────
  Float          ⌘J
─────────────────────
  Color Range...
─────────────────────
  Feather...
  Modify         ▶
  Matting        ▶
─────────────────────
  Grow           ⌘G
  Similar
─────────────────────
  Show Edges     ⌘H
─────────────────────
  Load Selection...
  Save Selection...
```

*Figure 6. Choose **Float** from the **Select** menu.*

To float a selection:

1. Click any selection tool (Marquee, Lasso, or Magic Wand) or the Move tool (**Figure 1**).

2. Make sure the Preserve Transparency box on the Layers palette is unchecked.

3. To move the selection and float it at the same time, position the cursor over the selection, then hold down Option and drag (**Figures 4-5**).

or

To float the selecion without moving it, choose Float from the Select menu (or hold down Command (⌘) and press "J") (**Figure 6**).

A new temporary layer called "Floating Selection" will appear on the Layers palette above the target layer name.

✔ Tips

■ Choose Defloat from the Select menu to merge the floating selection into the underlying layer, but keep the selection active. Click outside the selection to merge it into the underlying layer and deselect it. You can also restack a floating selection by dragging it up or down on the Layers palette so it floats above a different layer.

■ To delete the floating selection, choose Clear from the Edit Menu or press Delete.

■ Move the Opacity slider on the Layers palette to the left to make the Floating Selection less opaque.

Float a Selection

About the Clipboard

You can use the Cut and Copy commands to save a selection to a temporary storage area called the Clipboard. You then can use a Paste command (Paste or Paste Into) to paste the Clipboard contents onto the same layer, onto another layer, or in another picture. The Cut, Copy, and Paste Into commands are available only when an area of a layer is selected.

When a Paste command is chosen, the Clipboard contents appear in a temporary layer called Floating Selection. A floating selection can be repositioned and modified without affecting the underlying pixels in the layer below it.

To remove a floating selection, choose Cut or Clear from the Edit menu. The underlying layer's pixels will not be modified. If you use the Cut command, the selection will be placed on the Clipboard. The Clear command doesn't use the Clipboard.

Once deselected, a floating selection becomes part of the layer, replacing underlying pixels. If you Cut or Clear a nonfloating selection, the selection is removed from the layer and the exposed area fills with the Background color. If you remove pixels from any other layer, the area left behind will be transparent if the Preserve Transparency box on the Layers palette is unchecked, or will be filled with the Background color if the Preserve Transparency box is checked.

The Clipboard can contain only one selection at a time, which is replaced each time Cut or Copy is chosen. The same Clipboard contents can be pasted an unlimited number of times. The Clipboard will empty when you quit Photoshop, and if you switch to another application unless Export Clipboard is checked in the More Preferences dialog box. (Choose General from the Preferences submenu under the File menu, then check More in the General Preferences dialog box).

MORE ABOUT THE PASTE COMMANDS

The **Paste** command produces a temporary layer called **Floating Selection**. Parts of a floating, pasted selection may extend beyond the document window. The extended areas will not be deleted until you edit the layer. (To create a new layer, choose Make Layer from the Layers palette command menu or drag the Floating Selection layer over the New Layer icon at the bottom of the Layers palette.)

■

The **Paste Layer** command pastes the Clipboard contents into a new layer and preserves any areas that extend beyond the selection until you edit the new layer.

■

If you deselect a floating selection, it will merge with the layer below it, but the parts that extend beyond the selection will be preserved. You can move the entire layer to reveal the extended areas, and if you save your document, the extended areas will be saved with it. **If you edit the layer, however, the extended areas will be cropped.**

■

If you select another layer, the floating selection will merge with layer below it and the selection marquee will stay active, though now it will surround pixels on the new target layer. Deselect the marquee, so you don't confuse it with a marquee on another layer.

Clipboard Tips

■ If the selection on the Clipboard is large, the remaining available memory for processing is reduced. To increase the available memory, Cut or Copy a smaller selection when you're finished using the Clipboard.

■ Before using the Clipboard commands, compare the dimensions of the image to be Cut or Copied with the dimensions of the layer onto which it will be pasted (the "destination layer"). If the image on the Clipboard is larger than the destination layer (or larger than the selection on the destination layer), the Clipboard image will extend beyond the document window. You can use the Move tool to reposition the Floating Selection.

■ Follow the instructions on page 90 to paste into a smaller picture.

■ The size of an image may also change when pasted, because it is rendered in the resolution of the destination layer. If the resolution of the destination layer is higher than that of the image you are pasting, the Clipboard image will become smaller when pasted. Conversely, if the resolution of the destination layer is lower than the resolution of the Clipboard image, the Clipboard image will be enlarged when pasted. You can use the Image Size dialog box to choose the same resolution (and dimensions, if desired) for both pictures. (*See page 44*)

■ The opacity and mode of a pasted area is controlled by the settings of the layer it is pasted on.

■ A pasted image, like any other image, may become blurry if you enlarge it using the Scale command.

■ The dimensions in the New dialog box conform automatically to the dimensions of the current contents of the Clipboard.

Clipboard Tips

To copy and paste a selection:

1. Select an area of a picture (**Figure 7**). To feather the selection, enter a number in the Feather field on the Options palette.

2. Choose Copy from the Edit menu (**Figure 8**).

3. Choose None from the Select menu (**Figure 9**).

4. Leave the same layer selected, or choose a different layer, or choose a target layer in another document.

5. Choose Paste from the Edit menu. The Clipboard contents will appear as a floating selection layer above the current target layer (**Figure 10**). **Don't** select another layer name, or the floating selection will merge with the layer directly below it.

6. *Optional:* Defringe the selection. *(See page 80)*

7. *Optional:* To subtract from the selection, click any selection tool, then hold down Command (⌘) and drag around the area you wish to subtract.

8. *Optional:* Modify the selection: Move it, change its opacity and/or mode using the Layers palette, or apply any command or filter.

9. To merge the floating selection with the layer below it, choose None from the Select menu (**Figure 9**).

   or

   Hold down Command (⌘) and press "D."

✔ Tip

- ■ If you choose Cut instead of Copy for Step 2, the selection will be cut from the picture.

Figure 7. *Select an area of a picture.*

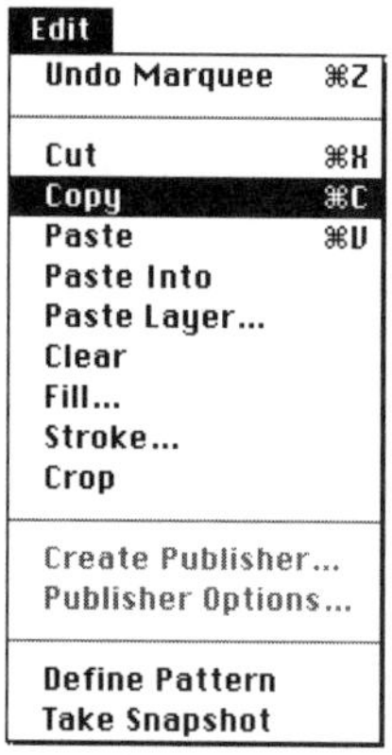

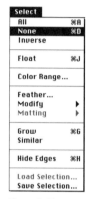

Figure 8. *Choose* **Copy** *from the* **Edit** *menu.*

Figure 9. *Choose* **None** *from the* **Select** *menu.*

Figure 10. *The pasted image appears as a floating selection.*

Figure 11. *Select an area of a picture, then choose Copy from the Edit menu.*

Figure 12. *The still life image was pasted into a selected area of the landscape image.*

Choose Paste Into to paste the Clipboard contents into a selection. The active marquee will then surround the Clipboard image. The pasted image can be repositioned within the boundary of the previous selection or otherwise modified.

To paste into a selection:

1. Select an area of a layer (**Figure 11**). *(See pages 66-70)* To feather the selection, enter a number in the Feather field on the Options palette.

2. Choose Copy from the Edit menu (**Figure 8**).

3. Leave the same layer selected, or choose a different layer, or choose a layer in another document.

4. Select an area (or areas) into which the Clipboard image will be pasted.

5. Choose Paste Into from the Edit menu (**Figure 12**). Beware: If you choose a different target layer, the floating selection will automatically merge with the layer directly below it.

6. *Optional:* To subtract from the selection, click the Lasso tool, then hold down Command (⌘) and drag around the area you wish to subtract.

7. *Optional:* Drag the selection to a new location within the original selected area or use any other feature to modify the selection.

8. Choose None from the Select menu (**Figure 9**)
   or
   Highlight a different layer on the Layers palette.

Paste Into a Selection

Note: Read page 87 before proceeding with the following instructions.

To paste into a smaller picture:

1. Click on the destination picture, then hold down Option and press and hold on the Sizes bar in the lower left corner of the document window. Jot down the picture's dimensions.

2. Create a selection on another (larger) picture. *(See pages 66-70)*

3. Choose Copy from the Edit menu (**Figure 13**).

4. Choose New from the File menu.

5. Enter a name in the Name field. From the Mode pop-menu, choose the mode of the picture from which the selection was copied. The Width and Height and Resolution will automatically conform to the settings of the Clipboard image.

6. Click OK or press Return.

7. Choose Paste from the Edit menu.

8. Choose Image Size from the Image menu.

9. Enter smaller numbers than the dimensions of the destination picture (Step 1, above) in the Width and Height fields (**Figure 14**). Make sure the File Size box is unchecked so the resolution doesn't change.

10. Click OK or press Return.

11. If you deselected the pasted image, Choose All from the Select menu (**Figure 15**).

12. Choose Copy from the Edit menu.

13. Click in the destination picture.

14. Follow steps 5-9 on page 88 or steps 4-8 on page 89.

Figure 13. *The **Edit** menu.*

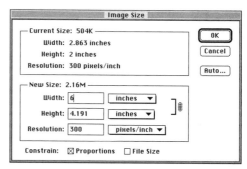

Figure 14. *In the **Image Size** dialog box, enter smaller numbers in the **Width** and **Height** fields and make sure the **File Size** box is unchecked.*

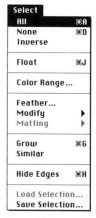

Figure 15. *Choose **All** from the **Select** menu.*

☞ **FOR THIS CHAPTER,** you'll need to open the **Layers palette.**

ALL NEW DOCUMENTS automatically have a Background layer, which can be White, the current Background color, or Transparent. Other layers can be added on top of the Background layer at any time using the **Layers palette.** You can only edit one layer at a time, so you can easily modify one part of a picture without changing the other layers.

In this chapter you will learn to use the Layers palette to create a new layer, turn a floating selection into a layer, move a layer within a document or to another document, restack a layer, delete a layer, and hide a layer.

In Chapter 13, *More Layers,* you will learn to blend between layers, create and modify layer masks, link layers to move them as a unit, use layers as a clipping group, merge layers, and flatten layers.

Layers are listed on the palette from topmost to bottommost, with the Background layer at the bottom of the list. The **target layer,** which is the layer currently highlighted on the palette, is the only layer that can be edited. **Click on a layer name to highlight it.** The target layer name will be listed on the document window title bar.

Layers take up storage space, so when your picture is finished, you can merge or flatten all the layers into one.

Notes: Click Don't Flatten to preserve layers in a multi-layered document if you change its color mode.

Only the PhotoShop 3.0 file format supports multi-layer documents. If you save your document in any other file format, all the layers will automatically be flattened.

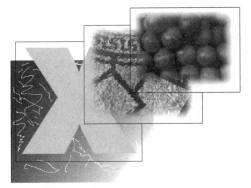

Figure 1. *Layers are like clear acetate sheets: opaque where there is imagery and transparent where there is no imagery.*

A document can have as many layers as memory and storage allow.

To create a new layer:

1. Choose New Layer from the Layers palette command menu (**Figure 2**).
or
Click the New Layers icon at the bottom of the palette.

Steps 2-4 are optional.

2. Enter a new name for the layer in the Name field (**Figure 3**).

3. Choose a different opacity and/or mode.

4. Click Group with Previous Layer to make the new layer a part of a clipping group. *(See page 152)*

5. Click OK or press Return. The new layer will appear directly above the previously highlighted layer.

✔ Tip

■ By default, a thumbnail of the layer is displayed next to the layer name. To change the size of the layer thumbnail, choose Palette Options from the Layers palette command menu, then click a different Thumbnail Size (**Figure 4**).

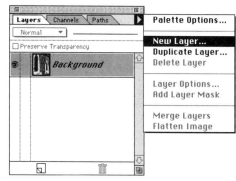

*Figure 2. Choose **New Layer** from the Layers palette command menu.*

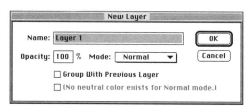

*Figure 3. The **New Layer** dialog box.*

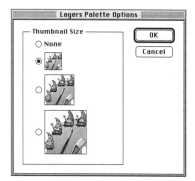

*Figure 4. You can click a different **Thumbnail Size** in the **Layers Palette Options** dialog box.*

*Figure 5. Before you add a new layer to your document, choose **Document Sizes** from the **Sizes** bar pop-up menu and note the current document size. Then note how much the file's storage size increases when you add a new layer. The picture in this figure contains three layers.*

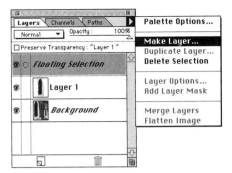

Figure 6. Choose **Make Layer** from the Layers palette command menu.

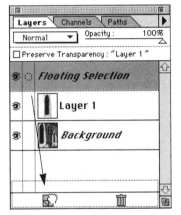

Figure 7. Or drag the **Floating Selection** layer over the **New Layer** icon.

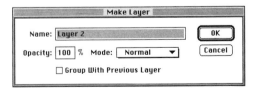

Figure 8. In the **Make Layer** dialog box, you can enter a new Name, change the Opacity prercentage, and choose a different Mode for the layer.

If you create a **floating selection** using the Paste or Float command or the Type tool, the selection will automatically be placed on a new temporary layer on top of the target layer (the layer currently highlighted on the Layers palette), and this layer will automatically be named "Floating Selection."

You can edit a floating selection, but if you are going to make extensive changes to it, it is best to place the floating selection on its own layer using the Layers palette, because once a floating selection is defloated or deselected or another layer name is highlighted, the floating selection will merge with the layer directly below it.

To turn a floating selection into a layer:

1. With a floating selection active in the document, choose Make Layer from the Layers palette command menu (**Figure 6**).

or

Drag the "Floating Selection" name over the New Layer icon on the Layers palette (**Figure 7**).

or

Double-click the floating layer name on the Layers palette.

Steps 2-4 are optional.

2. Enter a new name for the layer in the Name field (**Figure 8**).

3. Choose a different opacity and/or mode.

4. Click the Group with Previous Layer box to make the new layer a part of a clipping group. *(see page 152)*

5. Click OK or press Return.

To restack a layer:

1. Click on a layer name on the Layers palette.

2. Drag the layer name up or down on the palette, and release the mouse when a dark horizontal line appears under the layer name that you want to be on top of the one you're moving (**Figure 9**).

Figure 9. A layer being restacked.

To move a layer in the same document:

1. Click on a layer name on the Layers palette.

2. Choose the Move tool.

3. Drag the across the picture to move the target layer. The entire layer will move (**Figures 10a-b**).

✔ **Tips**

■ Press an arrow key to move a target layer one pixel at a time.

■ Any part of a layer other than the Background that is moved beyond the edge of the document will be saved with your document, but will be deleted if you modify pixels on the layer using an editing tool or an image editing command.

■ With the Move tool selected, hold down Command (⌘) and click on an object in the document window to quickly select that object's layer.

Figure 10a. The original picture.

Figure 10b. After moving the "cow toy" layer with the Move tool.

Restack a Layer, Move a Layer

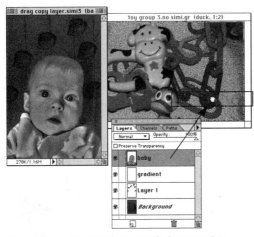

Figure 11. Choose a target layer. Drag the layer name into the destination document window.

Figure 12a. The destination document after dragging the "baby" layer name onto the picture.

To copy a layer to another document:

1. Open the document containing the layer you want to move and the document the layer is to be placed into (the "destination document").

2. Click in the source document window.

3. Click on the layer name you want to move on the Layers palette (**Figure 11**).

4. Drag the layer name from the Layers palette to the destination document window. The layer will appear where you release the mouse, and will be the topmost layer in the destination document (**Figures 12a-b**).

✔ Tip

■ If the dimensions of the layer being moved are larger than those of the destination document, the moved layer will extend beyond the edges of the destination document window. Use the Move tool to move the layer in the document window. The "hidden" parts will be saved with the document.

The parts of the layer beyond the edge of the destination document window will be saved with the document, but will be lost if you edit the layer or highlight another layer.

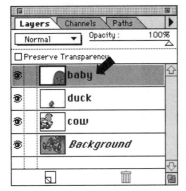

Figure 12b. The new layer name appears on the Layers palette, and is the topmost layer in the destination document.

Copy a Layer to Another Document

If you drag a whole selected layer or a selected area of a layer into another document window, you will create a floating selection — a selection that floats above the target layer.

Note: If you deselect a floating selection or highlight another layer name on the Layers palette, the floating selection will merge with the layer below it and you won't be able to move it independently.

To drag-and-drop a whole selected layer or a selected area to another document:

1. Open the document containing the layer or selection you want to move (the "source document") and the document the selection is to be moved to (the "destination document").

2. Click on the name of the layer on the Layers palette that you want to copy.

3. Select an area on the target layer.
or
Choose Select All from the Select menu.

4. *Optional:* Click in the destination document window, then click on the name of the layer on the Layers palette that you want the floating selection to appear on top of.

5. Choose the Move tool.

6. Click in the source document window. Drag the target layer or selection from the current document window to the destination document window (**Figure 13**). The layer or selection will be positioned where you release the mouse, and will be a temporary Floating Selection layer on top of the target layer in the destination document (**Figure 14**).

7. *Optional:* Use the Move tool to move the floating selection in the current document window.

8. *Optional:* Restack the floating selection among the layers *(see page 94).*

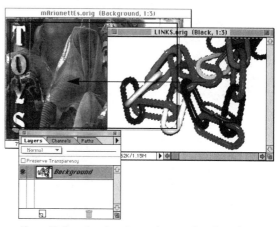

Figure 13. *Drag the selected target layer or selected area from the source document window into the destination document window.*

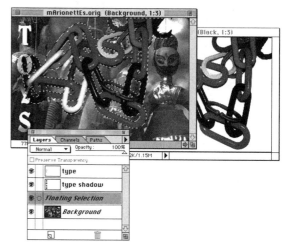

Figure 14. *The new layer or selection appears as a floating selection in the destination document window and is listed on the Layers palette.*

✔ **Tips**

■ If you highlight another layer, the floating selection will merge with the layer below it. If the selection marquee is still present, it is highlighting pixels on the new target layer.

■ To delete the temporary floating selection layer, drag the Floating Selection layer name over the trash icon on the Layers palette, or press Delete.

■ The mode and opacity of a Floating Selection is determined by the current settings for the layer below it.

(Instructions for turning a floating selection into its own layer are on page 93. See the second tip on page 94. See information about Paste commands on page 86.)

Figure 15. *The original picture.*

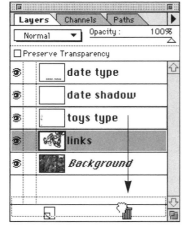

Figure 16. *Delete a layer by dragging its name over the **Trash** can icon.*

To delete a layer:

Drag the Layer name over the trash can icon on the palette (**Figures 15-17**).
or
Click on the layer name on the Layers palette that you wish to delete, then choose Delete Layer from the Layers palette command menu.

Figure 17. *The same picture after deleting the "toys type" layer.*

Delete a Layer

To display/hide a layer:

Click on the eye icon column (the left-most column) on the Layers palette for the layer you wish to display or hide. The eye icon indicates that layer is displayed **(Figure 18)**.

Note: Only currently displayed layers can be merged. When layers are flattened, hidden layers are discarded.

✔ Tip

■ Hold down Option and click an eye icon to hide all other layers. Option-click again to display all other layers.

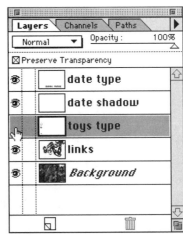

Figure 18. *Click the* **eye** *icon to hide a layer. Click again to display it.*

NOTES:

Painting and editing on layers.

You can use any painting or editing tool to edit pixels on the target layer, but keep in mind that in addition to the Options palette settings for each tool, tools are also affected by the target layer's current opacity and mode. For example, if a layer has an 60% opacity, a painting or editing tool will work at a maximum opacity of 60% on that layer, and less if the tool's opacity is below 100%.

The Preserve Transparency option.

With the Preserve Transparency box on the Layers palette checked, only areas of a layer that contain imagery can be edited. Blank areas will remain transparent. You can turn this option on or off for individual layers.

Figure 1. *To produce this picture, first the Marquee tool was used to select the center area. Then the Inverse command was used to reverse the selected and non-selected areas, and the Levels dialog box was used to screen back the selected area.*

T HIS CHAPTER covers the adjustment of light and dark values using dialog boxes opened from the Map and Adjust submenus under the Image menu, and using the Dodge or Burn tool.

You can make one-step modifications by choosing any command from the **Map** submenu under the Image menu. For example, you can Invert a layer to make it look like a film negative, Posterize it to decrease the number of shades, or change all the pixels to black and white to make it high contrast.

You can precisely adjust lightness or contrast in a layer's highlights, midtones, or shadows using dialog boxes opened from the **Adjust** submenu under the Image menu. All the Adjust dialog boxes are available for a picture in a color mode. Only the Levels, Curves, Brightness/Contrast, and Variations dialog boxes are available for a picture in Grayscale mode.

Finally, a large or small area of a layer can be darkened by dragging over it with the **Burn** tool or lightened by dragging over it with the **Dodge** tool.

All the commands discussed in this chapter can be applied to a color picture, but try applying them to a grayscale picture first to learn how they work.

(See "Appendix A: Glossary," for definitions of *Contrast, Film negative, Grayscale, Highlights, Histogram, Invert, Lightness, Luminosity, Midtones, Posterize, and Shadows*)

Note: The commands discussed in this chapter can be applied to a selected area of a target layer or to a whole layer.

THE PREVIEW CHECK BOX

Dialog boxes opened from the **Map** and **Adjust** submenus (Image menu) have a **Preview** box. Changes affect the entire screen with the Preview box unchecked. Changes preview only in the picture or in a selection with the Preview box checked. CMYK color displays more acccurately with Preview on.

TO RESET A DIALOG BOX

To undo changes made in a dialog box, hold down **Option** and click the **Reset** button.

Lights and Darks

Choose the **Invert** command to make the target layer look like a film negative. Each pixel will be replaced with its opposite brightness and color value.

To invert a layer's lights and darks:

Choose Invert from the Map submenu under the Image menu (**Figures 2-4**).
or
Hold down Command (⌘) and press "I."

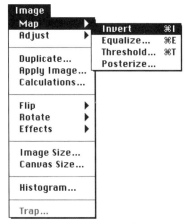

*Figure 2. Choose **Invert** from the **Map** submenu under the **Image** menu.*

Figure 3. The original picture.

Figure 4. After choosing the Invert command.

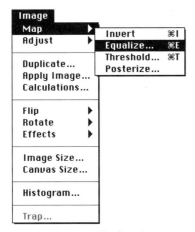

Figure 5. *Choose* **Equalize** *from the* **Map** *submenu under the* **Image** *menu.*

Use the **Equalize** command to redistribute the target layer's light and dark values. It may improve a picture that lacks contrast or is too dark.

To equalize a layer's lights and darks:

Choose Equalize from the Map submenu under the Image menu (**Figures 5-7**).
or
Hold down Command (⌘) and press "E".

✔ Tip

- To limit the Equalize effect to part of a layer, select the area, then click Select Area Only in the Equalize dialog box. To equalize the whole layer based on the values within the selected area, click Entire Image Based on Area.

Equalize

Figure 6. *The original picture.*

Figure 7. *After choosing the Equalize command.*

Use the **Threshold** dialog box to make the target layer high contrast by converting color or gray pixels into black and white pixels.

To make a layer high contrast:

1. Choose Threshold from the Map submenu under the Image menu (**Figure 8**).
or
Hold down Command (⌘) and press "T".

2. Move the slider to the right to increase the number of black pixels (**Figure 9**).
or
Move the slider to the left to increase the number of white pixels.
or
Enter a number between 1 and 255 in the Threshold Level field. Shades above this number will become white, shades below become black.

3. Click OK or press Return (**Figures 10-11**).

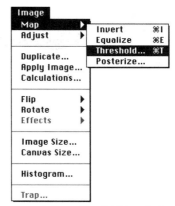

*Figure 8. Choose **Threshold** from the **Map** submenu under the **Image** menu.*

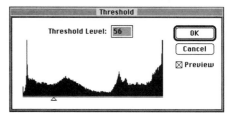

*Figure 9. Move the slider in the **Threshold** dialog box or enter a number in the **Threshold Level** field.*

Figure 10. The original picture.

Figure 11. After choosing the Threshold command.

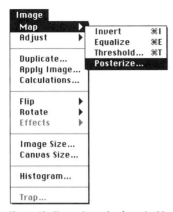

Figure 12. Choose *Posterize* from the *Map* submenu under the *Image* menu.

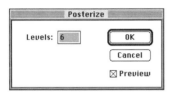

Figure 13. Enter a number between 2 and 255 in the *Levels* field in the *Posterize* dialog box.

Use the **Posterize** command to reduce the number of value levels in the target layer.

To posterize a layer:

1. Choose Posterize from the Map submenu under the Image menu (**Figure 12**).

2. Enter a number between 2 and 255 in the Levels field (**Figure 13**). To produce a dramatic effect, enter a number below 15.

3. Click OK or press Return (**Figures 14-15**).

✔ Tip

■ If the number of shades is reduced using the Posterize command and the picture is saved, the original shade information will be permanently lost. Choose Undo from the Edit menu to undo the Posterize command.

Figure 14. The original picture.

Figure 15. After choosing the Posterize command.

To adjust brightness and contrast (method 1):

1. Choose a target layer.

2. Choose Brightness/Contrast from the Adjust submenu under the Image menu (**Figure 16**).
   or
   Hold down Command (⌘) and press "B."

3. To lighten the layer, move the Brightness slider to the right (**Figure 17**).
   or
   To darken the layer, move the Brightness slider to the left.
   or
   Enter a number between -100 and 100 in the Brightness field.

4. To increase the contrast, move the Contrast slider to the right.
   or
   To lessen the contrast, move the Contrast slider to the left. With the slider in the leftmost position, the layer will be solid gray.
   or
   Enter a number between -100 and 100 in the Contrast field.

5. Click OK or press Return (**Figures 18-20**).

✔ Tip

■ When you move a slider in any of the Adjust submenu dialog boxes, note its position relative to the other sliders and how the layer changes.

Figure 16. *Choose* **Brightness/Contrast** *from the* **Adjust** *submenu under the* **Image** *menu.*

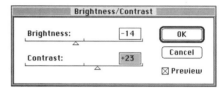

Figure 17. *In the* **Brightness/Contrast** *dialog box, move the sliders or enter numbers in the fields.*

Figure 18. *The original picture.*

Figure 19. *The Brightness slider moved right.*

Figure 20. *Brightness and contrast adjusted.*

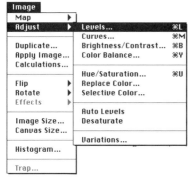

*Figure 21. Choose **Levels** from the **Adjust** sub-menu under the **Image** menu.*

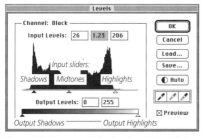

*Figure 22. Move any of the Input or Output sliders in the **Levels** dialog box.*

Figure 23. The original picture.

Figure 24. After Levels adjustments.

Use the **Levels** dialog box to make fine adjustments to a target layer's highlights, midtones, or shadows.

To adjust brightness and contrast (method 2):

1. Choose a target layer.

2. Choose Levels from the Adjust sub-menu under the Image menu (**Figure 21**).

or

Hold down Command (⌘) and press "L."

3. To increase contrast, brighten the highlights by moving the Input Highlights slider to the left (**Figure 22**).

and/or

To darken the shadows, move the Input Shadows slider to the right.

and/or

To lighten the midtones, move the Input Midtones slider to the left.

and/or

To darken the midtones, move the Input Midtones slider to the right.

4. To decrease contrast, move the Output Shadows slider to the right.

and/or

Move the Output Highlights slider to the left.

5. Click OK or press Return (**Figures 23-24**).

✔ Tip

■ To make a layer high contrast (black and white), move the Input Shadows and Highlights sliders very close together. Position them left of center to lighten the picture, right of center to darken the picture. You can use Threshold dialog box to produce the same effect. *(See page 102)*

To screen back a layer:

1. Choose a target layer.

2. Choose Levels from the Adjust submenu under the Image menu (**Figure 21**).
or
Hold down Command (⌘) and press "L."

3. To reduce the contrast, move the Output Highlights slider slightly to the left (**Figure 25**).
and
Move the Output Shadows slider to the right.

4. To lighten the midtones, move the Input Midtones slider to the left.

5. Click OK or press Return (**Figures 26-27**).

✔ **Tip**

■ To make a layer look like a film negative, reverse the position of the two Output sliders. The farther apart the sliders are, the more each pixel's brightness and contrast attributes will be reversed. The Invert command produces a similar effect. *(See page 100)*

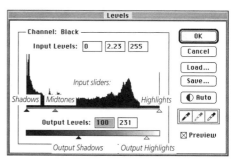

Figure 25. *The **Levels** dialog box.*

Figure 26. *The original picture.*

Figure 27. *The picture screened back.*

Screen Back a Layer

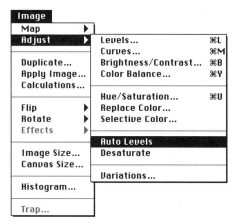

Figure 28. *Choose* **Auto Levels** *from the* **Adjust** *submenu under the* **Image** *menu.*

To adjust brightness and contrast automatically:

1. Choose a target layer.

2. Choose Auto Levels from the Adjust submenu under the Image menu (Figures 28-30).

✔ Tip

■ To execute the Auto Levels command from the Levels dialog box, click Auto.

Figure 29. *The original picture.*

Figure 30. *The levels adjusted automatically.*

Adjust Brightness and Contrast

Use the **Dodge** tool to lighten pixels in small areas or use the **Burn** tool to darken pixels. You can choose different Brushes palette settings for each tool. The Dodge and Burn tools can't be used on a picture in Bitmap or Indexed Color mode.

— *The **Dodge/Burn/Sponge** tool.*

Figure 31.

To lighten/darken using the Dodge/Burn tool:

1. Choose a target layer.

2. Double-click the Dodge/Burn/Sponge tool (**Figure 31**).

3. Choose Dodge or Burn from the Tool pop-up menu on the Toning Tools Options palette (**Figure 32**).

   and

   Position the Exposure slider between 1% (low intensity) and 100% (high intensity). Try a low exposure first (20%-30%) so the tool won't bleach or darken areas too quickly.

   and

   Choose Shadows, Midtones, or Highlights from the pop-up menu to Dodge or Burn those pixels.

4. Click the Brushes tab on the same palette, then click a hard-edged or soft-edged tip. A soft tip will produce the smoothest result.

5. Stroke on any area of the layer. Pause between strokes to allow the screen to redraw (**Figures 33-34**).

✔ Tips

- ■ If you Dodge or Burn an area too much, choose Undo from the Edit menu or choose Revert from the File menu. Don't use the opposite tool to fix it — the results will be uneven.

- ■ Option-click the Dodge/Burn/Sponge tool to switch between the three tools. They will retain their separate Brushes and Options palette settings.

- ■ To create a smooth, even highlight or shadow line, dodge or burn a path using the Dodge/Burn tool and the Stroke Path command *(see page 174)*.

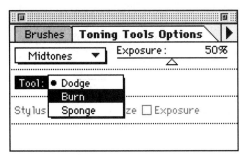

Figure 32. *Choose **Dodge** or **Burn** from the **Tool** pop-up menu on the **Toning Tools Options** palette.*

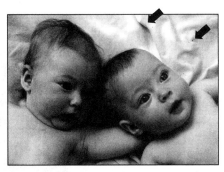

Figure 33. *The Dodge tool with Shadows chosen from the Toning Tools Options palette was used to eliminate dark spots in the background of this picture.*

Figure 34. *The final picture.*

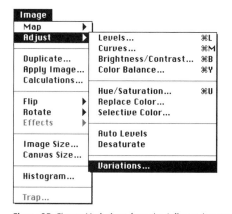

Figure 35. *Choose **Variations** from the **Adjust** submenu under the **Image** menu.*

You can adjust lights and darks on a target layer by clicking on thumbnails in the **Variations** dialog box.

(To adjust a color picture using the Variations dialog box, see pages 127-128)

To adjust lights and darks using thumbnail Variations:

1. Choose a target layer.

2. Choose Variations from the Adjust submenu under the Image menu (**Figure 35**).

3. Position the Fine/Coarse slider right of center to make major adjustments or left of center to make minor adjustments. Each notch to the right doubles the adjustment per click. Each notch to the left halves the adjustment per click (**Figure 36**).

4. Click the Lighter or Darker thumbnail in the Shadows, Midtones, or Highlights column. Compare the Current Pick thumbnail, which represents the modified picture, with the Original thumbnail.

5. *Optional:* Click the same thumbnail again to intensify the change, or click the opposite thumbnail to undo the modification.

6. Click OK or press Return (**Figures 37-38**).

✔ Tips

■ Click the Original thumbnail to undo changes made using the Variations dialog box.

■ Use the Levels or Brightness/Contrast dialog box to make more precise adjustments using the document window for previewing *(See pages 104 and 105)*

Adjust using Variations

Adjust using Variations

Click the **Original** thumbnail to undo all adjustments.

The **Current Pick** represents the modified picture.

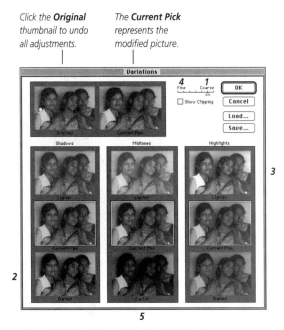

Figure 36. The **Variations** dialog box. The following steps were taken to produce the picture in Figure 38:

1 The Fine/Coarse slider was moved to the right 2 notches.
2 The Shadows-Darker box was clicked.
3 The Highlights-Lighter box was clicked.
4 The Fine/Coarse slider was moved to the left 4 notches.
5 The Midtones-Darker box was clicked.

Figure 37. The original picture.

Figure 38. After Variations adjustments.

☞ **FOR THIS CHAPTER,** you'll need to open the **Picker/Swatches/Scratch** palette.

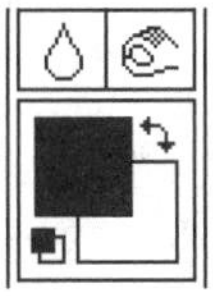

I N THIS CHAPTER you will learn how to choose colors using the **Picker** palette, how to add, delete, save, append, and load colors using the **Swatches** palette, and how to mix colors using the **Scratch** palette.

Foreground and Background colors:

When you use a fill command or a painting tool or create type, the current Foreground color is applied.

When you use the Eraser tool, add a border to a picture using the Canvas Size dialog box, or move a selection, the current Background color is applied — unless your document was created with a Transparent background. (If you move a floating selection, the underlying pixels don't change.) The Gradient tool produces blends with the Foreground and/or Background colors.

The Foreground and Background colors are displayed on the Toolbox and on the Picker palette in the Foreground and Background color squares (**Figures 1-2**). (When written with an uppercase "F" or "B," these terms refer to colors, not the foreground or background areas of a picture.)

Switch the Foreground and Background colors by clicking the Switch Colors icon on the Toolbox (**Figure 1**).

Restore the Foreground color to black and the Background color to white by clicking the Default Colors icon on the Toolbox.

Methods for choosing Foreground and Background colors are described on the next three pages.

Foreground color square. ——
Default Colors ——
icon.

Switch Colors icon.
Background color square.

Figure 1.

Foreground color square. The currently active square has a double frame.

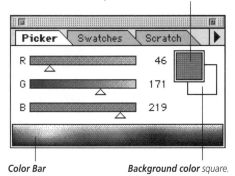

Color Bar   *Background color square.*

Figure 2. The **Picker** palette.

Foreground and Background Colors

To choose a process Foreground or Background color using the Color Picker:

1. Click the Foreground or Background color square on the Toolbox (**Figure 1**).

or

Click the Foreground or Background color square on the Picker palette if it is already active (**Figure 2**).

or

Double-click the Foreground or Background color square on the Picker palette if it is not active.

Note: If the color square you click on is a Custom color, the Custom Colors dialog box will open. Click Picker to open the Color Picker dialog box.

2. Click a color on the vertical color bar to choose a hue, then click a variation of that hue in the large rectangle (**Figures 3-4**).

or

Enter percentages from a matching guide in the C, M, Y, and K fields.

3. Click OK or press Return.

✔ Tips

■ To use the Photoshop Color Picker, Photoshop must be chosen from the Color Picker pop-up menu in the General Preferences dialog box, opened from the File menu.

■ You can enter numbers in the HSB, RGB, or Lab fields. RGB colors range from 0 (black) to 255 (pure R, G, or B).

New *color.* **Old** *color.*

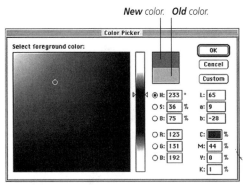

Figure 3. *In the **Color Picker** dialog box, click a color on the color bar, then click a color in the large rectangle, or enter numbers in the fields.*

Figure 4. *An **exclamation point** indicates there is no ink equivalent for the color you chose — it is **out of gamut** (nonprintable). Choose a different color or click the exclamation point to have Photoshop substitute the closest printable color (shown in the swatch below the exclamation point).*

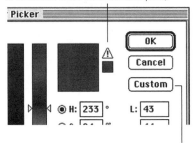

*Click **Custom** to choose a predefined color.*

Choose a Process Color

To choose a custom Foreground or Background color using the Custom Colors dialog box:

1. Click the Foreground or Background color square on the Toolbox (**Figure 1**).

or

Click the Foreground or Background color square on the Picker palette if it is already active (**Figure 2**).

or

Double-click the Foreground or Background color square on the Picker palette if it is not active.

Note: If the color square you click on is not a Custom color, the Color Picker dialog box will open. Click Custom to open the Custom Colors dialog box.

2. Choose a matching guide system from the Book pop-up menu (**Figure 5**).

3. Type a number (it will appear on the "Key #" line).

or

Click a color on the vertical color bar, then click a swatch.

4. Click OK or press Return.

✔ Tip

■ Follow the instructions on page 117 to load a predefined swatch palette onto the Colors palette.

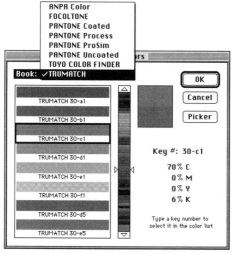

Figure 5. *In the **Custom Colors** dialog box, choose a matching system from the **Book** pop-up menu. Then type a number or click a color on the vertical color bar and click a swatch.*

To choose a Foreground or Background color from a picture:

1. On the Picker palette, click the Foreground or Background color square if it is not already active.

2. Click the Eyedropper tool (**Figure 6**).

3. Click on a color in the picture.

✔ Tip

■ Hold down Option and click to choose a Background color when the Foreground color square is active, or to choose a Foreground color when the Background color square is active.

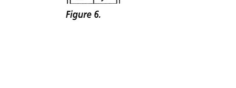

*The **Eyedropper** tool.*

Figure 6.

To choose a Foreground or Background color using the Picker palette:

1. Click the Foreground or Background color square if it is not already active (**Figure 7**).

2. Choose a color model for the sliders from the Picker palette command menu.

3. Move any of the sliders.
or
Click on the Color Bar.

✔ Tips

■ In RGB mode, white (the presence of all colors) is produced when all the sliders are in their rightmost positions. Black (the absence of all colors) is produced when all the sliders are in their leftmost positions. Gray is produced when all the sliders are vertically aligned in any other position.

■ The model you choose for the Picker palette does not have to match the current image mode. For example, you can choose the CMYK Color model from the Picker palette for a picture in RGB Color mode.

*1) Click the **Foreground** or **Background color** square.* *2) Choose a **model** for the sliders.*

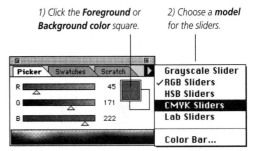

3) Click on the Color Bar or move any of the sliders. (Choose Color Bar from the command menu to choose a different Spectrum style.)

Figure 7. *The **Picker** palette.*

Choose a Color — Picture or Picker Palette

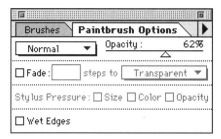

*Figure 8. Choose **Normal** from the mode pop-up menu on the **Options** palette, and move the **Opacity** slider to a medium opacity.*

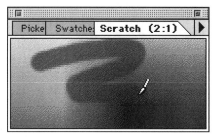

*Figure 9. Scribble on the **Scratch** palette with a painting tool.*

Other Scratch palette command menu options

Choose **Clear** to cover the Scratch palette with the current Background color.

Choose **Locked** to prevent the Scratch palette from being modified. Choose Locked again to unlock the palette.

Choose **Reset Scratch** to restore the default palette.

Choose **Load Scratch** to load an already saved Scratch palette.

Choose **Save Scratch** to save the current Scratch palette to a file.

To mix a color "by hand":

1. Choose a Foreground color.

2. Double-click a painting tool.

3. Choose Normal from the mode pop-up menu on the Options palette, and move the Opacity slider to a medium opacity (75% or lower) (**Figure 8**).

4. Click the Brushes tab to display the Brushes palette, then click a brush tip.

5. Click the Scratch tab to display the Scratch palette.

6. Scribble on the Scratch palette (**Figure 9**).

7. Choose a new Foreground color.

8. Scribble again on the Scratch palette.

9. *Optional:* Choose the Smudge tool, then drag across the Scratch palette to blend the colors.

10. Choose the Eyedropper tool.

11. To choose the new color as the Foreground color, click on the Scratch palette.
or
To choose the new color as the Background color, hold down Option and click on the Scratch palette.

✔ Tips

■ To clone an area of a picture onto the Scratch palette, double-click the Rubber Stamp tool, choose an Opacity and choose Clone (Aligned) from the Option pop-up menu on the Options palette, hold down Option and click on the picture, then drag across the Scratch palette.

■ To magnify the Scratch palette, click on it with the Zoom tool.

■ Choose Undo from the Edit menu to cancel the last change made to the palette.

Add, Delete Swatches

To add a color to the Swatches palette:

1. Mix a Foreground or Background color. *(See pages 112-114)*

2. Click the Swatches tab to display the Swatches palette.

3. Position the cursor in the white area below the swatches on the palette, and click with the bucket cursor (**Figure 10**).
The new color will appear next to the last swatch.

✔ Tips

■ To replace an existing swatch with the new color, hold down Shift and click on the color to be replaced.

■ To insert the new color between two swatches, hold down Option and Shift and click on either swatch (**Figure 11**).

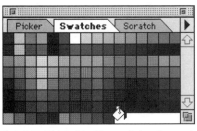

Figure 10. Click in the white area below the swatches.

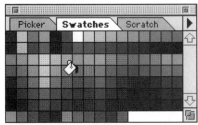

*Figure 11. Hold **Option** and **Shift** and click between two swatches to insert a color between them.*

To delete a color from the Swatches palette:

Hold down Command (⌘) and click on a swatch with the scissors cursor (**Figure 12**).

✔ Tip

■ To restore the default Swatch palette, choose Reset Swatches from the Swatches palette command menu.

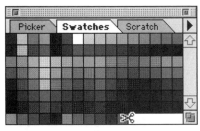

*Figure 12. Hold down **Command** (⌘) and click on a swatch to delete it.*

Nine preset color swatch palettes are supplied with Photoshop, and they can be loaded onto the Swatches palette. They include ANPA, Focoltone, Pantone (Coated, Process, ProSim, and Uncoated), System, Toyo, and Trumatch.

To load a swatch palette:

1. Choose Load Swatches from the Swatches palette command menu (**Figure 13**).

2. Open the Color Palettes folder in the Goodies folder in the Photoshop application folder.

3. Double-click a palette (**Figure 14**). The loaded swatches will appear on the Swatches palette.

or

Highlight a palette, then click Open.

✔ Tip

■ Choose Reset Swatches to restore the default palette.

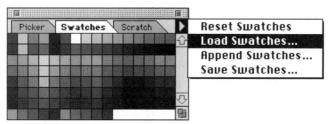

*Figure 13. Choose **Load Swatches** from the **Swatches** palette command menu.*

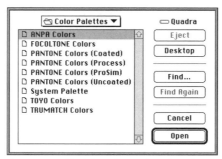

*Figure 14. Double-click a palette in the **Color Palettes** folder.*

Load a Swatch Palette

To save an edited swatch palette:

1. Choose Save Swatches from the Swatches palette command menu (**Figure 15**).

2. Enter a name for the edited palette in the "Save swatches in" field (**Figure 16**).

3. Choose a location in which to save the palette.

4. Click Save.

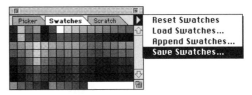

Figure 15. Choose *Save Swatches* from the *Swatches* palette command menu.

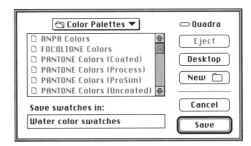

Figure 16. Enter a name in the *Save swatches in* field, choose a location in which to save the palette, then click *Save*.

You can append to an existing Swatch palette any swatch palette that you edit and save or any of the palettes that are supplied with Photoshop.

To append a swatch palette:

1. Choose Append Swatches from the Swatches palette command menu (**Figure 17**).

2. Open the Color Palettes or another palettes folder in the Goodies folder in the Photoshop application folder (**Figure 18**).

3. Double-click a palette.
or
Highlight a palette and click Open.

4. The appended swatches will appear below the existing swatches.

✔ Tip

■ To enlarge the palette to display the appended swatches, drag the palette resize box or click the palette zoom box.

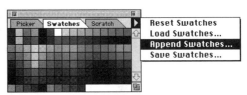

Figure 17. Choose *Append Swatches* from the *Swatches* palette command menu.

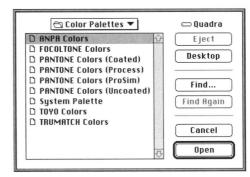

Figure 18. Open the Color Palettes or other folder, highlight a palette, then click *Open*.

Save or Append a Swatch Palette

I N THIS CHAPTER you will learn to fill a selection with color, color the edge of a selection, tint a Grayscale picture or adjust a color picture using the Hue/Saturation and Color Balance dialog boxes, adjust color using the Variations dialog box, replace color using the Replace Color command, and saturate or desaturate colors using the Sponge tool.

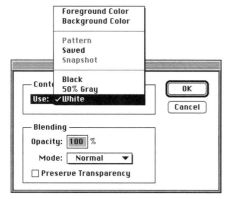

Figure 1. *Choose **Fill** from the **Edit** menu.*

Figure 2. *In the **Fill** dialog box, enter an **Opacity** and choose a **Mode**. You can choose a different Fill color from the **Contents** pop-up menu.*

To fill a selection with color:

1. Choose a target layer.

2. Use any method described in Chapter 5 to select the area or areas you want to fill with a new color.

3. Choose a Foreground color.

4. Choose Fill from the Edit menu (**Figure 1**).

5. Enter a number in the Opacity field (**Figure 2**).

6. Choose a mode from the Mode pop-up menu. *(See page 135)*

7. Click OK or press Return (**Gallery 1a-b**).

✔ Tips

■ If you don't like the new fill color, choose Undo from the Edit menu immediately so it won't blend with your next color or mode choice.

■ Press Delete to fill a selection with the Background color, 100% opacity.

■ Hold down Option and press Delete to fill a selection with the Foreground color, 100% opacity.

(To create a Fill pattern from a picture, see page 229)

To color the edge of a selection:

1. Choose a target layer.

2. Select an area of the layer (**Figure 3**)

3. Choose a Foreground color. *(See pages 112-114)*

4. Choose Stroke from the Edit menu (**Figure 4**).

5. Enter a number between 1 and 16 in the Width field (**Figure 5**).

6. Click Inside, Center, or Outside (the Location of the stroke on the selection edge).

7. Enter a number in the Opacity field.

8. Choose a mode from the Mode pop-up menu.

9. Click OK or press Return (**Gallery 1c-d**).

Figure 3. Select an area (or areas) of a picture.

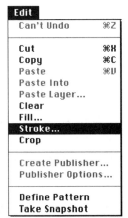

Figure 4. Choose **Stroke** from the **Edit** menu.

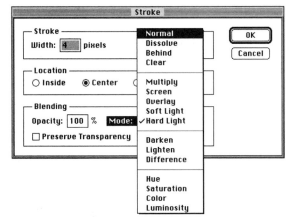

Figure 5. In the **Stroke** dialog box, enter a **Width** and **Opacity**, and choose a **Mode**.

Figure 6. *Choose* **Float** *from the* **Select** *menu.*

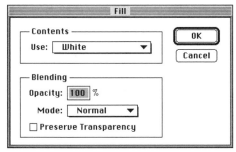

Figure 7. *In the* **Fill** *dialog box, enter an* **Opacity** *and choose a* **Mode**.

Figure 8. *Choose a* **mode** *and* **Opacity** *from the* **Layers** *palette.*

To fill a selection and preview fill options:

1. Choose a target layer.

2. Select an area of the layer. *(See pages 66-70)*

3. Choose Float from the Select menu (**Figure 6**).

4. Choose a Foreground color. *(See pages 112-114)*

5. Choose Fill from the Edit menu (**Figure 1**).

6. Enter 100 in the Opacity field (**Figure 7**).

7. Choose Normal from the Mode pop-up menu.

8. Click OK or press Return.

9. Choose a mode from the pop-up menu on the Layers palette (**Figure 8**).
and/or
Move the Opacity slider.

10. Choose None from the Select menu (**Gallery 1g-l**).
or
Click the selection with the Marquee tool or the Lasso tool.

✔ Tips

■ To remove the selection, choose Clear from the Edit menu or press Delete. The underlying pixels won't change.

■ Turn the Floating Selection into a permanent layer. Then you can modify it after it's deselected. *(See page 93)* You can also use the Layer Options dialog box, opened from the Layers palette, to try different options for blending the new layer with the layer below it.

Preview Fill Options

To colorize a grayscale picture using Hue/Saturation:

1. Open a Grayscale picture (**Figure 9**).

2. Choose RGB Color or CMYK Color from the Mode menu (**Figure 10**).

3. Choose a target layer.

4. Choose Hue/Saturation from the Adjust submenu under the Image menu (**Figure 11**).

5. Check the Colorize box. The picture will be tinted red (**Figure 12**).

6. Move the Hue slider left or right to apply a different tint. Pause to preview.

7. Move the Saturation slider.

8. Move the Lightness slider.

9. Click OK or press Return (**Gallery 1e-f**).

✔ Tips

- To restore the original dialog box settings, hold down Option and click Reset.

- You can also tint a Grayscale picture by converting it into a duotone *(see page 250)*.

- To colorize the picture, including pure black, move the Lightness slider to the right. To colorize the picture, including pure white, move the Lightness slider to the left.

Figure 9. The original Grayscale picture.

*Figure 10. Choose **RGB Color** or **CMYK Color** from the **Mode** menu.*

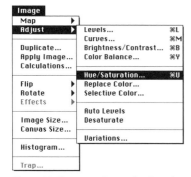

*Figure 11. Choose **Hue/Saturation** from the **Adjust** submenu under the **Image** menu.*

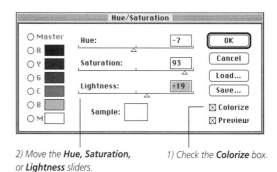

*2) Move the **Hue, Saturation**, or **Lightness** sliders.*

*1) Check the **Colorize** box.*

*Figure 12. The **Hue/Saturation** dialog box.*

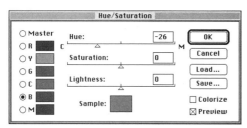

Figure 13. *In the* **Hue/Saturation** *dialog box, click* **Master** *or a click color button (R, Y, G, C, B, or M), then move the* **Hue, Saturation,** *or* **Lightness** *slider. In this figure, the B(Blue) button was clicked, and the Hue slider is moved to the left to add move C (Cyan) to the Blue.*

THE PREVIEW CHECK BOX

Dialog boxes opened from the Map and Adjust submenus (Image menu) have a Preview box. Changes affect the entire screen with the Preview box unchecked. Changes preview in just the picture (or selection) with the Preview box checked. CMYK color displays more acccurately with Preview on.

To display the unmodified picture in the document window, uncheck the Preview box, and press and hold on the title bar of the dialog box.

Color adjustments using the **Hue/Saturation** dialog box are easiest to see in a picture with clearly defined color areas.

To adjust a color picture using Hue/Saturation:

1. Choose a target layer.

2. Select an area of the layer to recolor only that area.

3. Choose Hue/Saturation from the Adjust submenu under the Image menu (**Figure 11**).

or

Hold down Command (⌘) and press "U."

4. Click Master to adjust all colors.

or

Click a color button to adjust only that color (**Figure 13**).

5. Move the Hue slider left or right. Pause to preview.

6. Move the Saturation slider to the left to decrease saturation or to the right to increase saturation.

7. Move the Lightness slider to the left to add Black or to the right to add White.

8. Click OK or press Return.

✔ Tips

■ Use the Save command in the Levels, Hue/Saturation, or Variations dialog box to save color adjustment settings, and then apply them to another layer or to another picture using the Load command.

■ To restore the original dialog box settings, hold down Option and click Reset.

Adjust a Color Picture

Use the **Replace Color** command to change colors in a picture without having to first select those areas.

To replace colors:

1. *Optional:* For an RGB picture, choose CMYK Preview from the Mode menu to see the actual picture and modifications to it in CMYK color. (The Sample swatch in the Replace Color dialog box will continue to display in RGB.)

2. Choose a target layer.

3. Choose Replace Color from the Adjust submenu under the Image menu (**Figure 14**).

4. Click on the color you want to replace in the Preview box in the Replace Color dialog box or in the document window (**Figure 15**).

5. *Optional:* Move the Fuzziness slider to the right to add related colors to the selection (**Figure 16**).

6. Move the Hue, Saturation, or Lightness Transform sliders to change the selected colors (Only the Lightness slider will be available for a Grayscale picture.) The Sample swatch will change as you move the sliders (**Figure 17**).

Note: Once you move the Transform sliders, they will stay in the same position while the dialog box is still open. The same color changes will affect each area of the picture you subsequently click on.

7. Click OK or press Return (**Figures 18-19**).

✔ Tips

■ To restore the original dialog box settings, hold down Option and click Reset.

■ Hold down Shift and click in the preview box or on the picture to add other colors areas to the selection (or

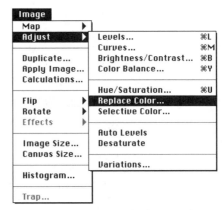

Figure 14. Choose **Replace Color** from the **Adjust** submenu under the **Image** menu.

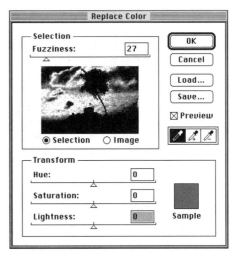

Figure 15. The **Replace Color** dialog box. The white areas in the Preview box are the active areas that will be modified.

Replace Color

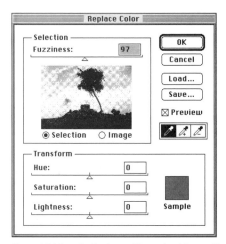

Figure 16. Move the Fuzziness slider to the right to add related colors to the selection. Now most of the sky is selected.

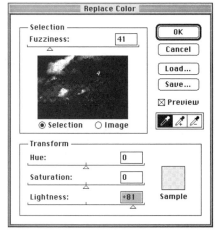

*Figure 17. Move the **Hue, Saturation,** and **Lightness** **Transform** sliders. The clouds were selected and lightened.*

Figure 18. The original picture.

just choose the **+** eyedropper icon before you click).

Hold down Command and click in the preview box or on the picture to subtract areas from the selection (or just choose the **–** eyedropper icon before you click).

■ Choose Undo from the Edit menu to restore the previous selection in the Preview box.

■ The Picker palette color squares and sliders display the colors and color breakdown you change using the Transform sliders. If the gamut alarm displays, you have produced a non-printable color using the Transform sliders. The Transform sliders don't change the amount of Black in a CMYK color because this component is set by Photoshop's Black Generation function.

■ Click the Selection button to preview the selection or click the Image button to display the entire image in the Preview box. Use the Command key to toggle between the two. If your picture extends beyond the edges of your monitor, turn the Image preview option on so you'll be able to sample from the entire picture with the eyedropper.

■ Select an area on a layer before opening the Replace Color dialog box to restrict color replacement to that area.

Figure 19. The picture after the Lightness adjustment.

Replace Color

Use the **Color Balance** dialog box to apply a warm or cool cast to a layer's highlights, midtones, or shadows. Color adjustments are easiest to see in a picture that has a wide tonal range.

To colorize or color correct using Color Balance:

1. To colorize a Grayscale picture, choose a color mode from the Mode menu.

2. Choose a target layer.

3. Choose Color Balance from the Adjust submenu under the Image menu (**Figure 20**).

4. Click Shadows, Midtones, or Highlights (**Figure 21**).

5. *Optional:* Check the Preserve Luminosity box to preserve brightness values.

6. Move any slider toward a color you want to add more of. Cool and warm colors are paired opposite each other. Pause to preview.

7. *Optional:* Repeat with any other button selected for step 4.

8. Click OK or press Return (**Figure 22** and **Gallery 1m-n**).

✔ Tips

■ Move sliders toward related colors to make a picture warmer or cooler. For example, move sliders toward Cyan and Blue to produce a cool cast.

■ Use a Paintbrush with a light opacity to recolor small areas.

■ With the Color Balance or any other Adjust dialog box open, the Info palette shows a color breakdown of the original and modified pixel directly under the cursor.

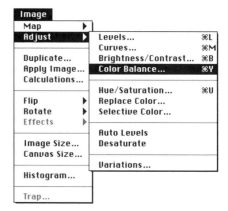

Figure 20. *Choose* **Color Balance** *from the* **Adjust** *submenu under the* **Image** *menu.*

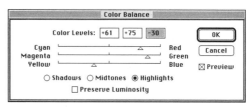

Figure 21. *In the* **Color Balance** *dialog box, click* **Shadows, Midtones,** *or* **Highlights,** *then move any of the sliders.*

Figure 22. *A Grayscale picture.*

Colorize or Color Correct

Thumbnail previews in the **Variations** dialog box represent how a picture will look with various color adjustments. To make more precise adjustments and preview changes in the document window, use the Color Balance dialog box.

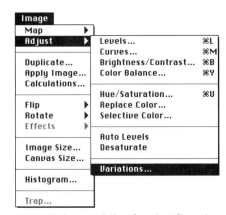

*Figure 23. Choose **Variations** from the **Adjust** submenu under the **Image** menu.*

To adjust color using thumbnail Variations:

1. Choose a target layer.

2. Choose Variations from the Adjust submenu under the Image menu (**Figure 23**).

3. Click Shadows, Midtones, or High-lights to modify only those areas (**Figure 24**).
or
Click Saturation to adjust only saturation.

4. Position the Fine/Coarse slider to the right of center to make major adjustments or to the left of center to make minor adjustments. Each notch to the right doubles the adjustment per click. Each notch to the left halves the adjustment per click.

5. Click any "More..." thumbnail to add more of that color to the layer. Pause to preview. The Current Pick thumbnail represents the modified layer.

6. *Optional:* Repeat steps 3 and 4.

7. Click OK or press Return (**Gallery 1o-r**).

Adjust Color using Variations

*Click the **Original**
thumbnail to restore the
unmodified layer.*

*The **Current Pick**
thumbnail represents
the modified layer.*

*First click **Shadows,
Midtones, Highlights,**
or **Saturation**.*

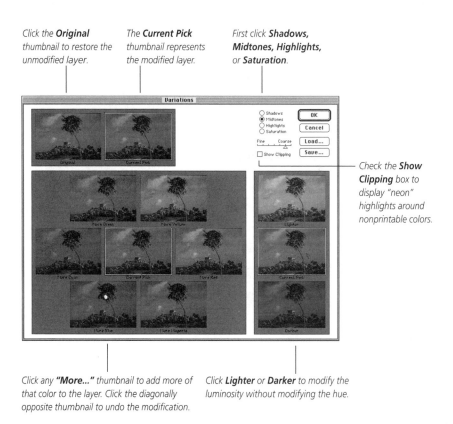

*Check the **Show
Clipping** box to
display "neon"
highlights around
nonprintable colors.*

*Click any **"More..."** thumbnail to add more of
that color to the layer. Click the diagonally
opposite thumbnail to undo the modification.*

*Click **Lighter** or **Darker** to modify the
luminosity without modifying the hue.*

Figure 24. *The **Variations** dialog box.*

— *The Sponge tool.*

Figure 25.

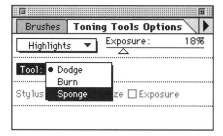

Figure 26. *Choose Sponge from the Tool pop-up menu on the Toning Tools Options palette.*

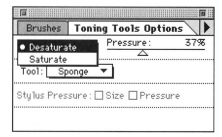

Figure 27. *Choose Desaturate or Saturate from the pop-up menu.*

Use the **Sponge** tool to make color areas on a target layer more or less saturated. Use the Sponge tool to desaturate out-of-gamut colors to make them printable.

Note: The Sponge tool can't be used on a picture in Bitmap or Indexed Color mode.

To saturate or desaturate colors using the Sponge tool:

1. Double-click the Dodge/Burn/Sponge tool (**Figure 25**).

2. Choose Sponge from the Tool pop-up menu on the Toning Tools Options palette (**Figure 26**).
and
Position the Pressure slider between 1% (low intensity) and 100% (high intensity). Try a low Pressure first (20%-30%) so the tool won't saturate or desaturate areas too quickly.
and
Choose Desaturate or Saturate from the pop-up menu (**Figure 27**).

3. Click the Brushes tab on the same palette, then click a hard-edged or soft-edged tip. A soft tip will produce the smoothest result.

4. Choose a target layer.

5. Stroke on any area of the layer, pausing to allow the screen to redraw. Stroke again to intensify the effect.

✔ Tips

■ If you Saturate or Desaturate an area too much, choose Undo from the Edit menu or choose Revert from the File menu. Don't use the opposite tool setting to fix it — the results will be uneven.

■ Hold down Option and click the Dodge/Burn/Sponge tool on the Toolbox to switch between the three tools. They will keep their separate Brushes palette and Options palette settings.

Use the **Gamut Warning** command to display out-of-gamut (non-printable) colors in gray on the picture. You can then use the Sponge tool to desaturate those areas to make them printable.

Use the **CMYK Preview** command to display an RGB Color file in CMYK Color without actually changing its color mode. In these instructions, a second document window is created to facilitate color correction.

Note: The Gamut Warning is only available for a picture in RGB Color or Lab Color mode.

To correct of out-of-gamut colors:

1. Open an RGB Color picture.

2. Choose Gamut Warning from the Mode menu (**Figure 28**).

3. *Optional:* To select the out-of-gamut areas and restrict color changes to those areas, choose Color Range from the Select menu, choose Out of Gamut from the Select pop-up menu (**Figure 29**), then click OK or press Return.

4. *Optional:* To preview the picture in a second window in CMYK color as you work, choose New Window from the Window menu. With the new window active, choose CMYK Preview from the Mode menu (**Figure 30**). Resize and move the new window so both pictures are visible on screen.

5. Follow steps 1 to 3 on the previous page, but choose Desaturate from the Toning Tools Options palette pop-up menu.

6. Choose a target layer.

7. Drag across the gray out-of-gamut areas (**Figure 31**). Colors will become desaturated and redisplay in color.

(Tips on the following page)

Figure 28. Choose **Gamut Warning** from the **Mode** menu.

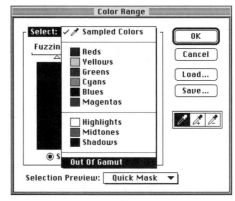

Figure 29. Choose **Out of Gamut** from the **Select** pop-up menu in the **Color Range** dialog box.

Figure 30. Choose **CMYK Preview** from the **Mode** menu.

Correct Out-of-Gamut Colors

Figure 31. For illustration purposes, the out-of-gamut colors in this picture are shown in White instead of Gray.

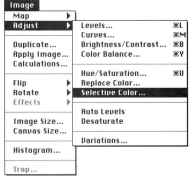

*Figure 32. Choose **Selective Color** from the **Adjust** submenu under the **Image** menu.*

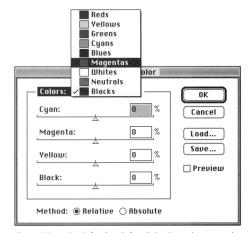

*Figure 33. In the **Selective Color** dialog box, choose a color from the **Colors** pop-up menu, then move the sliders to adjust printing ink percentages.*

✔ Tips

- ■ Don't desaturate colors too much — you will create muddy, uneven color.

- ■ To turn off the Gamut Warning, choose the command again from the Mode menu.

- ■ You can also use the Hue/Saturation dialog box (Adjust submenu under the Image menu) instead of the Sponge tool to correct out-of-gamut colors in the selected areas. Move the Saturation slider to the left to desaturate.

Use the **Selective Color** command to adjust the amount of ink used on press for specific colors. **Ask your print shop what ink percentages to use.**

To change printing ink percentages:

1. Make sure your picture is in CMYK Color mode.

2. Choose a target layer.
   or
   Flatten the picture to adjust the whole picture. *(See page 155)*

3. Choose Selective Color from the Adjust submenu under the Image menu (**Figure 32**).

4. Choose a color to adjust from the Colors pop-up menu (**Figure 33**).

5. Click Relative to add to or subtract a percentage of the current amount of a color or click Absolute to add to or subtract a fixed amount, then enter the percentages in the Cyan, Magenta, Yellow and/or Black fields that your print shop specifies.

☞ **FOR THIS CHAPTER,** you'll need to open the **Brushes** and **Options** palettes.

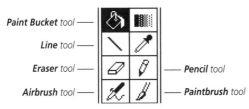

Paint Bucket *tool* ——
Line *tool* ——
Eraser *tool* ——
Airbrush *tool* ——
—— *Pencil* tool
—— *Paintbrush* tool

Figure 1. *Tools covered in this chapter.*

I N THIS CHAPTER you will learn to use Photoshop's Line, **Airbrush,** **Pencil** and **Paintbrush** tools (**Figure 1**). You can paint on a scanned image or you can paint a picture from scratch. You will learn how to create custom brush tips for the painting tools using the **Brushes palette,** how to save and load brush palettes, and about **Options palette** settings, such as mode and opacity. The **Paint Bucket** tool and the **Eraser** tool are also covered in this chapter.

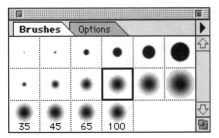

Figure 2. *Click a tip on the **Brushes** palette.*

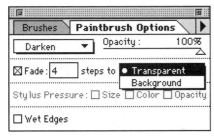

Figure 3. *On the **Options** palette, move the Pressure or Opacity slider and choose a mode. As an optional step, check the **Fade** box, enter a number of **steps**, then choose **Transparent** or **Background** from the **steps to** pop-up menu.*

To use the Paintbrush or Airbrush tool:

1. Choose a target layer.

2. Click the Paintbrush or Airbrush tool (**Figure 1**).

3. Choose a Foreground color. *(See pages 112-114)*

4. Click a hard-edged tip in the first row of the Brushes palette or a soft-edged tip in the second or third row (**Figure 2**). The number under a tip is the width of the tip in pixels.

5. Click the Options tab on the palette.

6. On the Options palette, move the Opacity/Pressure slider (**Figure 3**). At 100%, the stroke will completely cover the underlying pixels.
and
Choose from the mode pop-up menu. *(See "Paint, Fill, and Edit Modes" on page 135)*

(Continued on the following page)

Use the Paintbrush or Airbrush Tool

7. *Optional:* To create a stroke that fades as it finishes, check the Fade box, and enter a number of steps. The higher the number, the longer the stroke will be before it fades. Then choose Transparent from the "steps to" pop-up menu to fade from the Foreground color to no color, or choose Background to fade from the Foreground color to the Background color.

8. *Optional:* Check the Wet Edges box for the Paintbrush tool to produce a soft, "watercolor" stroke with a darker concentration of color at the edges. Use a soft-edged brush tip with this option (**Figures 4a-d**).

9. Drag across any area of the picture (**Gallery 2a-f**). If you press and hold on an area with the Airbrush tool without dragging, the "paint-drop" will gradually widen and become more saturated.

✔ Tips

■ To undo the last stroke, choose Undo from the Edit menu immediately. Only the last stroke can be undone.

■ To paint in a restricted area while protecting the rest of the picture, select the area before painting.

■ To draw a straight stroke, click once to begin the stroke, then hold down Shift and click in a different location to complete the stroke.

■ To choose a Foreground color from the picture with a painting tool selected, hold down Option and click on the picture.

■ With the Preserve Transparency box checked on the Layers palette, paint strokes will only affect existing pixels — transparent areas will remain transparent.

Figure 4a. *Strokes created with the Paintbrush tool with the **Wet Edges** box checked on the **Paintbrush Options** palette.*

Figure 4b.

Figure 4c. *The stroke on top was created with the **Paintbrush** tool, **Wet Edges** box **unchecked**. The stroke on the bottom was created with the **Wet Edges** box **checked.***

PAINT, FILL, AND EDIT MODES

The mode you choose for a tool affects how that tool modifies underlying pixels. You can select from 16 modes from the Options palette, the Layers palette, the Fill dialog box, or the Fill Path dialog box. When you choose a mode and opacity for a tool, factor in the mode and opacity of the target layer you're working on.

Notes: If the Preserve Transparency box is checked on the Layers palette for the target layer, only non-transparent areas will be modified.

NORMAL

Pixels of any color are modified.

DISSOLVE

Creates a chalky, dry brush texture with the paint color. The higher the pressure or opacity, the more solid the stroke.

BEHIND

Only areas of transparency are modified, not existing pixels. The effect is like painting on the reverse side of clear acetate. Good for creating shadows.

CLEAR

Makes pixels transparent where strokes are applied. Only available for a multi-layer document when using the Line tool, the Paint Bucket tool, the Fill command, or the Stroke command. Cannot be used on the Background layer.

MULTIPLY

Existing pixels and the paint color combine to produce a darker color.

SCREEN

Lightens (bleaches out) the inverse of the picture (pixel) color and paint color.

OVERLAY

Multiplies (darkens) dark pixels and screens (lightens) light pixels. Preserves luminosity (light and dark) values.

SOFT LIGHT

Lightens pixels if the paint color is light. Darkens pixels if the paint color is dark. Preserves luminosity values. Creates a soft lighting effect.

HARD LIGHT

Screens (lightens) pixels if the paint color is light. Multiplies (darkens) pixels if the paint color is dark. Good for painting highlights and shadows.

DARKEN

Pixels lighter than the paint color are modified; pixels darker than the paint color are not. Use with a paint color that is just darker than the colors you wish to modify.

LIGHTEN

Pixels darker than the paint color are modified; pixels lighter than the paint color are not. Use with a paint color that is just lighter than the colors you wish to modify.

DIFFERENCE

Subtracts the pixel color from the paint color, or vice versa, depending on which is brighter. Produces noticeable color shifts.

HUE

The paint color hue is applied. Saturation and luminosity values are not modified.

SATURATION

The paint color's saturation is applied. Hue and luminosity values are not modified.

COLOR

The paint color's saturation and hue are applied. Luminosity values are not modified.

LUMINOSITY

Only luminosity values are modified.

To modify a brush tip:

1. Double-click a brush tip on the Brushes palette (**Figure 5**).

or

Click a tip, then choose Brush Options from the palette command menu.

2. Move the Diameter slider (**Figure 6**).

or

Enter a number between 1 and 999 in the Diameter field.

3. Move the Hardness slider.

or

Enter a number between 0 and 100 in the Hardness field (the percentage of the diameter of the stroke that is opaque).

4. Move the Spacing slider.

or

Enter a number between 0 and 999 in the Spacing field. The higher the Spacing, the farther apart each "paintdrop" will be.

or

Uncheck the Spacing box to have the brush respond to mouse speed. The faster the mouse is dragged, the more "paintdrops" will skip.

5. Enter a number between 0 to 100 in the Roundness field. The higher the number, the rounder the tip.

or

Move either black dot up or down in the left preview box.

6. Enter a number between -180 and 180 in the Angle field.

or

Move the gray arrow in a circular direction in the left preview box.

7. Click OK or press Return (**Figure 7**).

✔ Tip

■ Only the Spacing percentage can be modified for the Assorted brushes and most of the Drop Shadow brushes.

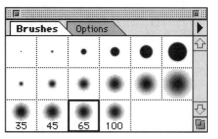

Figure 5. *Double-click a brush tip on the **Brushes** palette.*

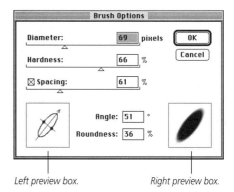

Left preview box.　　　　Right preview box.

Figure 6. *Choose **Diameter, Hardness, Spacing, Angle**, and **Roundness** values in the **Brush Options** dialog box.*

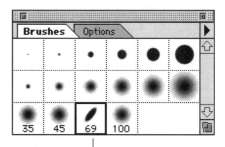

Figure 7. *The modified brush tip.*

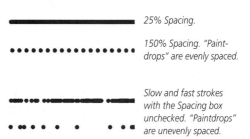

25% Spacing.

150% Spacing. "Paint-drops" are evenly spaced.

Slow and fast strokes with the Spacing box unchecked. "Paintdrops" are unevenly spaced.

Modify a Brush Tip

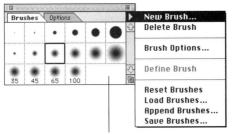

*Figure 8. Click on the white area at the bottom of the **Brushes** palette, or choose **New Brush** from the palette command menu.*

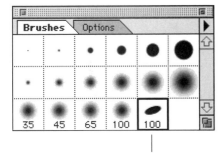

Figure 9. The new tip appears after the last tip.

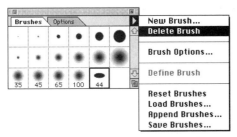

*Figure 10. Click a tip, then choose **Delete Brush** from the palette command menu.*

To create a new brush tip:

1. Click on the white area at the bottom of the Brushes palette (**Figure 8**).
or
Choose New Brush from the palette command menu.

2. Follow steps 2-7 on the previous page to customize the tip. The new tip will appear after the last tip on the palette (**Figure 9**).

To delete a brush tip:

1. Click a brush tip on the Brushes palette.

2. Choose Delete Brush from the palette command menu (**Figure 10**).

Create or Delete a Brush Tip

137

Monochromatic shades of the Foreground color are applied when you use a brush tip created from an area of a picture.

To create a brush tip from a picture:

1. Double-click the Marquee tool (**Figure 11**).

2. Choose Rectangular from the Shape pop-up menu on the Marquee Options palette.

3. Select an area of a picture. The selection cannot exceed 1,000 by 1,000 pixels (**Figure 12**).

4. Click the Brushes tab to display the Brushes palette, then choose Define Brush from the palette command menu. The new tip will appear after the last tip on the palette (**Figures 13-14** and **Gallery 2g**).

✔ Tips

■ Use the tip with the Paintbrush or Airbrush tool, and click (don't drag) on a white or monochromatic area so you can see the brush image clearly.

■ To smooth the edges of the stroke, double-click the custom brush tip, then check the Anti-aliased box. This option is not available for a large brush. You can also specify a Spacing value in the same dialog box. The higher the Spacing percentage, the greater the distance between "paint-drops."

*The **Marquee** tool.* ——

Figure 11.

Figure 12. *Select an area of a picture.*

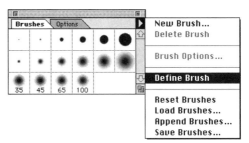

Figure 13. *Choose **Define Brush** from the **Brushes** palette command menu.*

Figure 14. *A custom brush tip.*

Create a Brush Tip from a Picture

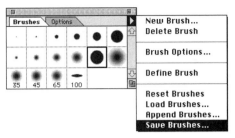

Figure 15. Choose **Save Brushes** from the **Brushes** palette command menu.

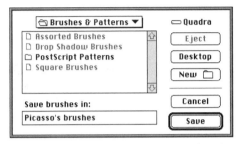

Figure 16. Enter a name in the **Save brushes in** field, choose a location in which to save it, then click **Save**.

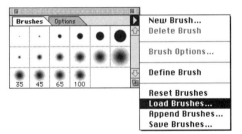

Figure 17. Choose **Load Brushes** from the Brushes palette command menu.

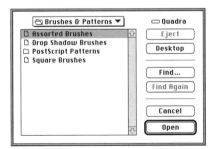

Figure 18. Highlight a palette, then click **Open**.

To save a Brushes palette:

1. Choose Save Brushes from the palette command menu (**Figure 15**).

2. Enter a name in the "Save brushes in" field (**Figure 16**).

3. Choose a location in which to save the palette.

4. Click Save or press Return.

To load a Brushes palette:

1. Choose Load Brushes from the palette command menu (**Figure 17**).

2. Open the Brushes & Patterns folder, which is in the Goodies folder in the Photoshop application folder.

3. Double-click a palette name (**Figure 18**).
or
Click a palette name, then click Open.

✔ Tips

■ Three Brushes palettes are supplied with Photoshop in addition to the Default Brushes: Assorted Brushes, which are special shapes and symbols, Drop Shadow Brushes, which are brush tips with soft edges you can use to make drop shadows, and hard-edged Square Brushes.

■ Choose Reset Brushes from the palette command menu to restore the default Brushes palette.

Save or Load a Brushes Palette

You can use the Pencil, Airbrush, or Paintbrush tool to create a linear element, such as a squiggly or a calligraphic line. Use different Angle and Roundness values to create your own line shapes.

To draw a calligraphic line:

1. Click the Pencil, Airbrush, or Paintbrush tool (**Figure 19**).

2. Choose a Foreground color. *(See pages 112-114)*

3. Double-click a hard-edged brush tip on the Brushes palette. (Only hard-edged tips are available for the Pencil tool).

4. Enter a number between 10 and 15 in the Diameter field (**Figure 20**).

5. Enter a number between 1 and 25 in the Spacing field.

6. Position the Hardness slider at 100%.

7. Enter 34 in the Angle field.

8. Enter 20 in the Roundness field. The brush will preview in the dialog box.

9. Click OK or press Return.

10. *Optional:* Click the Options tab to display the Options palette, then move the Opacity slider.

11. Draw shapes or letters (**Figure 21**).

— *The **Pencil** tool.*

Figure 19.

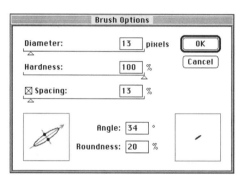

*Figure 20. The **Brush Options** dialog box.*

Figure 21. A calligraphic line added to a picture.

Draw a Calligraphic Line

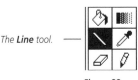

*The **Line** tool.*

Figure 22.

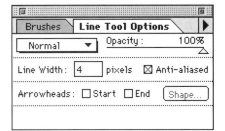

Figure 23. *Enter a number in the **Line Width** field on the **Line Tool Options** palette.*

Figure 24a. *Straight lines added to a picture using the Line tool.*

To draw a straight line:

1. Double-click the Line tool (**Figure 22**).

2. On the Line Tool Options palette (**Figure 23**):

Enter a number between 1 and 1000 in the Line Width field.
and
Choose a mode from the mode pop-up menu.
and
Choose an Opacity.

3. Choose a Foreground color. *(See pages 112-114)*

4. Draw a line. The line will fill with the Foreground color when the mouse is released (**Figure 24a**).

✔ Tips

■ Hold down Shift while dragging to constrain the line to the nearest 45° angle.

■ To draw a straight line with any other painting tool, click once to begin the stroke, then hold down Shift and click in a different location to complete the stroke (**Figure 24b**).

■ To create an arrow, click the Start and/or End box on the Line Tool Options palette. Click Shape, enter numbers in the Width, Length, and Concavity fields in the Arrowhead Shape dialog box, click OK, then draw a line.

Figure 24b. *A border created with the Pencil tool in Dissolve mode at 85% opacity.*

The **Paint Bucket** tool replaces pixels with the Foreground color, and fills areas of similar shade or color within a specified Tolerance range. Unlike the Fill command under the Edit menu, the Paint Bucket can be used without creating a selection.

To fill an area using the Paint Bucket tool:

1. Double-click the Paint Bucket tool (**Figure 25**).

2. On the Paint Bucket Options palette (**Figure 26**):

Enter a number up to 255 in the Tolerance field. The higher the Tolerance value, the wider the range of colors the Paint Bucket will fill. Try a low number first.
and
Choose a mode from the mode pop-up menu. Try Soft Light mode.
and
Choose an Opacity.
and
Make sure the Anti-aliased box is checked.

3. Choose a Foreground color. *(See pages 112-114)*

4. Click on the picture (**Figures 27-28**).

✔ Tip

■ To undo the fill, choose Undo from the Edit menu immediately.

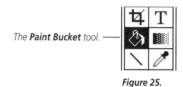
The *Paint Bucket* tool. ⸺

Figure 25.

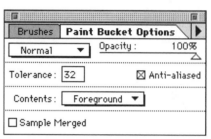

Figure 26. *Enter a number in the* **Tolerance** *field on the* **Paint Bucket Options** *palette.*

Figure 27. *The original picture.*

Figure 28. *After clicking with the* **Paint Bucket** *tool.*

Use the Paint Bucket

Default Colors button —

Figure 29.

Selection

Image

→

Figure 30. *Hold down Shift, then drag to the right. Do not release the mouse or Shift!*

↑

Figure 31. *Drag upward to create the second part of the drop shadow, then release Shift before you release the mouse.* **The vertical stroke won't appear until you release Shift.**

Figure 32. *The completed drop shadow.*

To create a drop shadow:

1. *Optional*: Follow the instructions on page 47 to add a white border to the picture.

2. To paint on a layer other than Background, choose the layer and uncheck the Preserve Transparency box.

3. Choose the Magic Wand tool.

4. Click on the white border.
   or
   Click on the transparent area of the target layer.

5. Double-click the Paintbrush tool.

6. On the Paintbrush Options palette, move the Opacity slider to 30%.

7. Click the Brushes tab to display the Brushes palette, then click a large, soft-edged tip.

8. Click the Default colors button on the Toolbox (**Figure 29**).

9. Position the cursor on the bottom edge of the image, then hold down Shift and drag slowly to the right until the cursor is slightly to the right of the image. **Don't release the mouse or the Shift key!** (**Figure 30**)

10. Keep Shift held down and drag upward along the right edge of the image. Release Shift when the cursor is just below the top of the image (**Figures 31-32**). **Release Shift, then release the mouse.**

   Note: To create a shadow for a non-rectangular shape, paint without holding down Shift.

✔ Tips

■ To delete the shadow, press Delete or choose Undo from the Edit menu.

■ Don't create two separate brush strokes. The area where they overlap will be darker.

■ You can also create shadows using Photoshop's Drop Shadow brushes. *(Instructions for loading brushes are on page 139)*

If you use the **Eraser** tool on the Background layer, the erased area will be replaced with the Background color — unless you created the document with a Transparent Background. If you use the Eraser tool on a layer with the Preserve Transparency box unchecked, the erased area will be transparent.

To erase part of a layer:

1. Double-click the Eraser tool (**Figure 33**).

2. Choose Paintbrush, Airbrush, Pencil, or Block from the pop-up menu on the Eraser Options palette (**Figure 34**), choose an Opacity.

3. Click a brush tip on the Brushes palette. (You can't choose a tip for the Block option.)

4. If you are going to erase over the Background layer of the picture or if the Preserve Transparency box is checked on the Layers palette, choose a Background color.

5. Click on or drag across any area of the layer (**Figures 35a-c**).

✔ Tips

■ To restore areas of the last saved version of a picture, use the Eraser tool with the Erase to Saved box checked on the Eraser Options palette. Erase to Saved will not work if you changed the mode, dimensions, or resolution of the picture, or added or deleted a layer or layer mask since it was last saved.

You can also use the Rubber Stamp tool with its From Saved Option and Options palette settings of your choice to restore areas of the last saved version. *(See page 207)*

■ Click Erase Image to erase the whole picture.

■ Choose Paintbrush from the pop-up menu and check the Wet Edges box to produce a wet-edge eraser effect.

The **Eraser** tool. ──

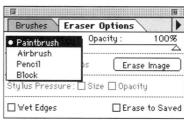
Figure 33.

Figure 34. Choose a tool from the pop-up menu on the **Eraser Options** palette. Move the **Opacity** slider to adjust the Eraser opacity.

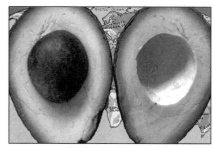

Figure 35a. The original picture.

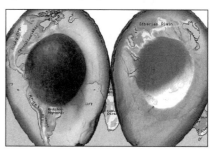

Figure 35b. After erasing part of the avocados layer (Airbrush option, 55% Opacity), and part of the map layer (Paintbrush option, 100% Opacity).

Figure 35c. A detail of the partially erased map layer.

Erase Part of a Layer

1a. The original picture.

1b. Three fill opacities and modes. Clockwise from lower left: untouched, 50% Normal, 90% Saturation, 40% Screen.

1c. The edge of a selection colored using the Stroke command (Edit menu).

1d. Edges colored using the Stroke command.

1e. A Grayscale picture colorized using Hue/ Saturation. Clockwise from lower left: Hue -26, Lightness -20; Hue -142, Lightness +8; Hue 15, Lightness 0; Hue 113, Lightness 0. A Saturation of 50 was used for all sections.

1f. Sections of a Grayscale picture colorized using Threshold and Hue/Saturation. The Hue/Saturation Lightness slider was moved to add color to darks (on the left) and lights (on the right).

1g. The original picture.

1h. Cyan fill — Normal mode, 50% Opacity.

1i. Orange fill — Normal mode, 60% Opacity.

1j. Yellow fill — Normal mode, 60% Opacity.

1k. Purple fill — Multiply mode, Opacity 60%.

1l. Cyan fill — Dissolve mode, Opacity 50%.

1m. A Grayscale picture colorized using the Color Balance dialog box.

1n. A Grayscale picture colorized using the Color Balance dialog box.

1o. Use the Variations dialog box to adjust color.

1p. The original picture.

1q. After adjustments using the Variations dialog box.

1r. After adjustments using the Color Balance dialog box. Use the Color Balance dialog box to see a full screen image when making color adjustments.

2a. The original picture.

2b. The Paintbrush tool — Normal mode, 75% Opacity, large soft-edged tip.

2c. The Paintbrush tool — Lighten mode, 60% Opacity.

2d. The Paintbrush tool — Hue mode, 100% Opacity.

2e. The Paintbrush tool — Dissolve mode, 40% Opacity.

2f. The Paintbrush tool — Normal mode, 75% Opacity, Fade-out Distance 20.

2g. Brush tip created from a picture, used with various Foreground colors and modes.

3a. Type filled with a linear blend.

3b. A linear, counterclockwise spectrum blend.

3c. A linear blend — red Foreground color, yellow Background color.

3d. A multicolor wash created with the Gradient tool. A low opacity blend was applied to the entire picture and a second light opacity blend was applied to the inner selection. The Rubber Stamp tool was used to restore some original colors.

4. A picture converted from RGB mode to Grayscale mode, then back to RGB mode. The Rubber Stamp tool was used with a 50% Opacity, Color mode to restore some of the original color.

5a. The Trace Contour and Minimum filters.

5b. The Find Edges filter without the Solarize filter step *(See 5c)*. The Rubber Stamp tool was used with a light opacity to restore color from the last saved version.

5c. The Find Edges filter, Invert command, and Solarize filter.

5d. The Color Halftone filter.

5e. A "watercolor" — Median and Minimum filters.

5f. Tiles filter — Inverse Image "grout."

5g. Tiles filter — Foreground color "grout."

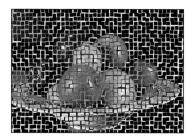

5h. Tiles filter — Inverse Image "grout."

5i. A woven texture.

6a. A picture converted to Indexed Color mode.

6b. A picture in Indexed Color mode, Spectrum Color Table.

6c. Indexed color image pasted using Paste Layer onto original, then modified using Layer Options — Normal mode, 50% Opacity.

6d. Indexed color image pasted using Paste Layer onto original, then modified using Layer Options — Normal mode, 90% Opacity, Underlying black slider moved to 30.

Peter Lourekas. *Memories.* Created using Adobe Dimensions, Photoshop and scanned images.

Phil Allen *Duck Wuck*

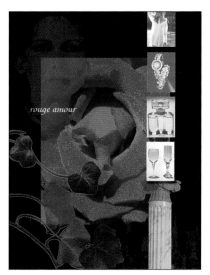

Leah Krivan

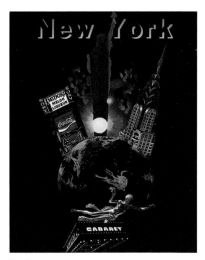

Jin Kim

Raisa Grubshteyn

I N THIS CHAPTER you will learn to blend between layers using the Layers Palette Opacity slider and mode pop-up menu and the Layer Options dialog box. You will also learn how to create, modify, and move layer masks, link layers to move them as a unit, save a copy of a layer in a separate document, use layers as a clipping group, merge layers, and flatten layers.

(Basic layer operations are covered in Chapter 8)

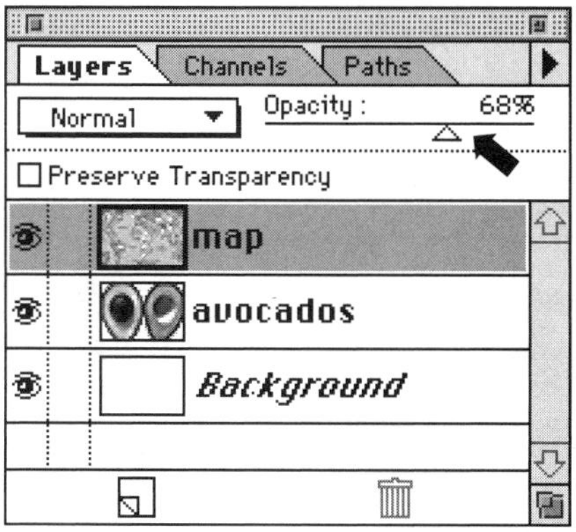

Figure 1. *Move the **Opacity** slider on the Layers palette.*

To modify the opacity of a target layer or a floating selection:

Move the Opacity slider on the Layers palette (**Figures 1-3**). The lower the Opacity, the more pixels from the layer below will show through the target layer.

✔ Tip
■ You can also choose an opacity for a layer or a floating selection using the Layer Options dialog box *(see the following page)*.

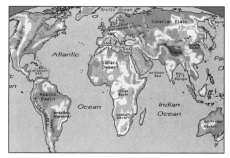

Figure 2. *The **map** layer, 100% Opacity, on top of the **avocados** layer.*

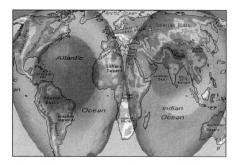

Figure 3. *The **map** layer Opacity reduced to 68%*

You can control which pixels in a pair of layers will be visible using the Underlying sliders in the **Layer Options** dialog box.

To blend pixels between two layers:

1. Choose a target layer, then choose Layer Options from the Layers palette command menu (**Figure 4**).
or
Double click a layer name.

2. Make sure the Preview box is checked, then move the black This Layer slider to the right to remove shadow areas from the target layer (**Figure 5**).
and/or
Move the white Underlying slider to the left to remove highlights from the target layer.
and/or
Move the black Underlying slider to the right to restore shadow areas from the layer below the target layer (**Figure 5**).
and/or
Move the white Underlying slider to the left to restore highlights from the layer below the target layer.

3. Click OK or press Return (**Figure 6**).

✔ Tips

■ To eliminate white in the topmost of the two layers, move the white This Layer slider to about 245.

■ To restore colors from one channel at a time, choose from the Blend If pop-up menu before moving the sliders.

■ To adjust the midtones independently of the shadows, hold down Option and drag the right part of the black slider (it will divide in two). To adjust the midtones independently of the highlights, hold down Option and drag the left part of the white slider.

Figure 4. *Click a layer name, then choose **Layer Options** from the Layers palette command menu.*

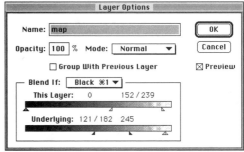

Figure 5. *To blend between layers, move the **This Layer** and/or **Underlying** sliders in the **Layer Options** dialog box. To produce Figure 6, the white **This Layer** slider and the black **Underlying** slider were divided and moved.*

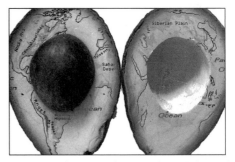

Figure 6. *The final picture. (Figure 2 is the original picture.)*

Figure 7. *Choose a* **mode** *for a layer from the Layers palette pop-up menu.*

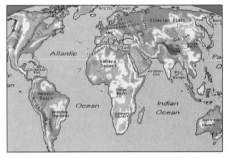

Figure 8. *The* **map** *layer on top of the* **avocados** *layer.*

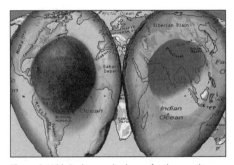

Figure 9. *With Darken mode chosen for the* **map** *layer.*

You can choose a **mode** for a layer from the mode pop-up menu on the Layers palette (**Figures 7-9**). *(Modes are described on page 135)*

✔ Tip

■ You can also choose a mode for a layer in the Layer Options dialog box (double-click a layer name to open it).

About layer masks

A layer mask is simply a channel that has White or Black as its Background color. By default, white areas on the layer mask permit pixels to be seen, black areas hide pixels, and gray areas partially mask pixels. You can use a mask to temporarily hide pixels on a layer so you can view the rest of the composite picture without them. Later, you can remove the mask and make the effect permanent or you can discard the mask.

The advantage of using a layer mask is that you can access it from both the Layers palette and the Channels palette. You'll see a thumbnail for the layer mask on the Layers palette and on the Channels palette when a layer that contains a mask is highlighted. Unlike an alpha channel selection, however, which can be loaded onto any layer, a layer mask can only be turned on or off for the layer or clipping group (group of layers) it is associated with.

Layer Modes, Layer Masks

To create a layer mask:

1. Click on a layer name on the Layers palette.

2. Choose Add Layer Mask from the Layers palette command menu (**Figure 10**).

✔ Tip

■ To display a thumbnail for the mask or layers on the Layers palette, choose Palette Options from the Layers palette pop-up menu, and click a Size button.

■ To turn a selection (or a type selection) into a layer mask, select an area on the layer that you want to remain visible, choose Save Selection from the Select menu, then choose "...Mask" from the Channel pop-up menu in the Save Selection dialog box (**Figures 11-12**).

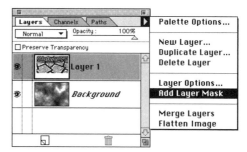

Figure 10. *Choose **Add Layer Mask** from the Layers palette command menu.*

To modify a layer mask:

1. Double-click the Paintbrush tool.

2. On the Options palette, choose 100% Opacity and Normal mode. (Or choose an Opacity below 100% to partially hide layer pixels.)

3. Click a brush tip on the Brushes palette.

4. Click on the Layer mask thumbnail on the Layers palette (don't click on the layer name). The selected thumbnail will have a dark border.

5. Paint on the picture with Black as the Foreground color to hide pixels on the layer.
and/or
Paint with White as the Foreground color to restore pixels on the layer.
and/or
Paint with Gray as the Foreground color to partially hide pixels on the layer.

Figure 11. *Layer 1 pixels are revealed through the White type in the layer mask.*

Figure 12. *The water layer is visible only through the letter shapes of the layer mask.*

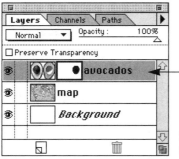

*Figure 13. The **avocados** layer contains a layer mask.*

The layer mask is also listed on the Channels palette.

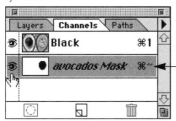

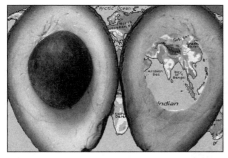

Figure 14. The center of the avocado on the right is blocked by a layer mask.

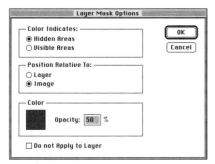

*Figure 15. Click **Position Relative To: Image** in the **Layers Mask Options** dialog box so the layer mask to can be moved independently of the layer.*

To display a layer mask as you paint on it:

1. Click on the layer mask thumbnail.

2. Click the Channels tab on the Layers/Channels palette.

3. Click in the eye icon column for the mask channel (it will have the same name as the layer) to display it (**Figures 13-14**).

4. Click on the Layers tab.

5. Paint with Black as the Foreground color to hide pixels on the layer.

and/or

Paint with White as the Foreground color to remove the mask and redisplay pixels on the layer.

(More about masks in Chapter 14)

✔ Tip

■ Hold down Option and click on the layer mask thumbnail on the Layers palette to display the mask channel by itself in the document window. (Hold down Option and click on the layer thumbnail on the Layers palette to redisplay the picture.)

By default, a layer and layer mask move together. Follow these steps to move a layer mask independently.

To move a mask without moving its layer:

1. Double-click the layer mask thumbnail on the Layers palette.

or

Double-click the Mask channel name on the Channels palette.

2. Click Position Relative To: Image (**Figure 15**).

3. Click OK.

4. Choose the Move tool.

5. Drag the layer mask in the document window.

Display/Move a Layer Mask

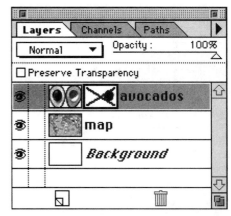

Figure 16. *To temporarily hide a mask effect, hold down Command (⌘) and click the layer mask thumbnail on the Layers palette. A red "X" will appear over the thumbnail.*

To temporarily remove the effects of a layer mask:

Hold down Command (⌘) and click the layer mask thumbnail on the Layers palette. A red "X" will appear over the thumbnail and the entire layer will be displayed (**Figure 16**).

(Hold down Command (⌘) and click again on the layer mask thumbnail to remove the "X" and restore the mask effect.)

✔ Tip

■ Make sure the mask channel is hidden (no eye icon for the mask on the Channels palette).

To apply or discard the effects of a layer mask:

1. Click the thumbnail on the Layers palette of the mask that you want to remove.

2. Choose Remove Layer Mask from the Layers palette command menu (**Figure 17**).

3. Click Apply to have the mask effect become permanent (**Figure 18**).
or
Click Discard to remove the mask without applying any changes.

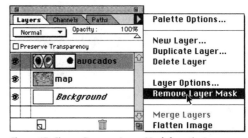

Figure 17. *Choose* **Remove Layer Mask** *from the Layers palette command menu.*

Figure 18. *Click* **Apply** *to permanently apply the mask effects or click* **Discard** *to discard the mask effects.*

If you link layers together, you can move them as a unit in the document window.

To link layers to move them as a unit:

1. Click on a layer name on the Layers palette.

2. Click in the second column for any other layer you want to link to the layer you chose in Step 1. The layers you link don't have be next to each other.

Cross icons will appear next to the linked layers (**Figure 19**).

3. Choose the Move tool.

4. Press and drag the linked layers in the document window.

✔ Tip

■ To unlink layers, click any cross icon. Click on a layer name to see if it's linked (a cross icon will appear).

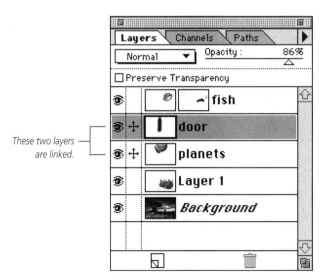

These two layers are linked.

Figure 19. *Click to display the cross icon in the second column on the Layers palette for any layers you want to link.*

A **clipping group** is a group of layers. The bottommost layer of a clipping group (the **base layer**) **clips** (limits) the display of pixels and controls the mode and opacity of the layers above it. Only pixels that overlap pixels on the base layer will be visible.

To create a clipping group:

1. Click on a layer name.

2. Hold down Option and click on the line between that layer name and the name just above it (the cursor will be two overlapping circles). A dotted line will appear between clipping group layer names, and the base layer name will be underlined (**Figures 20-21**).

✔ Tips

■ To remove a layer from a clipping group, hold down Option and click on the dotted line on the Layers palette. A solid line will appear.

■ The layers you choose for a clipping group must be listed consecutively on the Layers palette.

■ Create a type layer, and make it the base layer of a clipping group. The type layer shapes will fill with imagery from the layer(s) above it. To move the imagery inside the type, move the type layer or move the other clipping group layer(s). *(See page 185)*

■ To create a clipping group using the Layer Options dialog box, double-click the layer name on the Layers palette just above the layer you want to be the base (bottommost) layer, then check the Group with Previous Layer box.

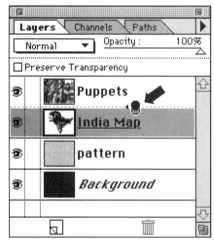

Figure 20. *Click between two layers to join them in a clipping group. A dotted line will appear, and the base layer will be underlined.*

Figure 21. *The map of India is clipping (limiting) the view of the puppets.*

Clipping Group

Use this technique to save individual layers in a new document whose resolution and size match the original "source" document. Follow these steps before you perform an operation that requires flattening, such as converting to Indexed Color mode (which does not support multiple layers), or saving your document in a file format other than Photoshop 3.0.

To save a copy of a layer in a separate document:

1. Choose a layer other than the Background layer.

2. Choose Duplicate from the Layers palette command menu (**Figure 22**).

3. Choose New from the Destination/Document pop-up menu (**Figure 23**).

4. Enter a name for the new document in the **Name** field.

5. Click OK or press Return.

6. Save the new document.

7. *Optional:* To delete the layer from the source document, click in the source document window, then drag the layer you duplicated over the Trash can icon.

✔ **Tip**

■ To move the layer back to its source document, drag the duplicate layer name from the duplicate document's Layers palette into the source document window. The layer will appear where you release the mouse in the document window, and will be the topmost layer in the document.

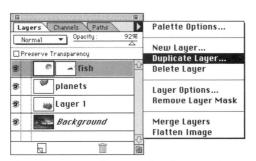

*Figure 22. Choose **Duplicate Layer** from the Layers palette command menu.*

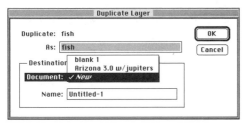

*Figure 23. Choose **New** from the **Destination/Document:** pop-up menu.*

In these instructions, a filter is applied to a duplicate layer and then the original and duplicate layers are blended using the Layers palette opacity and mode controls. This technique reduces the effect of a filter or other image editing command.

To blend a modified layer with the original layer:

1. Choose a target layer.

2. Choose Duplicate Layer from the Layers palette command menu.

3. Click OK.

4. Modify the duplicate layer. (Apply a filter or other image editing command.)

5. On the Layers palette, move the Opacity slider to achieve the desired degree of transparency between the original layer and the modified duplicate layer (**Figure 25-26**).
and/or
Choose a mode.

✔ Tips

■ For a beautiful textural effect, duplicate the Background in a color picture, highlight the new layer, then choose Desaturate (Adjust submenu under the Image menu) to make it grayscale. Next, apply the Add Noise filter or the Pointillize filter. Finally, choose a lower opacity and choose different modes for the new layer from the Layers palette.

■ To create a pure texture (no image), fill the Background with a solid color. Next, create a new layer, fill the new layer with a different solid color, and choose Add Layer Mask from the palette command menu. Click on the layer mask thumbnail and apply a filter or series of filters. Filters you might try include Add Noise, Pointillize, Add Noise/Crystallize, Add Noise/Pointillize, and Add Noise/Diffuse (try different Diffuse Modes).

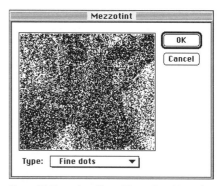

Figure 24. *To produce Figure 26, we chose Mezzotint from the Pixelate submenu under the Filter menu, chose Fine dots from the Type pop-up menu, then clicked OK.*

Figure 25. *The original picture.*

Figure 26. *The picture after applying the Mezzotint filter to the duplicate layer, then lowering the opacity of the duplicate layer.*

Blend Layers/Mezzotint filter

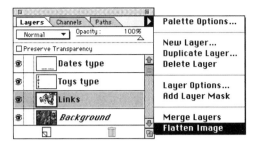

Figure 27a. *Choose* **Merge Layers** *or* **Flatten Image** *from the Layers palette command menu.*

Figure 27b. *The Layers palette for the merged or flattened document.*

Layers take up storage space, so when you're finished editing your picture, you should **Merge** or **Flatten** the layers to reduce the picture's storage size.

Note: Only the PhotoShop 3.0 file format supports multiple layers. To save your document in any other file format, you must first Merge or Flatten it.

The **Merge** command merges currently displayed layers into the **bottommost displayed layer. Hidden layers are preserved.**

To merge layers:

1. Display the layers you want to merge (all should have eye icons on the Layers palette), and hide the layers you *don't* want to merge. *Note:* Hide the Background if you don't want to merge into it.

2. Click on one of the layers to be merged.

3. Choose Merge Layers from the Layers palette command menu (**Figures 27a-b**).

The **Flatten** command merges currently displayed layers into the **bottommost displayed layer** and **discards hidden layers.**

To flatten layers:

1. Make sure all the layers you want to flatten are displayed (have eye icons).

2. Choose Flatten Image from the Layers palette command menu **Figures 27a-b**).

3. Click OK.

✓ **Tip**

■ Use the **Save a Copy** command (File menu) to save a flattened version of your picture. The layered version of the picture will stay open so you can continue to work on it.

☞ **FOR THIS CHAPTER,** you'll need to open the **Channels palette.**

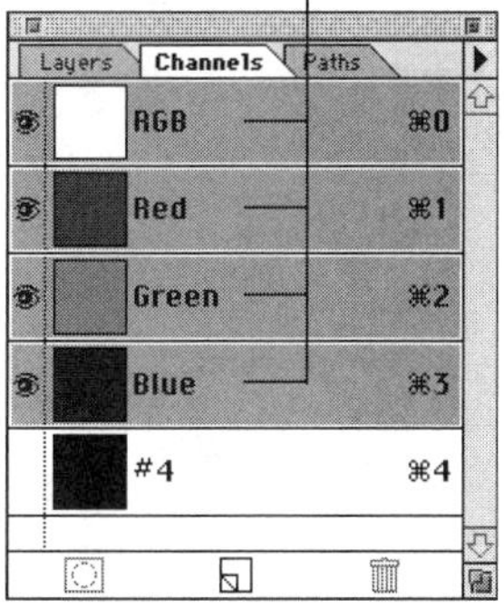

THIS CHAPTER covers two special selection techniques: saving a selection to an alpha channel and working in Quick Mask mode.

If you save a selection to a specially created grayscale channel, called an **alpha channel**, you can load the selection onto the picture at any time. For example, a selection with an irregular shape that would be difficult to reselect could be saved to an alpha channel. Up to 21 alpha channels can be created in a document. Keep in mind, though, that each channel increases a picture's storage size by approximately 25 to 30 percent. An alpha channel can be displayed or modified via the Channels palette (**Figure 1**), and saved or loaded onto a picture via Select menu commands or the Channels palette. *(See the "Tip" on page 168 to convert an alpha channel to a path to save file storage space)*

Using Photoshop's **Quick Mask** mode, the selected or unselected areas of a picture can be covered with a semi-transparent colored mask, which can then be modified using any editing or painting tool. Unlike an alpha channel, a Quick Mask cannot be saved, but the new selection can be saved when you return to Standard (non-Quick Mask) mode.

Note: If you are unfamiliar with Photoshop's basic selection tools, read Chapters 5 and 6 before reading this chapter.

(Layer masks are covered in Chapter 13)

Masks

*Only **highlighted** channels can be **edited.***

*An **eye** icon indicates that channel is **displayed.***

An Alpha channel. ──

Selection icon *New channel icon* *Trash icon*

Figure 1. The **Channels** palette.

To save a selection to a channel:

1. Select an area of a target layer (**Figure 2**). *(See pages 66-70)*

2. Choose Save Selection from the Select menu (**Figure 3**), then click OK (**Figure 4**).
or
Click the Selection icon on the Channels palette (the leftmost icon at the bottom of the palette).

✔ Tips

■ Choose an Operation option in the Save Selection dialog box to combine a current selection with an existing alpha channel that you choose from the Channel pop-up menu. (*Operations are discussed on page 160*)

■ Choose New from the Document pop-up menu in the Save Selection dialog box to save a selection to an alpha channel in a new, separate document.

■ You can save an alpha channel with a picture only in the Photoshop, TIFF or PICT (RGB) file formats.

■ If you save a floating selection to a channel, the selection will remain floating (it won't replace underlying pixels).

■ Choose "......Mask" from the Channel pop-up menu in the Save Selection dialog box to turn the selection into a layer mask for the target layer.

Figure 2. Select an area on a layer.

Figure 3. Choose Save Selection from the Select menu.

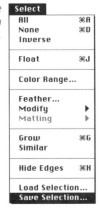

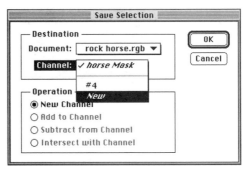

Figure 4. Choose New from the Channel pop-up menu in the Save Selection dialog box. If you are saving to an existing channel, choose an Operation option to add to or subtract from white areas on the channel.

Save a Selection to a Channel

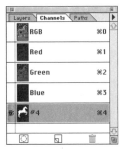

Figure 5. *Click an alpha channel number on the Channels palette.*

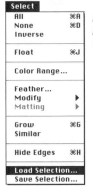

Figure 6. *An alpha channel. The selected area is white, the protected area is black.*

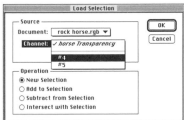

Figure 7. *Choose Load Selection from the Select menu.*

Figure 8. *Choose the channel name (number) from the Channel pop-up menu in the Load Selection dialog box.*

An alpha channel can be displayed without loading it onto the document as a selection.

To display a channel selection:

1. Click an alpha channel name on the Channels palette. The selected area will be white, the protected area will be black (**Figures 5-6**).

2. To restore the normal picture display, click the top channel name on the palette.

✔ Tips

■ If the selection has a Feather radius, the faded area will be gray and will only be partially affected by editing.

■ Modify the mask with any editing or painting tool using black, gray, or white "paint."

To load a channel selection onto the picture:

1. If the composite picture is not displayed, click the top channel name on the Channels palette.

2. Choose Load Selection from the Select menu (**Figure 7**).

3. Choose the channel name from the Channel pop-up menu (**Figure 8**).

4. Click OK or press Return.

✔ Tips

■ Choose Invert in the Load Selection dialog box to switch the selected and unselected areas in the loaded selection.

■ For a multi-layer document, you can choose "... Transparency" from the Channel pop-up menu to select only pixels on a layer, not the transparent areas.

Save Selection Operation Options

When a selection is saved to an existing channel, you can choose from these **Operation** options in the **Save Selection** dialog box:

Choose **Add to Channel** to add the new selection to the channel.

Choose **Subtract from Channel** to remove white or gray areas that overlap the new selection.

Choose **Intersect with Channel** to preserve only white or gray areas that overlap the new selection.

Save Selection shortcuts

With an active selection on the target layer, click the Selection icon on the Channels palette to create a new channel.

To replace the channel with the active selection, drag the Selection icon over an alpha channel name.

Hold down Shift and drag the Selection icon over an alpha channel name to add to the channel.

Hold down Command (⌘) and drag the Selection icon over an alpha channel name to subtract from the channel.

Hold down Command (⌘) and Shift and drag the Selection icon over an alpha channel name to intersect with the channel.

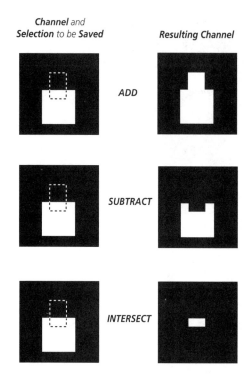

Channel and
Selection to be *Saved*   *Resulting Channel*

ADD

SUBTRACT

INTERSECT

Load Selection Operation Options

When a channel is loaded while an area of a layer is selected, you can choose from these **Operation** options in the **Load Selection** dialog box:

Choose **Add to Selection** to add the channel selection to the current selection.

Choose **Subtract from Selection** to remove areas of the current selection that overlap the channel selection.

Choose **Intersect with Selection** to preserve only areas of the current selection that overlap the channel selection.

Load Selection shortcuts

To load the selection, drag the alpha channel name over the Selection icon or hold down Option and click the channel name. This will replace the active selection with the channel.

Hold down Shift and drag the alpha channel name over the Selection icon to add the channel to the current selection.

Hold down Command (⌘) and drag the alpha channel name over the Selection icon to subtract the channel from the current selection.

Hold down Command (⌘) and Shift and drag the alpha channel name over the Selection icon to intersect the channel with the current selection.

Selection and *Channel* to be *Loaded*   *Resulting Selection*

ADD

SUBTRACT

INTERSECT

Load Selection Options and Shortcuts

You can superimpose an alpha channel selection as a colored mask over a picture, and then reshape the mask.

To reshape a mask:

1. Make sure there is no selection on the picture.

2. Click an alpha channel name on the Channels palette. An eye icon will appear next to it (**Figure 9**).

3. Click in the leftmost column at the top of the palette. An eye icon will appear. There should be only one highlighted channel — the alpha channel name (**Figure 10**).

4. Double-click the Pencil or Paintbrush tool on the Toolbox.

5. On the Options palette, choose Normal mode.
   and
   Choose 100% Opacity to create a full mask, or a lower Opacity to create a partial mask.

6. To enlarge the masked (protected) area, stroke on the cutout with Black as the Foreground color (**Figure 12**). (Click the Switch colors icon on the Toolbox to switch the Foreground color between Black and White.)
   or
   To enlarge the unmasked area, stroke on the mask with White as the Foreground color (**Figure 13**).

7. To hide the mask, click the Layers tab, then choose a target layer.

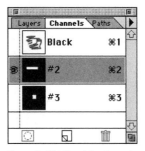

Figure 9. *Click the alpha channel name on the Channels palette.*

Figure 10. *Click in the leftmost column at the top of the palette. Make sure the alpha channel name stays highlighted.*

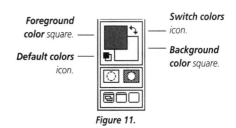

Foreground color square.
Default colors icon.
Switch colors icon.
Background color square.

Figure 11.

Figure 12. *Enlarge the masked area by stroking on the cutout with Black as the Foreground color.*

Figure 13. *Enlarge the unmasked area by stroking on the mask with White as the Foreground color.*

Reshape a Mask

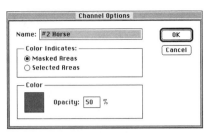

Figure 14. *In the **Channel Options** dialog box, enter a new name in the **Name** field.*

Figure 15. *The horse is the selected area.*

Figure 16. *The horse is still the selected area, but it is now black instead of white.*

To rename a channel:

1. Double-click a channel name on the Channels palette.

or

Click a channel name, then choose Channel Options from the palette command menu.

2. Enter a new name in the Name field (**Figure 14**).

3. Click OK or press Return.

✔ Tip

■ Normally, the selected areas of an alpha channel are white and the protected areas are black or colored. To reverse these colors without changing which area is selected, double-click an alpha channel name on the Channels palette, then click Selected Areas in the Color Indicates box (**Figures 15-16**).

To delete a channel:

Drag the channel name over the Trash icon on the palette (**Figure 17**).

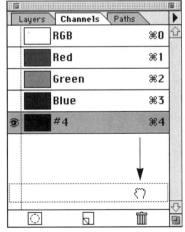

Figure 17. *Drag the channel to be deleted over the Trash can icon.*

If you choose **Quick Mask** mode when an area of a target layer is selected, a semi-transparent tinted mask will cover the unselected areas and the selected areas will be revealed in a cutout. The cutout or mask can be modified with the Pencil or Paintbrush tool.

Note: You can't save a Quick Mask while your document is in Quick Mask mode, but you can save your selection to an alpha channel.

To create a Quick Mask:

1. Select an area of a target layer (**Figure 18**).

2. Click the Quick Mask mode icon. A mask will cover part of the picture (**Figures 19-20**).

3. Double-click the Pencil or Paintbrush tool.

4. On the Options palette, move the Opacity slider to 100%.
and
Choose Normal from the Mode pop-up menu. Make sure all check boxes on the palette are unchecked.

5. Click the Brushes tab, then click a tip on the Brushes palette.

6. Stroke on the cutout with Black as the Foreground color to enlarge the masked (protected) area.
or
Stroke on the mask with White as the the Foreground color to enlarge the cutout (unmasked area). (Click the Switch Colors icon on the Toolbox to switch the Foreground and Background colors.)

7. Click the Standard mode icon to turn off Quick Mask (**Figure 19**). The selection will still be active.

8. Modify the layer. Only the unmasked area will be affected.

9. *Optional:* Save the selection to an alpha channel so you can use it later *(see page 158)*.

Figure 18. *Select an area on a layer.*

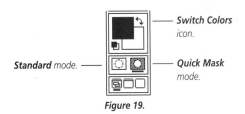

Standard *mode.*

Switch Colors *icon.*

Quick Mask *mode.*

Figure 19.

Figure 20. *The unselected area is covered with a mask.*

Create a Quick Mask

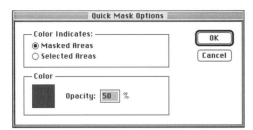

Figure 21. *In the* **Mask Options** *dialog box, choose whether* **Color Indicates Masked Areas** *or* **Selected Areas***. Click the* **Color** *square to choose a different mask color.*

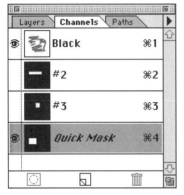

Figure 22. *"Quick Mask" appears on the* **Channels** *palette. To open the Quick Mask Options dialog box, double-click "Quick Mask" or double-click the Quick Mask icon on the Toolbox.*

✔ **Tips**

■ To create a Quick Mask without first creating a selection, click the Pencil or Paintbrush tool, double-click the Quick Mask icon, click Selected Areas, then stroke on the layer. Use a soft-edged brush to produce a soft-edged mask.

■ To cover the Selected Areas with a mask instead of the protected areas, double-click the Quick Mask icon on the Toolbox, then click Selected Areas (**Figure 21**). To quickly switch the mask Color between the selected and masked areas, hold down Option and click the Quick Mask icon on the Toolbox.

In the Quick Mask Options dialog box, you can also click the Color box and choose a new mask color or change the Opacity of the mask color.

■ "Quick Mask" will be listed on the Channels palette and on the document window title bar while Quick Mask mode is on (**Figure 22**).

■ If you modify a Quick Mask using a tool with a low opacity, that area will be partially affected by modifications.

Create a Quick Mask

☞ **FOR THIS CHAPTER,** you'll need to open the **Paths palette.**

LIKE THE PEN TOOL in Adobe Illustrator, the Pen tool in Photoshop creates outline shapes, called paths, consisting of anchor points connected by curved or straight line segments. A path can be reshaped by adding, deleting, or moving its anchor points. A curved line segment can also be reshaped by adjusting its Bezier direction lines.

The Pen tool and its variations are chosen from, and paths are displayed, using the Paths palette (**Figure 1**). There is no Pen tool in the Toolbox.

A path can be saved, converted into a selection, or exported to Adobe Illustrator, where it can be used as a path. You can also convert a selection into a path.

Paths

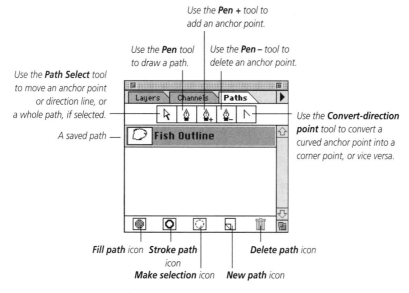

Use the **Pen +** tool to add an anchor point.

Use the **Pen** tool to draw a path.

Use the **Pen –** tool to delete an anchor point.

Use the **Path Select** tool to move an anchor point or direction line, or a whole path, if selected.

A saved path

Use the **Convert-direction point** tool to convert a curved anchor point into a corner point, or vice versa.

Fill path icon Stroke path icon

Make selection icon New path icon

Delete path icon

Figure 1. The **Paths** palette.

To convert a selection into a path:

1. Select an area of a picture (**Figure 2**).

2. Choose Make Path from the Paths palette command menu (**Figure 3**).

3. Enter 3, 4, or 5 in the Tolerance field. The minimum is 0.5; the maximum is 10. At a low Tolerance value, many anchor points will be created and the path will conform precisely to the selection marquee. At a high Tolerance value, fewer anchor points will be created and the path will be smoother, but it will conform less precisely to the selection (**Figure 4**).

4. Click OK or press Return (**Figure 5**).

✔ Tips

■ When a path is saved with a picture, the storage size of the picture does not increase, unlike when an alpha channel is saved with a picture. To save storage space, you can convert an alpha channel into a selection and then into a path, save the path, delete the alpha channel, then save the picture. Later on you can convert the path back into a selection and save the selection to a new alpha channel.

Follow the instructions on page 159 to load an alpha channel selection. Follow steps 2-4 on this page and the steps on page 171 to save the path. Then click the alpha channel name on the Channels palette, choose Delete Channel from the pop-up menu on the right side of the palette, and save the picture. Follow the instructions on page 172 later if you need to convert the path back into a selection.

■ You can also convert a selection into a path using the last used Tolerance setting by dragging the Make Selection icon at the bottom of the Paths palette over the New Path icon at the bottom of the Paths palette.

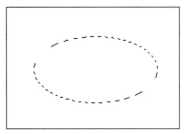

Figure 2. *Select an area of a picture.*

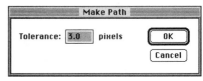

Figure 3. *Choose **Make Path** from the **Paths** palette.*

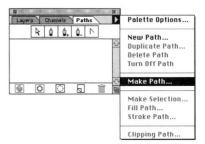

Figure 4. *Enter a number in the **Tolerance** field in the **Make Path** dialog box.*

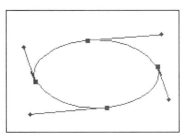

Figure 5. *A selection converted into a path.*

*Double-click the **Pen** tool on the Paths palette.*

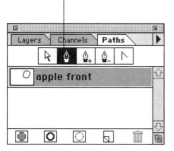

Figure 6.

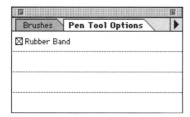

Figure 7. *Check the **Rubber Band** box on the **Pen Tool Options** palette.*

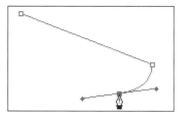

Figure 8. *Click to create straight sides.*

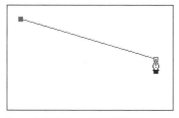

Figure 9. *Press and drag to create a curved segment.*

Click with the Pen tool to create anchor points connected by straight line segments. Press and drag with the Pen tool to create anchor points connected by curved line segments (Bezier curves).

To create a path using the Pen tool:

1. Double-click the Pen tool on the Paths palette (**Figure 6**).

2. Check the Rubber Band box on the Options palette to preview the line segments as you draw (**Figure 7**).

3. Click, move the mouse, then click again to create a straight segment.
or
Press and drag to create a curved segment, then release the mouse. Direction lines will appear (**Figures 8-12**).

4. Repeat step 3 as many times as necessary to complete the shape.

5. To leave the path open, click the Path Select tool on the Paths palette or double-click the Pen tool.
or
To close the path, click on the starting point (a small circle will appear next to the Path Select cursor).

✔ Tips

■ Hold down Shift while clicking to constrain a straight line segment to the nearest 45° angle.

■ Press Delete to erase the last anchor point created. Press Delete twice to delete the entire path.

Create a Path using the Pen Tool

Figure 10. *Press and drag to create curved segments around a shape.*

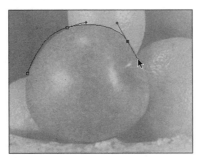

Figure 11. *A third anchor point is created.*

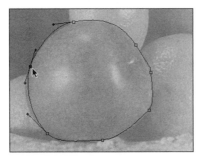

Figure 12. *The completed path.*

Figure 13. *Choose* **Save Path** *from the Paths palette command menu.*

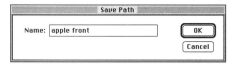

Figure 14. *Enter a* **Name** *in the* **Save Path** *dialog box. All currently displayed paths will be saved under one name.*

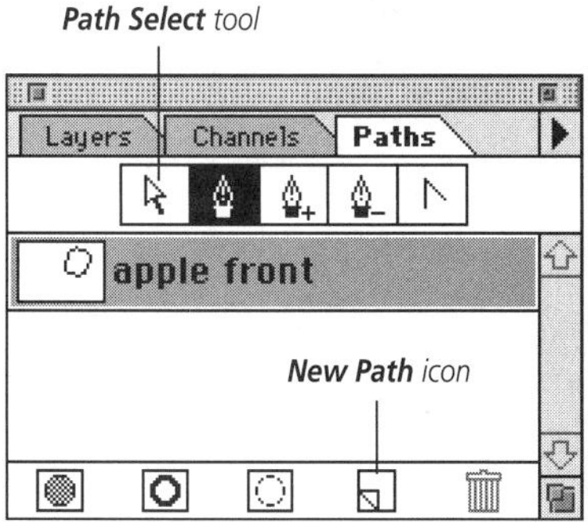

Path Select tool

Figure 15. *To display a saved path, click its name on the Paths palette.*

A new path will be automatically labeled Work Path, and it will save with the file. Any additional Work Path you create, though, will replace the prior Work Path. Follow these instructions to save a path so it won't be deleted.

To save a path:

1. Choose Save Path from the Paths palette command menu (**Figure 13**).
or
Double-click the path name on the palette.

2. Enter a name (**Figure 14**).

3. Click OK or press Return (**Figure 15**).

✔ Tip

■ To save a path with the default name, drag the path name over the New Path icon at the bottom of the Paths palette (**Figure 15**).

To display a path:

Click a path name on the Paths palette (**Figure 15**).

To hide a path:

Click on the white area on the Paths palette below the path name.
or
Choose Turn Off Path from the palette command menu.

To select a path:

1. Click a path name on the Paths palette.

2. Click the Path Select tool (**Figure 15**).

3. Click on the path.

✔ Tip

■ To select all the anchor points on a path, hold down Option and click on the path. An entire path can be moved when all its points are selected.

Save, Display, Hide, Select a Path

To deselect a path:

1. Click the Path Select tool.

2. Click outside the path.

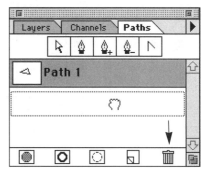

Figure 16. *To delete a path, drag the path name over the Trash can icon.*

To delete a path:

Drag the path name over the Trash can icon on the palette (**Figure 16**).

To convert a path into a selection:

1. Create a new path or display a saved path.

2. Drag the path name over the Make Selection icon at the bottom of the Paths palette (**Figure 17**). The selection will appear on top of the path.

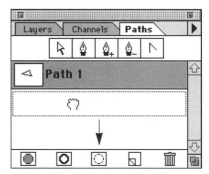

Figure 17. *To turn a path into a selection, drag the path name over the **Make Selection** icon.*

✔ Tips

■ If you convert a path into a selection by choosing Make Selection from the palette command menu, you can add a Feather Radius to the selection (enter a low number to soften the edge slightly), and you can add, subtract, or intersect the path with an existing selection on the picture by clicking an Operation option (**Figure 18**).

■ To move the selection, click any selection tool, then hold down Command (⌘) and Option and drag the selection.

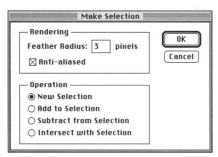

Figure 18. *To feather the edge of the selection, enter a number in the **Feather Radius** field in the **Make Selection** dialog box.*

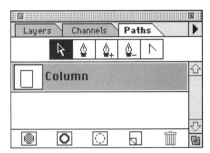

*Figure 19. Click a path name, then click the **Path Select** tool.*

Figure 20. Drag an anchor point.

Figure 21. Pull or rotate a direction line of a curved anchor point.

You can drag, add, or delete an anchor point to reshape a path. To modify the shape of a curved line segment, move a direction line toward or away from its anchor point or rotate it around its anchor point.

To reshape a path:

1. To reshape a saved path, click the path name on the Paths palette (**Figure 19**).

2. Click the Path Select tool on the Paths palette.

3. Click on the path to select it.

4. Drag an anchor point (**Figure 20**).
and/or
Drag or rotate a direction line (**Figure 21**).

5. Click outside the path to deselect it.

✔ Tips

■ To add an anchor point to a path, click the Pen + tool, then click on a line segment.

■ To delete an anchor point from a path, click the Pen – tool, then click on the anchor point.

■ Use the Convert-direction point tool to rotate half of a direction line independently. Once the Convert-direction point tool has been used on part of a direction line, you can use the Path Select tool to move the other part.

■ To convert a curved point into a corner point, click the Convert-direction point tool, then click the anchor point (deselect the Convert-direction point tool by clicking another tool). To convert a corner point into a curved point, click the Convert-direction point tool, then drag the anchor point.

■ Once a path has been saved, it is resaved automatically each time it is modified.

Reshape a Path

Use the Stroke Path command to apply color to the edge of a path.

To stroke a path:

1. Create a new path or display an existing path.

2. Double-click the Pencil, Paintbrush, Airbrush, Rubber Stamp, Smudge, Blur/Sharpen, or Dodge/Burn/Sponge tool.

3. On the Options palette, choose a mode *(see page 135)* (**Figure 22**).
and
Choose an Opacity (or Pressure).

4. Click the Brushes tab on the palette, then click a Brush tip.

5. Choose a Foreground color *(see pages 112-114)*.

6. Choose Stroke Path (or Stroke Subpath for a Work Path) from the Paths palette command menu (**Figure 23**).

7. Choose the tool you double-clicked in step 2 from the Stroke Path pop-up menu (**Figure 24**).

8. Click OK. The path will be stroked with the tool you chose and its current attributes (**Figure 25**).

✔ Tip

■ To stroke a path using the current Stroke Path dialog box tool choice, drag the path name over the Stroke Path icon at the bottom of the Paths palette. To open the Stroke Path dialog box, hold down Option as you drag.

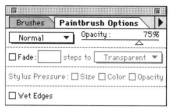

Figure 22. On the **Options** *palette, choose a mode and Opacity (or Pressure).*

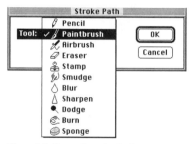

Figure 23. Choose **Fill Path** *or* **Stroke Path** *from the pop-up menu on the* **Paths** *palette.*

Figure 24. Choose from the **Tool** *pop-up menu in the* **Stroke Path** *dialog box.*

Figure 25. This glowing line was created by creating a path, double-clicking the Paintbrush tool, moving the Opacity slider to 30%, and choosing Stroke Path from the Paths palette.

Stroke a Path

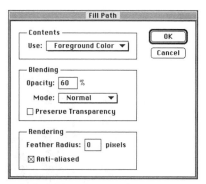

*Figure 26. In the **Fill Path** dialog box, choose **Foreground Color** from the **Use** pop-up menu, enter an **Opacity**, and choose a **Mode**.*

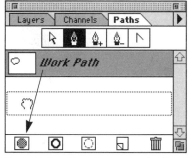

Figure 27. The left column was filled with white, 40% Opacity.

*Figure 28. Drag the path name over the **Fill Path** icon.*

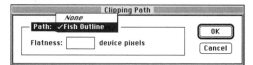

*Figure 29. In the **Clipping Path** dialog box, choose a **Path** name, enter a **Flatness** value or leave the Flatness field blank, and click a **Fill Rule** button.*

Use the Fill Path command to fill an open or closed path with the Foreground color.

To fill a path:

1. Create a new path or display an existing path.

2. Choose a Foreground color.

3. Choose Fill Path (or Fill Subpath for a Work Path) from the palette command menu (**Figure 23**).

4. Choose Foreground Color from the Use pop-up menu (**Figure 26**).

5. Enter an Opacity.

6. Choose a Mode.

7. *Optional:* Enter a number in the Feather Radius field.

8. Click OK or Press Return (**Figure 27**).

✔ Tip

■ To fill a path using the current Fill Path dialog box settings, drag the path name over the Fill Path icon at the bottom of the Paths palette (**Figure 28**). To open the Fill Path dialog box, hold down Option as you drag.

You can silhouette an image in Photoshop, then open or import it in another application, such as Adobe Illustrator or QuarkXPress. The area outside the image will be transparent, so it can be layered over other page elements, such as text.

To silhouette an image to use in another application:

1. Create a path around the portion of the image you wish to keep.

2. Save the path.

3. Choose Clipping Path from the Paths palette command menu.

4. Choose the path name from the Path pop-up menu (**Figure 29**).

5. Enter a number in the Flatness field. Leave this field blank to use the

(Continued on the following page)

printer's default setting. The higher
the Flatness value, the less precisely
the clipping path will match the
curves of the original path. Enter 8,
9, or 10 for high-resolution printing;
enter 1, 2, or 3 for low resolution
printing (300 to 600 dpi).

6. Click OK or press Return.

7. Save the document in the EPS file
format *(see page 52).*

Open or import the file in another
application. Only the area inside the
clipping path will display and print.

✔ Tip

■ In Adobe Illustrator, if you move or
scale the silhouetted image, the area
outside it will remain transparent.
However, if you rotate, reflect, or
shear the image, the area outside
it will become opaque.

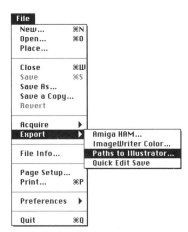

Figure 30. To create this illustration, a path was exported to Adobe Illustrator, where type was added to it. The type was then added to the Photoshop picture using the Place command.

You can create a path in Photoshop,
export it to Adobe Illustrator, and use it
as a path in that program. If you like,
you can then place it back in Photoshop
(**Figure 30**) *(see "Place an Adobe Illustrator picture" on page 43).*

To export a path to Adobe Illustrator:

1. Create and save a path.

2. Choose Paths to Illustrator from the
Export pop-up menu under the File
menu (**Figure 31**).

3. *Optional:* Modify the name in the
"Export paths to file" field.

4. Choose a location in which to save
the path file (**Figure 32**).

5. Click Save. The path can be opened
as an Adobe Illustrator document.

✔ Tip

■ To ensure the picture fits when you
reimport it into Photoshop, don't alter
the picture's crop marks in Illustrator.

*Figure 31. Choose **Paths to Illustrator** from the **Export** pop-up menu under the **File** menu.*

*Figure 32. Choose a location in which to save the path, then click **Save**.*

☞ **FOR THIS CHAPTER,** you'll need to open the **Layers palette.**

Figure 1. The side of a character with the Anti-aliased box unchecked in the Type Tool dialog box.

Figure 2. The Anti-aliased box checked in the Type Tool dialog box.

Figure 3. Adobe Type Manager turned off or not installed.

I N PHOTOSHOP, type is composed of pixels. Newly created type appears on a picture as a floating selection, and it can be modified. If you deselect the type, it will replace the underlying pixels of the target layer. If you make the type into its own layer, you can continue to modify it, like any other layer.

This chapter covers how to create, move, deselect, and delete a type selection, how to place type on its own layer, how to screen back type and screen back a picture behind type in a single- or multi-layer picture, how to fill type with imagery, how to use type in a clipping group of layers, and how to emphasize type with a drop shadow.

Type can also be rotated, imported from Adobe Illustrator, filled with a gradient, filled with a pattern, or modified by applying a filter. You'll learn these techniques in other chapters.

The resolution of type is the picture's resolution. To create the smoothest possible type for high-resolution output, choose 200 dpi or higher as the picture's resolution. Unfortunately, increasing a file's resolution causes its file size to increase. If you want to superimpose type over a picture for a particular design and are not creating a special Photoshop type effect, import your Photoshop picture into a page layout program or into an illustration program, like Adobe Illustrator, and layer PostScript type over it.

Check the Anti-aliased box in the Type Tool dialog box for smooth rendering (**Figures 1-2**). Photoshop uses Adobe Type Manager when rendering Adobe PostScript fonts (**Figure 3**). TrueType fonts can also be used with System 7 or later.

Type

Note: **You can restyle a floating type selection only while it is selected.** If you unintentionally deselect a floating type selection, immediately choose Undo from the Edit menu. **If you save type to its own layer, you'll be able to modify it after you deselect it.** *(See the following page)*

— *Click the **Type** tool.*

Figure 4.

To create a type selection:

1. Choose a target layer.

2. Click the Type tool (**Figure 4**).

3. Click on the picture where you want the type to appear.

4. *Optional:* Check the Show Font and Show Size boxes to preview the type in the dialog box (**Figure 5**).

5. Enter characters in the text field in the Type Tool dialog box. Press Return when you want to start a new line, otherwise all the type will appear in one line on the picture.

6. Choose a typeface from the Font pop-up menu.

7. Choose Points or Pixels from the pop-up menu next to the Size field, then enter a number between 4 and 720 in the Size field.

Steps 8-11 are optional.

8. If you enter more than one line of type, enter a number between 0 and 1000 in the Leading field (the space between lines of type).

9. Enter a number between -99.9 and 999.9 in the Spacing field (the space between characters).

10. Check a Style.

11. Click a different Alignment icon.

12. Check the Anti-aliased box to smooth the type (this is checked by default).

13. Click OK. The floating type selection will automatically fill with the Foreground color (**Figure 6**).

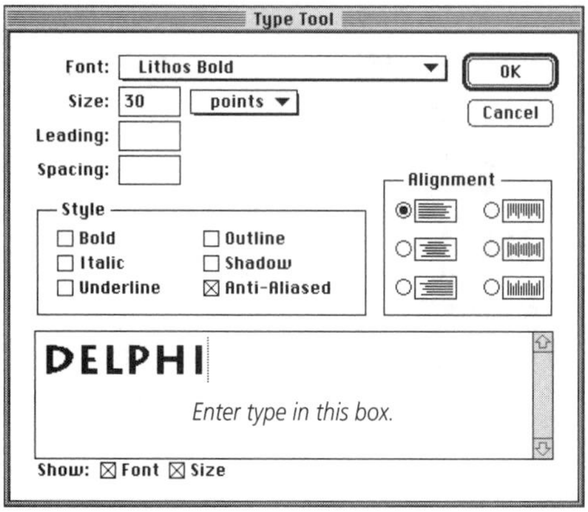

Figure 5. *The **Type Tool** dialog box. Don't double Style a font. For example, if you choose Garamond Italic from the Font menu, don't apply the Italic style to it. And don't use city-name fonts (Chicago, Monaco, etc.) unless they are TrueType fonts.*

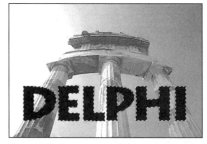

Figure 6. *Type appears as a floating selection.*

Create a Type Selection

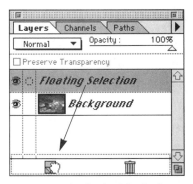

Figure 7. *Drag the* **Floating Selection** *layer over the* **New Layer** *icon on the* **Layers** *palette.*

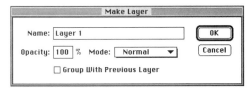

Figure 8. *The* **Make Layer** *dialog box.*

Figure 9. *The type layer is on top of other layers.*

Figure 10. *A floating type selection being moved.*

To place type on its own layer:

1. Follow steps 1-13 on the previous page. The type will automatically be a floating selection in the picture and be listed as "Floating Selection" on the Layers palette.

2. Drag the Floating Selection layer name over the New layer icon at the bottom of the Layers palette (**Figure 7**).
   or
   Double-click the Floating Selection layer name.

3. *Optional:* Enter a new name for the layer in the Name field (**Figure 8**).

4. Click OK or press Return (**Figure 9**).

5. *Optional:* To restack the type layer, drag the type layer name up or down on the Layers palette.

✔ Tips

■ Move the Opacity slider on the Layers palette to make the type less opaque. You can also choose a different mode for the type layer from the Layers palette.

■ With the type layer selected, check the Preserve Transparency box on the Layers palette to restrict painting, editing, and filter effects to the letter shapes. The transparent areas of the layer won't be modified.

To move type:

If the type is a floating selection, position the pointer over the type, then drag with the arrow pointer (**Figure 10**), or choose the Move tool, then drag.

If the type is on its own layer, click the layer name on the Layers palette, choose the Move tool, then drag in the document window.

To recolor a type selection:

1. If the type is a floating selection, make sure the Floating Selection layer is highlighted on the Layers palette.

If the type is on its own layer, click the type layer name on the Layers palette (**Figure 11**), and check the Preserve Transparency box so only the type pixels on the layer will be recolored.

2. Choose a Foreground color.

3. Choose Fill from the Edit menu.

4. Choose Foreground Color from the Contents/Use pop-up menu (**Figure 12**).

5. Enter a number between 1 and 100 in the Opacity field.

6. Choose a mode from the Mode pop-up menu. *(See page 135)*

7. Click OK or press Return.

✔ Tips

■ You can also choose a fill opacity and a mode for a type selection from the Layers palette.

■ For a painterly effect, choose the Paintbrush tool and a Foreground color, make sure the type layer is highlighted on the Layers palette, then drag across the type layer in the document window. With the Preserve Transparency box checked on the Layers palette, only existing pixels will be repainted.

To paint behind the type on the same layer, as in **Figure 13**, make sure the type layer is highlighted on the Layers palette and uncheck the Preserve Transparency box, choose a Foreground color, double-click the Paintbrush tool, choose Behind from the Mode pop-up menu on the Paintbrush Options palette, then paint on the picture.

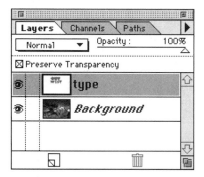

*Figure 11. Click the **type** layer on the **Layers** palette, and check the **Preserve Transparency** box.*

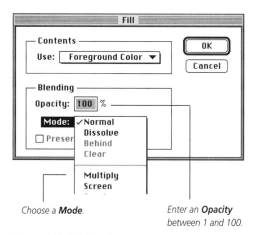

*Choose a **Mode**.*

*Enter an **Opacity** between 1 and 100.*

*Figure 12. The **Fill** dialog box.*

Figure 13. Paint behind type.

Figure 14. Move the **Opacity** slider to 1% on the Layers palette.

Figure 15. Choose **Defloat** from the **Select** menu.

You can fill type with a screened back version of a picture.

To screen back a type selection in a one-layer picture:

1. Make sure the Floating Selection layer name is highlighted on the Layers palette, then move the Opacity slider to 1% (**Figure 14**).

2. Make sure the type is in the desired position, then choose Defloat from the Select Menu (**Figure 15**). The Defloat command will merge the Floating Selection pixels with the layer below it, but the type will remain selected.

3. Choose Levels from the Adjust submenu under the Image menu.

4. Move the Input Midtones slider to the left. Pause to preview (**Figure 16**).

5. Move the Output Shadows slider to the right. Pause to preview.

6. Click OK or press Return (**Figure 17**).

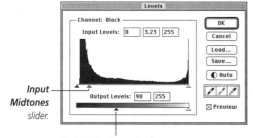

Input Midtones slider.

Output Shadows slider.

Figure 16. In the **Levels** dialog box, move the **Input Midtones** slider to the **left**, and move the **Output Shadows** slider to the **right**.

Figure 17. Screened back type.

To screen back a one-layer picture with type:

1. Follow the steps on page 178 to create a type selection, and reposition the type, if desired.

2. Make sure the Floating Selection layer name is highlighted on the Layers palette, then move the Opacity slider to 1% (**Figure 14**).

3. Choose Inverse from the Select menu to select the background of the picture (**Figure 18**).

4. Choose Levels from the Adjust sub-menu under the Image menu.

5. Move the Input Midtones slider to the left to lighten the picture's midtones. Pause to preview (**Figure 16**).

6. Move the Output Shadows slider to the right to reduce the picture's contrast. Pause to preview.

7. Click OK or press Return (**Figure 19**).

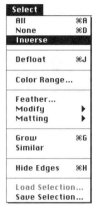

Figure 18. *Choose* **Inverse** *from the* **Select** *menu.*

Screen Back a Picture

Figure 19. *A screened back picture with type.*

Figure 20. *The original picture with a Background layer and a type layer.*

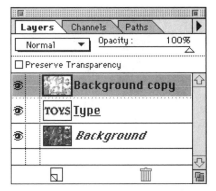

Figure 21. *The type layer and the Background copy layer are combined in a clipping group. The type layer is underlined and there is a dotted line between the type layer and the Background copy layer.*

Figure 22. *The type layer is clipping the Background copy layer. The Background copy layer was screened back using the Levels command.*

To screen back type in a multi-layer picture:

1. Follow the steps on page 178 to create a type layer (**Figure 20**).

2. Click the name of the layer that is to be the backdrop image behind the type.

3. Choose Duplicate from the Layers palette pop-up menu.

4. *Optional:* Enter a new name for the duplicate layer in the Name field.

5. Click OK or press Return.

6. On the Layers palette, drag the duplicate layer name above the type layer.

7. Hold down Option and click on the line between the two layer names to create a clipping group. A dotted line will appear and the name of the base (bottom) layer of the group will be underlined (**Figure 21**).

8. Click on the duplicate layer name.

9. Choose Levels from the Adjust submenu under the Image menu.

10. Move the Input Midtones slider to the left to lighten the midtones in the type. Pause to preview.

11. Move the Output Shadows slider to the right to reduce the contrast in the type. Pause to preview.

12. Click OK or press Return (**Figure 22**).

✔ Tips

■ The opacity and mode for the base layer (the underlined name on the Layers palette) will automatically be the opacity and mode for all the layers in the clipping group.

■ To screen back a picture with type, follow the steps above, but for step 8, click on the layer that is the backdrop image behind the type (not the duplicate).

To fill type with an image:

1. Follow the steps on page 178 to create a type selection. Reposition the type, if desired.

2. Open another picture.

3. Choose All from the Select menu.
   or
   Select an area of the picture. *(See pages 66-70)*

4. Choose Copy from the Edit menu.

5. With the picture containing the type selection active, choose Paste Into from the Edit menu (**Figures 23-24**). The pasted image will be selected; the type will be deselected.

6. *Optional:* Drag within the selection to reposition the image.

   (See options for modifying a pasted image on page 89)

Figure 23. *Choose* **Copy,** *then* **Paste Into** *from the* **Edit** *menu.*

Figure 24. *Type filled with a picture using the Paste Into command.*

Other ways to modify a type selection:

- **Flip** it *(instructions on page 74)*.

- **Rotate** it *(instructions on page 75)*.

- Apply a **filter** to it *(instructions on pages 209-236). (And see "Apply the Wind filter to type" on page 216)*

- Paste a **pattern** or **texture** into it *(instructions on page 229)* (**Figure 25**).

- Fill it with a **gradient** *(instructions on pages 195-198)* (**Figure 26**).

Figure 25. *Type filled with a pattern.*

✔ Tips

- You can import an Adobe Illustrator file containing type. It will automatically be rasterized (rendered as bitmapped pixels) in the Photoshop picture's resolution.

- Type will become distorted if you resize it using the Scale command (including type imported from Adobe Illustrator).

Figure 26. *Type filled with a gradient.*

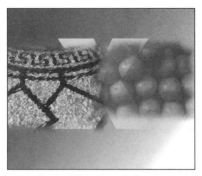

Figure 27. The different layers before the type layer becomes a clipping group.

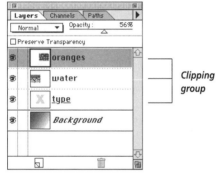

*Figure 28. The **Layers** palette after Option-clicking on the lines above the type layer. The type layer (the underlined name) is the clipping group base layer. There are dotted lines between layers in the clipping group.*

To fill type with a picture using a clipping group:

1. Create a type layer. *(See page 179)*

2. Move the type layer on the Layers palette just below the layer or layers that are to become the type fill (**Figure 27**).

3. Hold down Option and click on the line between the type layer name and the next layer up the list to create a clipping group. A dotted line will display and the base (bottom) layer of the group will be underlined. Only pixels that overlap the letter shapes will be visible (**Figures 28-29**).

4. *Optional:* Highlight the type layer and use the Move tool to reposition the letter shapes in the document window.

5. *Optional:* Option-click on the lines between other layers just above the clipping group to incorporate them into the group.

✔ Tips

■ To release a layer from a clipping group, hold Option and click on the dotted line.

■ The opacity and mode for the clipping group are determined by those settings for the base layer (the underlined name on the Layers palette in our example). Readjust this layer's settings to change the whole group.

Figure 29. The final image using the clipping group.

Figure 30. The separate layers in order.

To delete a type selection:

Choose Clear from the Edit menu
(**Figure 31**).

or

Press Delete.

or

Drag the Floating Selection layer over
the trash can icon on the Layers palette.

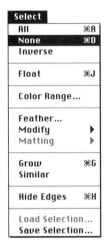

Figure 31. Choose **Clear**
from the **Edit** *menu.*

To deselect a type selection:

Click outside the selection.

or

Choose None from the Select menu
(**Figure 32**). The type will replace the
underlying pixels of the layer below it.

✔ Tip

■ To replace the underlying pixels *and*
create a copy of the floating selection,
choose Defloat from the Select menu.
To create a hard-edged shadow for
the type, choose a Background color
for the shadow, choose Defloat, then
move the type selection slightly to the
left and upward (**Figure 33**).

Figure 32. Choose **None**
from the **Select** *menu.*

Figure 33. *Type with a shadow.*

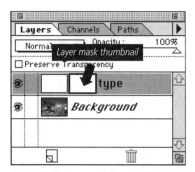

Figure 34. The layer mask thumbnail is highlighted.

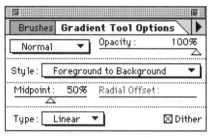

*Figure 35. The **Gradient Tool Options** palette.*

To create "fading" type:

1. Create type on its own layer, and leave the type layer selected.

2. Choose Add Layer Mask from the Layers palette command menu. A second thumbnail will appear next to the layer name (**Figure 34**).

3. Double-click the Gradient tool.

4. Choose 100% Opacity, Normal mode, and Foreground to Background from the Gradient Tool Options palette (**Figure 35**).

5. Click the Switch Colors icon on the Toolbox, if necessary, to make Black the Foreground color.

6. Drag from the top or bottom of the selection at least halfway across the type. The type layer mask will fill with a black-to-white gradient (**Figures 36**).

7. Choose None from the Select menu.

✔ Tip

■ Click on the layer thumbnail on the Layers palette to modify the layer; click on the layer mask thumbnail to modify the layer mask. (*More about layer masks in Chapter 13*)

Fading Type

The layer mask for the fading type.

Figure 36. Fading type.

You can follow these instructions to create a shadow for any object on its own layer.

To create shadow type:

1. Open a picture.

2. Create type, and put it on its own layer. (*See page 179*)

3. With the type layer selected, choose Duplicate Layer from the Layers palette command menu.

4. *Optional:* Enter a new name in the "As" field.

5. Click OK or press Return

6. Click on the original type layer name on the Layers palette (the layer below the duplicate) (**Figure 37**).

7. Choose the Move tool, then drag the type slightly away from the duplicate type. You can reposition it later, if you wish (**Figure 38**).

8. Choose a Foreground color for the shadow color from the Picker palette. (We chose Black for our illustration.)

9. Check the Preserve Transparency box on the Layers palette so only existing layer pixels will be recolored, not the transparent areas on the layer.

10. Choose Fill from the Edit menu.

11. Choose Foreground color from the Content/Use pop-up menu, and enter 100 in the Opacity field.

12. Click OK or press Return (**Figure 39**).

13. *Optional:* Press any of the arrow keys to move the type layer in small increments.

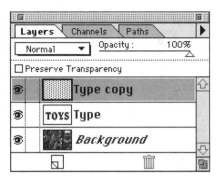

Figure 37. *The Layers palette showing the two type layers that were used to create the shadow type.*

Figure 38. *Move the original type layer to create a shadow.*

Figure 39. *The shadow type with a hard edge.*

Shadow Type

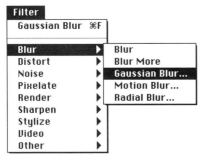

*Figure 40. Choose **Gaussian Blur** from the **Blur** submenu under the **Filter** menu.*

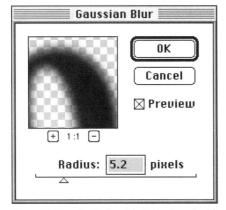

*Figure 41. Move the **Radius** slider in the **Gaussian Blur** dialog box to blur the type.*

14. Uncheck the Preserve Transparency box on the Layers palette.

15. Choose Gaussian Blur from the Blur submenu under the Filter menu (**Figure 40**).

16. Check the Preview box (**Figure 41**).

17. Move the Radius slider to the right to blur the type.

(Drag in the Preview window to move the picture inside it. Click the **+** button to zoom in or click the **–** button to zoom out).

18. Click OK or press Return (**Figure 42**).

✔ **Tip**

■ To create shadow type on a textured background, make the texture the Background, then follow the instructions for shadow type on this page and the previous page, but choose a color other than Black for step 8. After step 18, choose Multiply mode from the Layers palette. Move the Layers palette Opacity slider to lighten or darken the shadow.

(Shadow type instructions continue on the following page.)

Shadow Type

Figure 42. Shadow type with a soft edge.

Follow these steps below to heighten the contrast between the shadow type and the Background layer.

To screen back the background:

1. Click the Background layer name on the Layers palette. If there is more than one layer below the shadow type layer, highlight each layer individually and perform the following steps for each.

2. Choose Levels from the Adjust submenu under the Image menu.

3. Check the Preview box.

4. Move the gray Input slider a little to the left (**Figure 43**).

and

Move the black Output slider a little to the right.

5. Click OK or press Return (**Figures 44-45**).

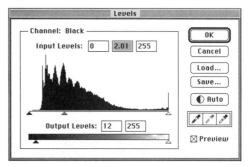

Figure 43. Move the **Input** sliders in the **Levels** dialog box to intensify the contrast between the shadow type and the background.

Figure 44. Soft-edged shadow type. The Background layer was screened back using the **Levels** dialog box.

Figure 45. Another variation of shadow type. The **Clouds** filter was applied to the type on the left.

☞ **FOR THIS CHAPTER,** you'll need to open the **Brushes palette.**

THIS CHAPTER covers two Photoshop editing tools: Blur/Sharpen and Smudge.

The **blur** function of the **Blur/Sharpen tool** decreases contrast between pixels. Use it to soften edges between shapes.

The **sharpen** function of the Blur/Sharpen tool increases contrast between pixels. Use it to delineate edges between shapes.

The **Smudge tool** smudges colors into each other, and can be used to create painterly effects. When used with the tool's Finger Painting option, the smudge starts with the Foreground color.

Double-click the ——
Blur/Sharpen *tool.*

Figure 1.

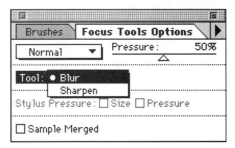

Figure 2. *Choose* ***Blur*** *or* ***Sharpen*** *from the* ***Tool*** *pop-up menu on the* ***Focus Tools Options*** *palette, then choose a* ***mode*** *and a* ***Pressure*** *percentage.*

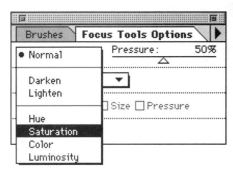

Figure 3. *Choose a mode from the pop-up menu on the* ***Focus Tools Options*** *palette.*

The **Blur** tool decreases contrast between pixels. The **Sharpen** tool increases contrast between pixels.

Note: the Blur/Sharpen tool can't be used on a picture in Bitmap or Indexed Color mode.

To sharpen or blur edges:

1. Double-click the Blur/Sharpen tool (**Figure 1**).

2. On the Focus Tools Options palette:
Choose Blur or Sharpen from the Tool pop-up menu (**Figure 2**).
and
Move the Pressure slider left or right. You can try a setting of around 30% first.
and
Choose a mode from the mode pop-up menu (**Figure 3**). Choose Normal to sharpen or blur pixels of any shade or color. Choose Darken to sharpen

(Continued on the following page)

Sharpen or Blur

or blur only pixels darker than the Foreground color. Choose Lighten to sharpen or blur only pixels lighter than the Foreground color. *(A full description of modes is on page 135)*

3. *Optional:* Click the Sample Merged box on the Options palette to edit all the layers in the document. Leave it unchecked to edit only the target layer.

4. Click the Brushes tab on the palette, then click a hard-edged or soft-edged tip (**Figure 4**).

5. Drag across any area of the picture (**Figures 5-6**). (Stroke again to intensify the effect.)

✔ **Tips**

■ Hold down Option and click the Blur/Sharpen tool to switch between its Blur and Sharpen functions. Each function will retain its own Options palette settings.

■ Hold down Option to switch between the Blur and Sharpen functions without clicking on the Toolbox. When the Blur or Sharpen function is accessed using this shortcut, the current Focus Tools Options palette settings apply.

■ Use the Sharpen tool with a medium Pressure setting and stroke only once on an area to avoid creating a grainy texture.

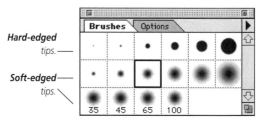

Hard-edged tips. ——

Soft-edged tips.

*Figure 4. The **Brushes** palette.*

Figure 5. The original picture.

Figure 6. After using the Sharpen tool on the strawberry in the center, and the Blur tool on the rest of the picture.

Sharpen or Blur

— *Double-click the **Smudge** tool.*

Figure 7.

Figure 8. *Choose a mode from the pop-up menu on the **Smudge Tools Options** palette, and choose a Pressure. To smudge with the Foreground color, check the **Finger Painting** box.*

Note: The Smudge tool can't be used on a picture in Bitmap or Indexed Color mode.

To smudge edges:

1. Double-click the Smudge tool (**Figure 7**).

2. On the Smudge Tool Options palette (**Figure 8**):

Move the Pressure slider to under 100%.

and

Choose a mode.

Normal to smudge all shades or colors.

or

Darken to push dark colors into lighter colors.

or

Lighten to push light colors into darker colors.

3. *Optional:* Click the Sample Merged box on the Options palette to edit all the layers in the document. Leave it unchecked to edit only the target layer.

4. Click the Brushes tab on the palette, then click a hard-edged or soft-edged tip (**Figure 4**).

5. Drag across any area of the picture (**Figures 9-13**). Pause to allow the screen to redraw.

✔ Tip

■ To Smudge with the Foreground color, check the Finger Painting box on the Smudge Tool Options palette. Hold down Option with the Smudge tool selected to temporarily turn on its Finger Painting option. The higher the Pressure percentage, the more Foreground color will be applied.

Smudge

Figure 9. The original picture.

Figure 10. Smudge (Normal mode, 100% Pressure).

Figure 11. Smudge (Normal mode, 50% Pressure).

Figure 12. Smudge (Darken mode, 100% Pressure). Only the light side of the pot is modified.

Figure 13. Smudge (Lighten mode, 100% Pressure). Only the dark side of the pot is modified.

☞ **FOR THIS CHAPTER,** you'll need to open the **Picker/Swatches/Scratch palette**.

I N THIS CHAPTER you will learn to create linear and radial gradients, fill type with a gradient, fill a layer or the background of a layer with a gradient, and layer multiple gradients.

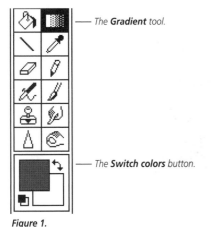

— The **Gradient** tool.

— The **Switch colors** button.

Figure 1.

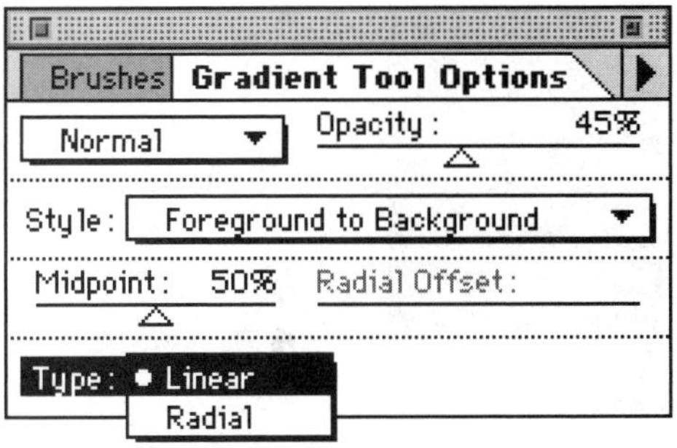

*Figure 2. On the **Gradient Tool Options** palette, choose **Normal** mode, choose an **Opacity**, and choose **Linear** from the **Type** pop-up menu.*

To create a linear gradient:

1. *Optional:* Select an area of a layer to confine the gradient to that area.

2. Double-click the Gradient tool (**Figure 1**).

3. On the Gradient Tool Options palette, choose Normal from the mode pop-up menu (**Figure 2**).
and
Choose an Opacity.
and
Choose Linear from the Type pop-up menu.
and
Choose from the Style pop-up menu.

4. Choose Foreground and/or Background colors if the gradient Style you chose uses them.

5. Drag from one side of the document or selection to the other (**Figures 3a-b**).
or
To produce a diagonal gradient, drag from corner to corner (**Figures 3c-d**).

(Illustrations on the following two pages)

Linear Gradient

In the illustrations below, the arrow shows where the mouse was dragged.

Figure 3a. *The Gradient tool dragged from the middle to the right.*

Figure 3b. *The Gradient tool dragged a short distance in the middle with the same colors.*

Figure 3c. *The Gradient tool dragged from upper left to lower right.*

Figure 3d. *The Gradient tool dragged from lower right to upper left with the same colors.*

Figure 3e. *The Gradient tool dragged from left to center using the Foreground to Transparent Style.*

Figure 3f. *The Gradient tool dragged from left to right using the Counterclockwise Spectrum Style.*

Figure 4a. *The original picture.*

Figure 4b. *Type was created, then filled with a gradient.*

GRADIENT TIPS

■ To delete a gradient, choose Undo from the Edit menu immediately.

■ To reverse the order of colors for a Foreground to Background gradient, drag in the opposite direction. Or, click the Switch colors button on the Toolbox before dragging (**Figure 1**).

■ The distance you drag defines the width of the transition area. Drag a long distance to produce a subtle transition; drag a short distance to produce an abrupt transition (**Figures 3a-b**).

■ To produce more of the Foreground color than the Background color, move the Midpoint slider on the Gradient Tool Options palette above 50%. To produce more of the Background color than the Foreground color, move the Midpoint slider below 50%.

■ Test the gradient on the scratch pad on the Scratch palette. To test a light opacity gradient, choose White as the Background color and choose Clear from the palette command menu to create a white scratch pad.

■ To create a gradient in type, create a type selection, then follow the instructions on page 195 (**Figures 4a-b** and **Gallery 3a**). To temporarily hide the selection marquee while keeping the type selected, choose Hide Edges from the Select menu. Choose Show Edges to restore the marquee.

■ To produce a "rainbow" in a gradient, choose Clockwise Spectrum or Counterclockwise Spectrum from the Style pop-up menu on the Options palette (**Figure 3f** and **Gallery 3b**).

Gradient Tips

To create a radial gradient:

1. *Optional:* Select an area of a layer to confine the gradient to that area.

2. Double-click the Gradient tool (**Figure 1**).

3. On the Gradient Tool Options palette, choose Normal from the mode pop-up menu (**Figure 5**).
and
Choose an Opacity.
and
Choose Radial from the Type pop-up menu.
and
Choose from the Style pop-up menu.

4. To produce more of the starting color as solid color, move the Radial Offset slider above 25%. To produce less of the starting color, move the Radial Offset slider below 25%. (25% is the default.)

5. Choose Foreground and/or Background colors if the gradient Style you chose uses them.

6. Press to establish a center point, then drag outward (**Figures 6-7**).

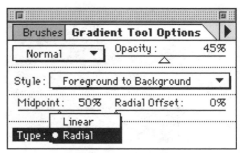

Figure 5. *Choose* **Radial** *from the* **Type** *pop-up menu on the* **Gradient Tool Options** *palette.*

Figure 6. *The original picture.*

Figure 7. *A radial gradient in the background. The arrow shows where the mouse was dragged.*

Radial Gradient

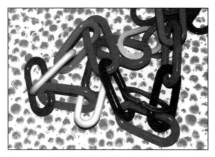

Figure 8. *The original three-layer picture.*

In the following instructions, a gradient is placed behind a layer using Behind mode without creating a separate layer for the gradient.

To create a gradient behind "objects" on a layer:

1. Choose a target layer that contains pixel "objects" on a transparent background (**Figure 8**).

2. Make sure the Preserve Transparency box on the Layers palette is unchecked (**Figure 9**).

3. Follow steps 1-5 on page 195, but choose **Behind** from the mode pop-up menu (**Figures 10-11**).

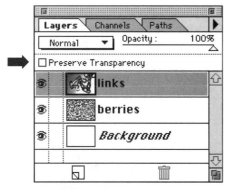

Figure 9. *Uncheck the **Preserve Transparency** box on the **Layers** palette for the target layer.*

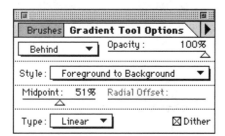

Figure 10. *Choose **Behind** mode from the **Gradient Tool Options** palette.*

Figure 11. *The final picture with a gradient behind the links on the top layer.*

To fill the background of a picture, first select it with the Magic Wand tool. The fewer colors or shades the background contains, the easier it will be to select.

Note: In the following instructions, the terms "foreground" and "background" refer to areas of the picture, not the Foreground and Background color squares.

To create a background gradient on a one-layer picture:

1. Double-click the Magic Wand tool (**Figure 12**).

2. Enter a number between 1 and 10 in the Tolerance field on the Magic Wand Options palette (**Figure 13**). The fewer shades or colors in the background of the picture, the lower the Tolerance value needed. If the background contains only one flat color, enter 1.

3. Click on the background of the picture (**Figure 14**). If the entire background does not select, enter a higher number in the Tolerance field and use the Magic Wand tool again with Shift held down or choose Grow from the Select menu. Make sure the entire background is selected and no part of the foreground is selected.

4. *Optional:* To soften the edge between the foreground and the gradient, choose Feather from the Select menu, enter 1 in the Feather Radius field (**Figure 15**), then click OK or press Return.

5. Follow steps 2-5 on page 195 (**Gallery 3c**).

✔ Tip

■ Use the Lasso tool with the Shift key to add to or subtract from the Magic Wand selection.

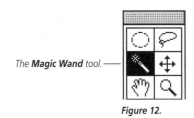
The **Magic Wand** tool.

Figure 12.

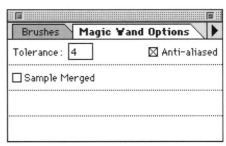
Figure 13. *Enter a number between 1 and 10 in the* **Tolerance** *field on the* **Magic Wand Options** *palette.*

Figure 14. *The original picture with the background selected.*

Figure 15. *Enter 1 in the* **Feather Radius** *field in the* **Feather Selection** *dialog box.*

Background Gradient

— The **Gradient** tool.

Figure 16.

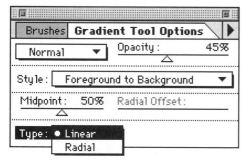

*Figure 17. On the **Gradient Tool Options** palette, choose **Normal** mode, choose an **Opacity** between 40% and 50%, choose **Linear** from the **Type** pop-up menu, and choose **Foreground to Background** from the **Style** pop-up menu.*

Figure 18. A soft-edged gradient in a feathered selection over another gradient in the background. To produce this effect, select an area of the picture, choose Feather from the Select menu, enter 15 in the Feather Radius field, then drag across the selection with the Gradient tool. Choose Inverse from the Select menu, choose a different Foreground color, then drag across the background of the picture.

To achieve similar results on multiple layers, create a gradient on the Background layer, select an area of the picture on a new layer, drag over the selection with the Gradient tool, then deselect. Uncheck the Preserve Transparency box on the Layers palette, choose Gaussian Blur from the Blur submenu under the Filter menu, move the gradient area in the Preview box so you can see its edge, move the Radius slider to choose an edge softness, then click OK.

To create a soft, multicolor wash, apply a translucent gradient, then apply a second gradient over the first one in another direction.

To create a multicolor wash:

1. Open a picture.

2. Choose a warm-toned Foreground color as the starting color.

3. Choose a cool-toned Background color for the ending color.

4. Double-click the Gradient tool (**Figure 16**).

5. On the Gradient Tool Options palette, choose Normal from the mode pop-up menu (**Figure 17**).
and
Move the Opacity slider to 40% or 50%.
and
Choose Linear from the Type pop-up menu.
and
Choose Foreground to Background from the Style pop-up menu.

6. Drag across the picture from left to right.

7. Repeat steps 5-6 above, but choose a different warm-toned Foreground color. Don't change the Background color.

8. Drag across the picture from top to bottom (**Gallery 3d**).

✔ Tip

■ To restore part of the original picture, double-click the Rubber Stamp tool, choose From Saved from the Option pop-up menu on the Options palette, and move the Opacity slider to about 50%. Choose a soft, medium-sized tip from the Brushes palette, then drag over any area of the picture you want to restore.

Multicolor Wash

For the greatest flexibility in positioning and editing multiple washes, place each wash on a separate layer.

To create a multicolor wash on multiple layers:

1. Choose a target layer (not the Background).

2. *Optional:* Select an area of a layer to confine the gradient to that area.

3. Double-click the Gradient tool.

4. On the Gradient Tool Options palette (**Figure 19**):

Choose an Opacity.
and
Choose Normal or Dissolve mode.
and
Choose Foreground to Transparent from the Style pop-up menu.

5. Drag from left to right in the document window.

6. Choose another target layer.

7. Repeat step 4.

8. Drag right to left in the document window.

9. *Optional:* Move the Opacity slider on the Layers palette to change the opacity for either gradient layer (**Figures 20-21**).

10. *Optional:* Restack the gradient layers using the Layers palette.

✔ Tip

■ For added flexibility, create a gradient fill on its own layer with Normal mode and 100% Opacity selected from the Options palette. Then adjust the mode and/or Opacity of the gradient fill using the Layers palette.

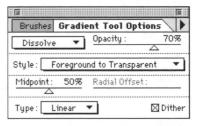

Figure 19. *The* **Gradient Tool Options** *palette.*

Figure 20. *The Layers palette after gradient fills were applied to two of the layers. The thumbnails show where the gradient fills are on the layers.*

Figure 21. *The final picture. The gradient on the Wash 1 layer was created by dragging from the lower left corner toward the center. The gradient on the Wash 2 layer was created by dragging from the upper right toward the center.*

☞ **FOR THIS CHAPTER,** you'll need to open the **Brushes palette.**

The Rubber Stamp tool. —

Figure 1.

I N THIS CHAPTER you will learn to use the Rubber Stamp tool to clone and rearrange imagery within a picture or clone imagery from one picture to another. You will also learn how to use the Rubber Stamp tool's From Saved option to restore part of the last saved version of a picture.

To clone a shape within a picture:

1. Double-click the Rubber Stamp tool (**Figure 1**).

2. Choose "Clone (aligned)" from the Option pop-up menu on the Rubber Stamp Options palette (**Figure 2**).

3. Click the Brushes tab, then click a small brush tip to clone a small detail or a medium- to large-sized tip to duplicate larger areas.

4. Choose a target layer.

5. Hold down Option and click on the area of the layer you wish to clone from to establish a source point.

6. Drag the mouse back and forth where you want the clone to appear (**Figure 3**).
or
Select another target layer, then drag the mouse.

Two cursors will appear on the screen: a crosshair cursor over the source point and a Rubber Stamp cursor where you drag the mouse. Imagery from the source point will appear where the mouse is dragged, and replace the underlying pixels.

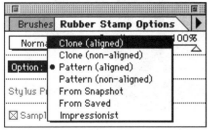

*Figure 2. Choose **Clone (aligned)** from the **Option** pop-up menu on the **Rubber Stamp Options** palette.*

(Continued on the following page)

Clone a Shape Within a Picture

Clone a Shape Within a Picture

✔ **Tips**

■ Using the Rubber Stamp tool with the Clone (aligned) Option, you can clone the entire layer, as long as you don't change the source point. The distance between the source point cursor and the Rubber Stamp cursor will remain constant, so you can release the mouse and drag in another area. To establish a new source point to clone from, hold down Option and click on a different area.

■ Choose Clone (non-aligned) for the Rubber Stamp tool to create multiple clones from the same source point. The crosshair cursor will return to the same source point each time you release the mouse. You can create a pattern with Clone (non-aligned) chosen by cloning a picture element multiple times (**Figure 4**).

■ You can modify Option palette settings for the Rubber Stamp tool between strokes. To create a "double exposure" on one layer, choose a low Opacity percentage so the underlying pixels will partially show through the cloned pixels (**Figure 5**).

Transparency and cloning

When the Preserve Transparency box is checked on the Layers palette, cloning will only appear where existing pixels are on that layer. If you choose a source point on the transparent part of a layer, nothing will be cloned.

The Sample Merged option

Check the Sample Merged box on the Options palette to have the Rubber Stamp tool sample pixels from all the layers you Option-click on.

Uncheck the Sample Merged box to sample pixels from only the current target layer. With this option unchecked, you can choose a source point from one layer and select another layer to clone pixels to.

Figure 3. *Drag the mouse where you want the clone to appear. To produce this illustration, Clone (aligned) was chosen for the Rubber Stamp tool.*

Figure 4. *Choose Clone (non-aligned) for the Rubber Stamp tool to create multiple clones from the same source point.*

Figure 5. *An Opacity of 45% was chosen for the Rubber Stamp tool to create this double exposure effect.*

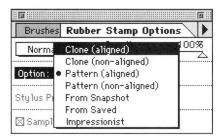

*Figure 6. Choose **Clone (aligned)** from the **Option** pop-up menu on the **Rubber Stamp Options** palette.*

Destination picture.   Source picture.

Figure 7. Option-click on the non-active picture to establish a source point. Drag back and forth in short strokes on the active (destination) picture to make the clone appear.

Figure 8. To create this effect, a picture was cloned to a new document with a white background.

To clone a shape from picture to picture:

1. Open two pictures, and position the two windows side by side.

2. If both pictures are color, choose the same mode from the Mode menu for both pictures. *Note:* Choose the Don't Flatten option to preserve layers. You can also clone between a color picture and a Grayscale picture.

3. Double-click the Rubber Stamp tool.

4. From the Rubber Stamp Options palette, choose Clone (aligned) from the Option pop-up menu to reproduce a continuous area from the source point (**Figure 6**).
or
Choose Clone (Non-aligned) to produce multiple clones from the source point.
and
Choose an Opacity.

5. Click the Brushes tab, then click a brush tip.

6. Click on the picture where the clone is to appear, and choose a target layer for the clone.

7. Hold down Option and click on an area of the source (non-active) picture that you want to clone from.

8. Drag back and forth on the destination (active) picture to make the clone appear (**Figure 7**).

✔ Tips

■ To create a brush stroke version of a picture, clone to a new document with a white or solid-colored background (**Figure 8**).

■ You can choose any mode for the Rubber Stamp tool. To test a mode, create a new document with a white background, make part of the background black, choose Clone

(Continued on the following page)

Clone a Shape from Picture to Picture

(non-aligned) in the Rubber Stamp Options dialog box, choose a mode from the Options palette, then clone to the new document (**Figure 9**).

Choose Darken to clone onto a white background, choose Lighten to clone onto a black background, choose Luminosity to produce a grayscale clone from a color picture, or choose Dissolve with an opacity of less than 100% to produce a grainy, chalky clone (**Figures 10-12**).

Figure 9. *The image on the left was cloned with Luminosity mode selected and 50% Opacity. The image on the right was cloned with Lighten mode chosen and 85% Opacity.*

Figure 10. *The original picture.*

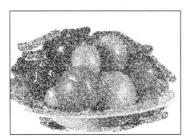

Figure 11. *The same image cloned with Dissolve mode chosen for the Rubber Stamp tool.*

Figure 12. *The same image was cloned on the left side on a light gray background with Darken mode chosen and on the right side on a dark gray background with Lighten mode chosen. The darkness of the background colors prevented some shades from being cloned.*

*The **Rubber Stamp** tool.* —

Figure 13.

If you save a picture and then modify a layer, you can restore portions of the saved version to contrast with the modifications using the Rubber Stamp tool with its From Saved option. Remember to save your document at a stage you would like to restore.

Note: The From Saved option cannot be used if you cropped the picture, changed its mode, or changed its dimensions or resolution since it was saved, or if you added or deleted a layer or a layer mask.

To restore part of the last saved version of a picture:

1. Save the document.

2. Modify a layer.

3. Double-click the Rubber Stamp tool (**Figure 13**).

4. Choose From Saved from the Options palette pop-up menu (**Figure 14**).
and
Choose an Opacity.
and
Choose a mode.

5. Click the Brushes tab, then click a brush tip.

6. Drag across any area of the layer (**Figure 15**).

✔ Tips

■ To undo the last stroke, choose Undo from the Edit menu immediately.

■ Choose a low Opacity to restore a light impression of the saved picture. Each subsequent stroke over the same area will restore it more.

■ Choose the Impressionist Option with a small brush tip to produce a soft rendition of the last saved version.

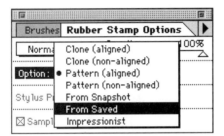

Figure 14. *Choose **From Saved** from the **Option** pop-up menu on the **Rubber Stamp Options** palette.*

Figure 15. *Part of this picture was restored. The Rubber Stamp tool was used with 100% Opacity on the left side and 40% Opacity on the right side.*

To convert a color layer to grayscale and selectively restore its color:

1. Choose a target layer.

2. Choose Hue/Saturation from the Adjust submenu under the Image menu (**Figure 16**).

3. Move the Saturation slider all the way to the left (to -100) (**Figure 17**).

4. Click OK or press Return.

5. Double-click the Rubber Stamp tool (**Figure 13**).

6. On the Rubber Stamp Options palette, choose From Saved from the Option pop-up menu (**Figure 18**).
and
Choose a mode.
and
Choose an Opacity.

7. Drag across any area of the layer (**Gallery 16**).

✔ Tips

■ Try any of the following mode/opacity combinations:

Dissolve with a 40%-50% Opacity to restore color with a chalky texture.

Multiply with a 100% Opacity to darken and intensify the color in the restored areas.

Color at 100% Opacity to restore only the hues from the last saved version of the picture while retaining the light and dark values and any modifications made while the picture was in Grayscale mode.

■ To achieve the same results on an entire RGB Color or CMYK Color picture, convert the picture to Grayscale mode, convert it back to RGB Color or CMYK Color mode, then follow steps 5-8 above to restore the original colors. **Click Don't Flatten when you change image modes!**

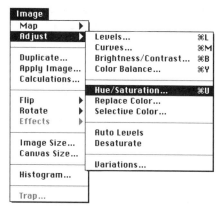

*Figure 16. Choose **Hue/Saturation** from the **Adjust** submenu under the **Image** menu.*

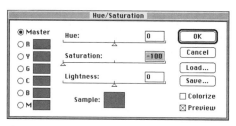

*Figure 17. In the **Hue/Saturation** dialog box, move the **Saturation** slider all the way to the left to remove the color from the layer.*

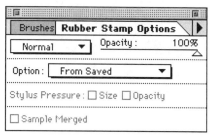

*Figure 18. On the **Rubber Stamp Options** palette, choose **From Saved** from the **Option** pop-up menu, and choose a **mode** and **Opacity**.*

Figure 1. *Filters are grouped into submenu categories under the **Filter** menu. Choose the top entry to reapply the last filter applied. To open the dialog box of the last filter applied, hold down **Command (⌘)** and **Option** and press "**F**." (See page 265 for a list of shortcuts for applying filters)*

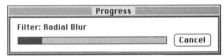

Figure 2. *A **Progress** dialog box appears while some filters are processing.*

Figure 3. *Some filter dialog boxes have sliders and a preview box. Drag in the preview box with the hand cursor to move the picture in the box. Click the "+" button to zoom in on the picture in the preview box, or click the "–" button to zoom out. Move the slider to increase or decrease the amount the filter is applied. Check the Preview box to display filter effects in both the document window and in the preview box.*

THIS CHAPTER covers some of Photoshop's many filters. Filters are grouped into nine submenu categories under the Filter menu (**Figure 1**). Any third-party filter added to the program will have its own submenu. *(See the Photoshop User Guide for information about installing third-party filters)*

You can use some filters for retouching, such as Blur, Blur More, Sharpen, and Sharpen More. You can use the "arty" filters, such as Color Halftone, Find Edges, Emboss, Mosaic, Tiles, Trace Contour, and Wind, to stylize an image. You can completely transform a picture into curves, twists, and spiral patterns by applying a "wild & wavy" filter, like Ripple or Twirl. And you can create a wide variety of beautiful lighting illusions using the Lighting Effects filter. Later in this chapter we'll show you how to create patterns and textures you can use in a Photoshop picture or in a document in another application.

Filters can be applied to the whole target layer or to a selected area of the target layer. Some filters are applied in one step by selecting them from a submenu. Other filters are applied via dialog boxes in which one or more variables are specified. Highlight the top entry under the Filter menu to reapply the last filter chosen using the same variables. Choose the filter from its submenu to modify its variables. A filter cannot be applied to a picture in Bitmap or Indexed Color mode.

Use the instructions in this chapter as a foundation to create your own formulas. Choose different variables in a filter dialog box, or apply more than one filter to the same picture. The stronger the amount you specify for a filter, the more abstract your image will become.

Like the Blur tool, the **Blur** filter subtly blends colors. Apply the Blur filter to evenly blur an entire target layer or a selected area on the target layer.

To apply the Blur filter:

1. Choose Blur from the Blur submenu under the Filter menu (**Figures 4-6**).

2. *Optional:* Choose Blur again to magnify the effect.
   or
   Choose Blur More to produce an effect about four times stronger.

✔ Tip

■ Use the Blur tool to blend small areas on a target layer.

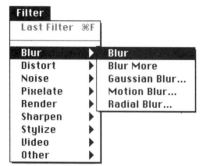

Figure 4. Choose **Blur** from the **Blur** submenu under the **Filter** menu.

Figure 5. The original picture.

Figure 6. The Blur filter applied.

Filter	
Last Filter ⌘F	

Blur	▶
Distort	▶
Noise	▶
Pixelate	▶
Render	▶
Sharpen	▶
Stylize	▶
Uideo	▶
Other	▶

Sharpen
Sharpen Edges
Sharpen More
Unsharp Mask...

Figure 7. Choose **Sharpen** *from the* **Sharpen** *submenu under the* **Filter** *menu.*

Like the Sharpen tool, the Sharpen filter increases contrast between pixels on a target layer or in a selected area of a target layer. Apply it to an image that was blurry before it was scanned or became blurry as a result of scanning to improve overall contrast.

To apply the Sharpen filter:

1. Choose Sharpen from the Sharpen submenu under the Filter menu (**Figures 7-9**).

2. *Optional:* Choose Sharpen again to magnify the effect.
or
Choose Sharpen More to produce an effect about four times stronger. Be careful not to over sharpen.

✔ Tip

■ Use the sharpen tool to sharpen small details on the target layer.

Figure 8. The original picture.

Figure 9. The Sharpen filter applied.

Apply the **Find Edges** filter to transform a continuous tone image into a line art drawing. The lines are stroked with complementary colors to those in the original pixels on the target layer and the space between edges turns white.

A method for applying the Find Edges filter:

1. Save your document.

2. Choose a target layer.

3. Choose Find Edges from the Stylize submenu under the Filter menu (**Figure 10**).

4. *Optional:* Choose Hue/Saturation from the Adjust submenu under the Image menu, move the Saturation slider all the way to the left to remove the target layer's color (**Figure 11**), then click OK or press Return.

5. Choose Solarize from the Stylize submenu under the Filter menu.

6. Double-click the Rubber Stamp tool.

7. On the Rubber Stamp Options palette (**Figure 12**):

Choose From Saved from the Option pop-up menu.
and
Move the Opacity slider to 50%.
and
Choose Normal or Color mode.

8. Drag over any area to restore that area's original color or shade (**Figure 13** and **Gallery 5b**).

✔ Tips

■ To produce colored lines on a dark background, choose Find Edges, then choose Invert from the Map submenu under the Image menu (**Gallery 5c**).

■ Apply the Solarize filter by itself to create the illusion of a partial film negative.

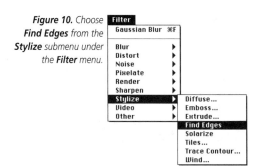

Figure 10. Choose *Find Edges* from the *Stylize* submenu under the *Filter* menu.

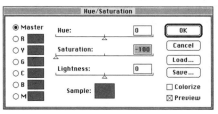

Figure 11. Move the *Saturation* slider all the way to the left in the *Hue/Saturation* dialog box.

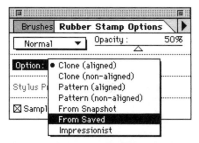

Figure 12. Choose *From Saved* from the *Option* pop-up menu on the *Rubber Stamp Options* palette.

Figure 13. Drag across any area to restore that area's original colors or shades.

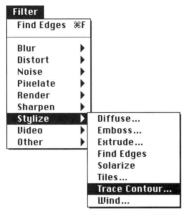

Figure 14. *Choose* **Trace Contour** *from the* **Stylize** *submenu under the* **Filter** *menu.*

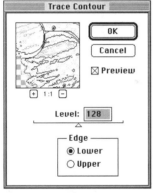

Figure 15. *Enter a number in the* **Level** *field in the* **Trace Contour** *dialog box.*

Figure 16. *The Trace Contour filter with a Level value of 50 was applied to produce this picture.*

The **Trace Contour** filter transforms a continuous tone image into a contour drawing on a white background. The lines are colored with the channel colors of the current image mode. Apply the Trace Contour filter to a target layer that has a lot of shapes and colors.

To apply the Trace Contour filter:

1. Choose Trace Contour from the Stylize submenu under the Filter menu (**Figure 14**).

2. Move the Level slider to between 0 and 255. At one extreme more yellow lines will be created; at the other extreme more red and blue lines will be created (**Figure 15**).

3. Click OK or press Return (**Figure 16**).

4. *Optional:* To make the picture look like a magic marker drawing, choose Minimum from the Other submenu under the Filter menu, enter 1 or 2 in the Radius field, then click OK (**Gallery 5a**).

✔ Tip

■ To recolor the lines on a dark background, after step 3 or 4, choose Invert from the Map submenu under the Image menu. To thicken the lines on a dark background, choose Maximum from the Other submenu under the Filter menu.

Trace Contour Filter

The **Emboss** filter removes most of the color from a target layer and makes it look as if it is stamped onto porous paper or fossilized in stone.

To apply the Emboss filter:

1. If the target layer is low contrast, choose Levels from the Adjust submenu under the Image menu, move the black Input slider to the right and the white Input slider to the left to increase the contrast, then click OK.

2. Choose Emboss from the Stylize submenu under the Filter menu (**Figure 17**).

3. Enter a number in the Angle field, or move the dial in the circle (**Figure 18**).

4. Enter a number between 1 and 10 in the Height field. Try 3 first.

5. Enter a number between 1 and 500 in the Amount field. The lower the number, the more color will be removed from the picture.

6. Click OK or press Return (**Figures 19a-b**).

✔ Tip

■ To recolor the layer after applying the Emboss filter, choose Hue/Saturation from the Adjust submenu under the Image menu, check the Colorize box, then move the Hue, Saturation, or Lightness sliders.

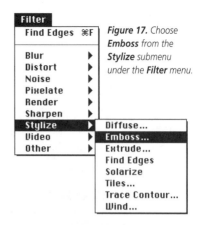

Figure 17. Choose **Emboss** from the **Stylize** submenu under the **Filter** menu.

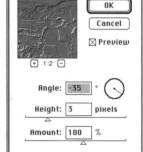
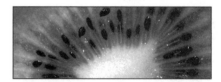

Figure 18. Where the dial is positioned in this illustration, highlights will appear on the left and shadows will appear on the right.

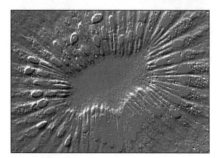

Figure 19a. To produce this picture, the Emboss filter was applied with an Angle of -35, Height of 3, and Amount of 100.

Figure 19b. Another embossed image (from a close-up of a kiwi). (A detail of the original image above)

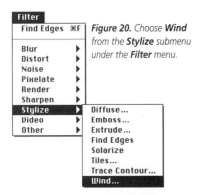

Filter
Find Edges ⌘F

Blur ▶
Distort ▶
Noise ▶
Pixelate ▶
Render ▶
Sharpen ▶
Stylize ▶
Video ▶
Other ▶

Diffuse...
Emboss...
Extrude...
Find Edges
Solarize
Tiles...
Trace Contour...
Wind...

Figure 20. Choose **Wind** *from the* **Stylize** *submenu under the* **Filter** *menu.*

The **Wind** filter produces an illusion of wind blowing across the target layer.

To apply the Wind filter:

1. Choose Wind from the Stylize submenu under the Filter menu (**Figure 20**).

2. Click Wind to produce a light breeze (**Figure 21**).
   or
   Click Blast to produce a hurricane force wind. Blast will slightly diminish a picture's saturation.
   or
   Click Stagger to create an Impressionistic effect with the picture's original colors.

3. Click Left or Right (the Wind direction).

4. Click OK or press Return (**Figures 22-24**).

Figure 21. In the **Wind** *dialog box, click* **Wind, Blast,** *or* **Stagger,** *and click* **Left** *or* **Right.**

Figure 22. The Wind filter was applied to this picture with the Wind Method and Left Direction chosen.

Figure 23. The Wind filter was applied to this picture with the Blast Method and Left Direction chosen.

Figure 24. The Wind filter was applied to this picture with the Stagger Method and Left Direction chosen.

Wind Filter

Use the following instructions as a starting point. You can experiment with other Layers palette Opacity settings, other Hue/Saturation box settings, and other filters, such as Emboss, Facet, and Pointillize. Choose Undo from the Edit menu to undo a filter.

To apply the Wind filter to type:

1. Create type. Choose a bold font in a large size relative to the picture.

2. Click the New Layer icon on the Layers palette, then click OK (**Figure 25**).

3. With the new type layer highlighted on the Layers palette, move the Opacity slider to the left.

4. If your picture is in a color mode, choose Hue/Saturation from the Adjust submenu under the Image menu, move the Saturation slider to the right (**Figure 26**), then click OK.

5. Make sure the Preserve Transparency box on the Layers palette is unchecked.

6. Choose Wind from the Stylize submenu under the Filter menu (**Figure 27**).

7. Click a Method and Direction (**Figure 28**).

8. Click OK or press Return.

9. *Optional:* Follow steps 6-8 again, but click the opposite Direction button. (**Figure 29**).

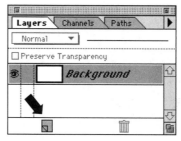

Figure 25. With the type as a floating selection, click the **New Layer** icon on the **Layers** palette.

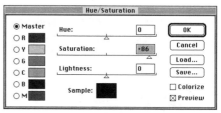

Figure 26. Move the **Saturation** slider to the right in the **Hue/Saturation** dialog box.

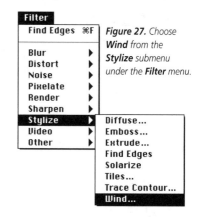

Figure 27. Choose **Wind** from the **Stylize** submenu under the **Filter** menu.

Figure 28. Click **Blast** or **Stagger** and click a **Direction** in the **Wind** dialog box.

Figure 29. The Wind filter applied to type.

*Figure 30. Choose **Add Noise** from the **Noise** submenu under the **Filter** menu.*

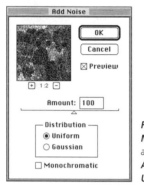

*Figure 31. In the **Add Noise** dialog box, enter a number in the **Amount** field, and click **Uniform** or **Gaussian**.*

Figure 32. The Add Noise filter was applied to this picture with an Amount of 60 and Gaussian Distribution.

The **Add Noise** filter randomly recolors pixels on the target layer. Apply it to a new document with a solid white background to create a speckled, grainy pattern. You can then use the pattern as an element in another Photoshop picture or in a document in another application. Apply the Add Noise filter to an existing target layer to create a grainy, high-speed film effect.

(To save a pattern to use in another application, see pages 52-53)

To apply the Add Noise filter:

1. Choose Add Noise from the Noise submenu under the Filter menu (**Figure 30**).

2. Enter a number between 1 and 999 (the intensity of the filter) in the Amount field (**Figure 31**).

3. Click Uniform or Gaussian.

4. Click OK or press Return (**Figure 32**).

✔ Tips

■ To create a subtler effect, add pixels of a single color by applying the Add Noise filter to only one of a target layer's channels. Click a channel color name on the Channels palette (**Figure 33**), apply the Add Noise filter following the steps above, then click the top channel on the palette to redisplay the composite picture.

■ Check the Monochromatic box in the Add Noise dialog box to produce only grayscale dots.

*Figure 33. Click a channel name on the **Channels** palette.*

Add Noise Filter

Note: For drama, apply the Ripple, Zigzag, or Twirl filter to a picture with a wide, white border. Follow the instructions on page 221 to create a "wrinkled" edge using the Ripple filter.

The **Ripple** filter will make a target layer look as if it is reflected on water.

To apply the Ripple filter:

1. Choose Ripple from the Distort submenu under the Filter menu (**Figure 34**).

2. Enter a number between -999 and 999 in the Amount field (**Figure 35**). The further the number is from 0, the more distortion will be produced.

3. Click Small, Medium or Large. Large produces the most distortion.

4. Click OK or press Return (**Figures 36-38**).

Figure 34. *Choose* **Ripple** *from the* **Distort** *submenu under the* **Filter** *menu.*

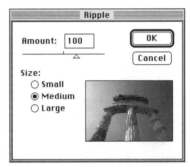

Figure 35. *In the* **Ripple** *dialog box, enter a number in the* **Amount** *field, and click* **Small**, **Medium**, *or* **Large**.

Figure 36. *The original picture.*

Figure 37. *The Ripple filter — Amount 150, Large.*

Figure 38. *The Ripple filter — Amount 100, Medium.*

Figure 39. *Choose* **ZigZag** *from the* **Distort** *submenu under the* **Filter** *menu.*

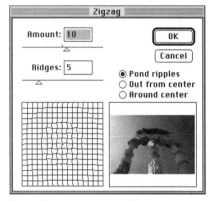

Figure 40. *In the* **Zigzag** *dialog box, enter an* **Amount**, *a number of* **Ridges**, *and click* **Pond ripples, Out from center**, *or* **Around center**.

The **Zigzag** filter produces an illusion of patterns on the surface of water, as if a stone was thrown into it or a canoe passed by. The distortion is greatest in the center of the target layer or selection.

To apply the Zigzag filter:

1. Choose Zigzag from the Distort submenu under the Filter menu (**Figure 39**).

2. Enter a number between 100 and -100 in the Amount field (**Figure 40**). The further the number is from 0, the more distortion will be produced.

3. Enter a number between 1 and 20 in the Ridges field (the number of zigzags or rings).

4. Click Pond Ripples to distort pixels diagonally.
or
Click Out from Center to produce patterns radiating from the layer's center.
or
Click Around Center to produce zigzags around the layer's center.

5. Click OK or press Return (**Figures 41-42**).

Zigzag Filter

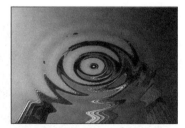

Figure 41. *The Zigzag filter applied to a picture with an Amount of -100, 5 Ridges, and Pond ripples chosen.*

Figure 42. *The Zigzag filter applied to a picture with an Amount of 10, 5 Ridges, and Pond ripples chosen.*

The **Twirl** filter spirals the middle of a target layer around its center.

To apply the Twirl filter:

1. Choose Twirl from the Distort pop-up menu under the Filter menu (**Figure 43**).

2. Enter a number between -999 and 999 in the Angle field (**Figure 44**). The further the number is from 0, the more distortion will be produced.

3. Click OK or press Return (**Figures 45-46**).

Figure 43. *Choose* **Twirl** *from the* **Distort** *sub-menu under the* **Filter** *menu.*

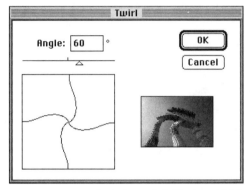

Figure 44. *Enter a number in the* **Angle** *field in the* **Twirl** *dialog box.*

Figure 45. *The Twirl filter applied at a 60° Angle.*

Figure 46. *The Twirl filter applied at a 180° Angle.*

Twirl Filter

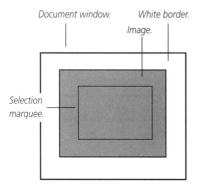

Document window. — *White border.*
Image.

Selection marquee.

Figure 47. *A selection before choosing the Inverse command.*

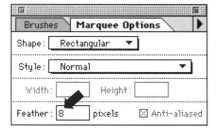

Figure 48. *Enter 8 in the **Feather** field on the **Marquee Options** palette.*

Apply the **Ripple, Twirl,** or **Zigzag** filter to a target layer with a white border to produce a "warped paper" texture.

To create a "wrinkled" edge:

1. Follow the steps on page 47 to create a white border around a picture.

2. Choose the Background layer as the target layer.

3. Double-click the Marquee tool.

4. Choose Rectangular from the Shape pop-up menu on the Marquee Options palette (**Figure 48**).
and
Enter 8 in the Feather field.

5. Drag a selection marquee across about three quarters of the layer (**Figure 47**).

6. Choose Inverse from the Select menu. The border will become the active selection.

7. Follow the steps on page 218, 219, or 220 (**Figures 49-51**).

Figure 49. *A "wrinkled edge" produced using the Ripple filter — Amount 100, Medium.*

Figure 50. *A "wrinkled edge" produced using the Twirl filter — Angle -300.*

Figure 51. *A "wrinkled edge" produced using the Zigzag filter — Amount 40, Ridges 8, Around center.*

Create a "Wrinkled" Edge

The **Color Halftone** filter transforms pixels on a target layer into enlarged "halftone screen" dots. You can specify the size of the dots.

Note: Despite its name, the Color Halftone filter can be applied to a picture in Grayscale mode.

To apply the Color Halftone filter:

1. Choose Color Halftone from the Pixelate submenu under the Filter menu (**Figure 52**).

2. Enter a number between 4 and 8 in the Max. radius field (**Figure 53**). The higher the Radius value, the larger the dots. The minimum is 4, the maxiumum is 127.

3. *Optional:* To produce a different "rosette" pattern, change the numbers in the Screen Angle fields.

4. Click OK or press Return (**Figure 54** and **Gallery 5d**).

Figure 52. *Choose* **Color Halftone** *from the* **Pixelate** *submenu under the* **Filter** *menu.*

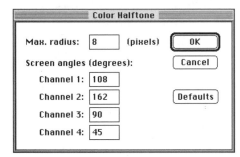

Figure 53. *Enter a number in the* **Max. radius** *field in the* **Color Halftone** *dialog box.*

Figure 54. *The original picture.*

Color Halftone Filter

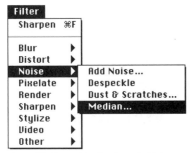

Figure 55. Choose **Median** from the **Noise** submenu under the **Filter** menu.

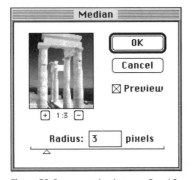

Figure 56. Enter a number between 3 and 8 in the **Radius** field in the **Median** dialog box.

Apply the **Median Noise** and **Minimum** filters to a picture to transform it into a "watercolor."

To create a "watercolor":

1. Choose Median from the Noise submenu under the Filter menu (**Figure 55**).

2. Move the Radius slider to a number between 2 and 8 (**Figure 56**).

3. Click OK or press Return (**Figure 57**).

4. Choose Minimum from the Other submenu under the Filter menu (**Figure 58**).

5. Move the Radius the slider to 1, 2, or 3 (**Figure 59**).

6. Click OK or press Return (**Gallery 5e**).

✔ Tip

■ The Minimum filter applied by itself will darken and blur a picture.

Figure 57. The Median filter applied with a Radius value of 3.

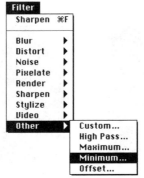

Figure 58. Choose **Minimum** from the **Other** submenu under the **Filter** menu.

Figure 59. Enter 3 or 4 in the **Radius** field in the **Minimum** dialog box.

Create a "Watercolor"

Apply the **Tiles** filter to transform a target layer into unevenly spaced tiles. You can specify the "grout" color to appear between the tiles.

To apply the Tiles filter:

1. Choose Tiles from the Stylize sub-menu under the Filter menu (**Figure 60**).

2. Enter the Number of Tiles to appear across the narrowest dimension of the picture (**Figure 61**). The fewer the tiles, the larger each tile will be. The minimum is 1, the maximum is 99.

3. Enter a number in the Maximum Offset field (the maximum distance between tiles as a percentage of tile size). The minumum is 1, the maximum is 90.

4. Click an option to fill the background area ("grout") between the tiles: Background Color, Foreground Color, Inverse Image, or Unaltered Image.

5. Click OK or press Return (**Figures 62-63** and **Gallery 5f-h**).

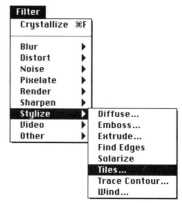

Figure 60. *Choose **Tiles** from the **Stylize** submenu under the **Filter** menu.*

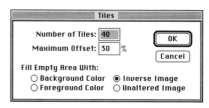

Figure 61. *In the **Tiles** dialog box, enter a **Number of Tiles**, a **Maximum Offset**, and click a "grout" color.*

Figure 62. *The original picture.*

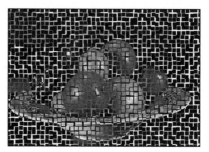

Figure 63. *To produce this illustration, 30 was entered in the Number of Tiles field and Inverse Image was clicked. This picture is 2 inches wide.*

Tiles Filter

*Figure 64. Choose **Add Noise** from the **Noise** submenu under the **Filter** menu.*

*Figure 65. In the **Add Noise** dialog box, enter a number between 1 and 999 in the **Amount** field and click **Uniform** or **Gaussian**.*

*Figure 66. Choose **Motion Blur** from the **Blur** submenu under the **Filter** menu.*

*Figure 67. In the **Motion Blur** dialog box, enter -17 in the **Angle** field and 40 in the **Distance** field.*

A variety of textures can be created using the Add Noise filter as the starting point. Earlier in this chapter the Add Noise filter was applied to an image. On this page and on the next page, it is applied to a blank picture.

To create a woven texture:

1. Create a new document, Contents White.

2. Choose Add Noise from the Noise submenu under the Filter menu (**Figure 64**).

3. Enter a number between 1 and 999 (the amount of noise) in the Amount field (**Figure 65**).

4. Click Uniform or Gaussian.

5. Click OK or press Return.

6. Choose Motion Blur from the Blur submenu under the Filter menu (**Figure 66**).

7. Enter -17 in the Angle field (**Figure 67**).

8. Enter 40 in the Distance field.

9. Click OK or press Return.

10. To heighten contrast, choose Levels from the Adjust submenu under the Image menu (**Figure 68**).

11. Move the black Input slider to the right and move the white Input slider to the left (**Figure 69**).

12. Click OK or press Return (**Figure 70** and **Gallery 5i**).

13. *Optional:* To add a wave to the texture, choose Twirl from the Distort submenu under the Filter menu, enter 72 in the Amount field, then click OK (**Figures 71-72**).

✔ **Tip**

■ Use the Hue/Saturation dialog box (Adjust submenu under the Image menu) to recolor the texture. Check the Colorize box, then move the Hue, Saturation, or Lightness sliders.

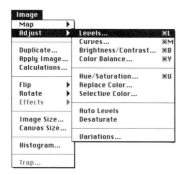

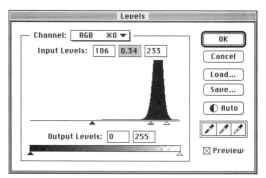

Figure 68. *Choose **Levels** from the **Adjust** submenu under the **Image** menu.*

Figure 69. *In the **Levels** dialog box, move the **black Input** slider to the **right** and move the **white Input** slider to the **left**.*

Figure 70. *A woven texture.*

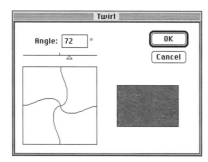

Figure 71. *Enter 72 in the **Angle** field in the **Twirl** dialog box.*

Figure 72. *A woven texture with the Twirl filter applied.*

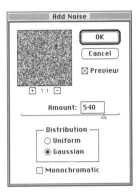

Figure 73. *Move the Amount slider to between 400 and 700 in the **Add Noise** dialog box.*

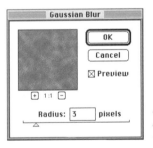

Figure 74. *A new document with the Add Noise filter applied.*

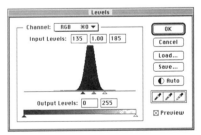

Figure 75. *Enter 3 in the **Radius** field in the **Gaussian Blur** dialog box.*

To create a spaghetti texture:

1. Create a new document, Contents White.

2. Choose Add Noise from the Noise submenu under the Filter menu.

3. Move the Amount slider to a number between 400 and 700 (**Figure 73**).

4. Click Gaussian.

5. Click OK or press Return (**Figure 74**).

6. Choose Gaussian Blur from the Blur submenu under the Filter menu.

7. Enter 3 in the Radius field (**Figure 75**).

8. Click OK or press Return.

9. Choose Find Edges from the Stylize submenu under the Filter menu.

10. Choose Levels from the Adjust submenu under the Image menu.

11. Move the black Input slider to the right and move the white Input slider to left (**Figure 76**). Pause to preview.

12. Click OK or press Return (**Figure 77**).

13. *Optional:* Choose Sharpen Edges from the Sharpen submenu under the Filter menu.

Create a Spaghetti Texture

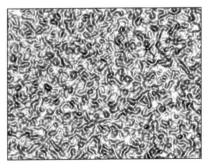

Figure 76. *Move the black **Input** slider to the right and move the white **Input** slider to left in the **Levels** dialog box.*

Figure 77. *Spaghetti.*

In the following instructions, the **Mosaic** filter is applied to multiple selections to break the target layer into pixel blocks that gradually enlarge from left to right.

To apply the Mosaic filter:

1. Choose a target layer.

2. Double-click the Marquee tool, then choose Rectangular from the Shape pop-up menu on the Marquee Options palette.

3. Drag a marquee across about a quarter of the picture (**Figure 78**).

4. Choose Mosaic from the Pixelate submenu under the Filter menu (**Figure 79**).

5. Enter 6 in the Cell Size field (**Figure 80**).

6. Click OK or press Return.

7. With the selection still active, hold down Command (⌘) and Option and drag the marquee to the right (**Figure 78**).

8. Repeat steps 4-7 three more times, entering 12, then 24, then 30 in the Cell Size field.

9. Hold down Command (⌘) and press "D"(**Figure 81**).

✔ Tip

■ To create larger pixel blocks, enter higher numbers — like 8, 16, 28, and 34 — in the Cell Size field.

Figure 78. *Select an area with the Marquee tool. After you apply the Mosaic filter, move the marquee to the right.*

Figure 79. *Choose **Mosaic** from the **Pixelate** submenu under the **Filter** menu.*

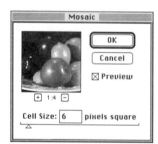

Figure 80. *Enter a number in the **Cell Size** field in the **Mosaic** dialog box. Enter progressively higher numbers when you repeat steps 4 and 5.*

Figure 81. *The Mosaic filter applied to a picture.*

Figure 82. *Select an area of a picture.*

Figure 83. *Choose Define Pattern from the Edit menu.*

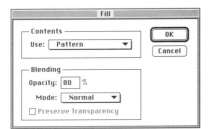

Figure 84. *In the Fill dialog box, click Pattern, enter an Opacity value, and choose from the Mode pop-up menu.*

Figure 85. *A pattern created using a shape as a Fill.*

Follow the instructions on this page to create a **pattern** from a selected area of a target layer and use the pattern as a Fill. Then follow the instructions on the next page to enhance the pattern using filters.

To create a pattern from a picture:

1. Choose a target layer.

2. Double-click the Marquee tool.

3. Choose Rectangular from the Shape pop-up menu on the Marquee Options palette.

4. Select an area to become the fill pattern (**Figure 82**).

5. Choose Define Pattern from the Edit menu (**Figure 83**).

6. Create a New document in the same picture mode as the picture from which the pattern was created.
   or
   Choose a target layer.

7. Choose Fill from the Edit menu.

8. In the Fill dialog box, choose Pattern from the Contents/Use pop-up menu (**Figure 84**).
   and
   Enter a number in the Opacity field.
   and
   Choose a mode from the Mode pop-up menu. Try Normal.

9. Click OK (**Figure 85**).

   Note: To texturize the pattern, follow the instructions on the next page.

✔ Tip

■ To fill an area with a pattern using strokes, follow steps 1-5 above. Double-click the Rubber Stamp tool, choose Pattern (aligned) or Pattern (non-aligned) from the Option pop-up menu on the Rubber Stamp Options palette, choose a mode, and choose an Opacity. Then drag back and forth across a picture.

Create a Pattern from a Picture

To texturize a pattern:

1. Follow the instructions on the previous page.

2. Choose Duplicate Layer from the Layers palette pop-up menu. Rename the layer, if you like.

3. Click OK or press Return.

4. Choose Find Edges from the Stylize submenu under the Filter menu (**Figure 86**).

5. Choose a light Foreground color. *(See pages 112-114)*

6. Choose Fill from the Edit menu.

7. In the Fill dialog box, choose Foreground Color from the Contents/Use pop-up menu (**Figure 87**).
and
Enter 60 in the Opacity field.
and
Choose Color from the Mode pop-up menu.

8. Click OK or press Return.

9. On the Layers palette:

Move the Opacity slider to the left to decrease the opacity of the duplicate layer (**Figures 88-89**).
and
Choose a mode from the Mode pop-up menu. Try Difference, Overlay, or Luminosity mode.

*Figure 86. Choose **Find Edges** from the **Stylize** submenu under the **Filter** menu.*

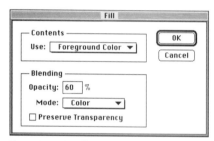

*Figure 87. In the **Fill** dialog box, click **Foreground**, enter 60 in the **Opacity** field, and choose **Color** from the **Mode** pop-up menu.*

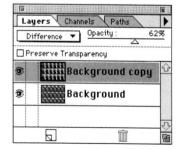

*Figure 88. Choose an **Opacity** and a **mode** from the Layers palette.*

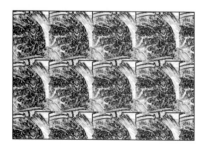

Figure 89. A texturized pattern.

Texturize a Pattern

Figure 90. *Create a copy of the Background layer by choosing* **Duplicate** *from the Layers palette command menu.*

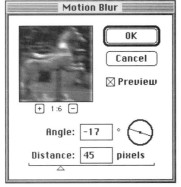

Figure 91. *Enter numbers in the* **Angle** *and* **Distance** *fields in the* **Motion Blur** *dialog box.*

Figure 92. *Select an object in a picture.*

To create an illusion of motion, select an object on a duplicate of the Background layer to be the "stationary" object, and then apply the **Motion Blur** filter to the Background layer.

To apply the Motion Blur filter:

1. Choose Duplicate Layer from the Layers palette command menu. Rename the layer, if you like.

2. Click OK or press Return (**Figure 90**).

3. Choose the Background layer as the target layer. Hold down Option and click the Eye icon for that layer to hide all the other layers.

4. Choose Motion Blur from the Blur submenu under the Filter menu.

5. Enter a number between -360 and 360 in the Angle field (**Figure 91**). We entered -17 to produce Figure 95. *or* Drag the axis line.

6. Enter a number between 1 and 999 in the Distance field (the amount of blur). We entered 50 to produce Figure 95.

7. Click OK or press Return.

8. Hold down Option and click the Eye icon for the Background layer on the Layers palette to display all the other layers.

9. Choose the duplicate layer.

10. Select an object on the Duplicate layer that is to remain "stationary" (**Figure 92**).

11. Choose Feather from the Select menu.

12. Enter 5 in the Feather Radius field.

13. Click OK or press Return.

14. Choose Inverse from the Select menu.

15. Uncheck the Preserve Transparency box on the Layers palette.

16. Press Delete (**Figure 93**).

(Tips on following page)

Motion Blur Filter

✔ **Tips**

- ■ Use the Move tool to reposition the "stationary" image on the duplicate layer.

- ■ Move the Layers palette Opacity slider to change the opacity of the duplicate layer.

Figure 93. *The completed* **Motion Blur**.

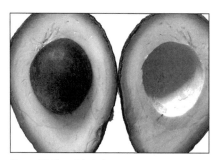

Figure 94. *The original picture.*

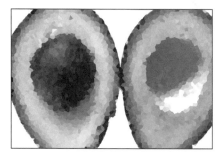

Figure 95. *After applying the* **Crystallize** *filter, Cell Size 15.*

Figure 96. *The Groucho filter, one of many third-party filters.*

Figure 97. *The Zapatista filter, by Oroz Co.*

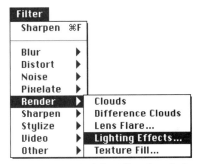

Figure 98. Choose *Lighting Effects* from the *Render* submenu under the *Filter* menu.

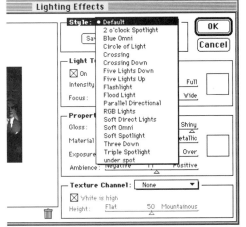

Figure 99. Choose a preset lighting effect from the *Style* pop-up menu in the *Lighting Effects* dialog box.

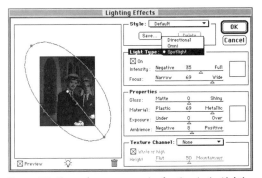

Figure 100. Choose from a cornucopia of options in the *Lighting Effects* dialog box to create your own lighting effects.

The **Lighting Effects** filter produces a tremendous variety of lighting effects. You can choose from up to 16 different light sources and you can assign to each light source a different color, intensity, and angle.

Note: For the Lighting Effects filter to work, there must be at least 6 MB of RAM allocated to Photoshop.

To cast a light:

1. Make sure your picture is in RGB Color mode.

2. Choose a target layer.

3. *Optional:* Select an area on the layer to limit the filter effects to that area.

4. Choose Lighting Effects from the Render submenu under the Filter menu (**Figure 98**).

5. Choose Default or choose a preset lighting effect from the Style pop-up menu (**Figure 99**).

Follow any of the following optional steps to adjust the light (**Figure 100**)*:*

6. Choose from the Light Type pop-up menu. Choose Spotlight to create a narrow, elliptical light.

7. Move the Intensity slider to adjust the brightness of the light. Full creates the brightest light. Negative creates a black light effect.

8. Move the Focus slider to adjust the size of the beam of light that fills the ellipse shape. The light source starts from where the radius touches the edge of the ellipse.

9. Click on the color swatch to change the color of the light.

10. In the preview window:

Drag the center point of the ellipse to move the whole light.

(Continued on the following page)

Lighting Effects Filter

Drag either endpoint toward the center of the ellipse to increase the intensity of the light.

Drag either side point of the ellipse to change the angle of the light and to widen or narrow it.

11. Move the Properties sliders to adjust the surrounding light conditions on the target layer.

The **Gloss** property controls the amount of surface reflectance on the lighted surfaces.

The **Material** property controls which parts of the picture reflect the light source color — Plastic (the light source color is like a glare) or Metallic (the object surface glows).

The **Exposure** property lightens or darkens the whole ellipse.

The **Ambience** property controls the balance between the light source and the overall light in the picture. Move this slider in small increments.

Click the **Properties** color swatch to choose a different color from the Color Picker dialog boxfor the ambient light around the spotlight.

12. Click OK or press Return (**Figures 101a-l**).

Figure 101a. The default spotlight ellipse with **Full Intensity**.

Figure 101b. The default spotlight ellipse with **Wide Focus**. The light is strongest at the sides of the ellipse.

Figure 101c. The default spotlight ellipse with **Narrow Focus**.

Figure 101d. The default spotlight ellipse after dragging the end points inward to narrow the light beam.

Figure 101e. The spotlight ellipse rotated to the left by dragging a side point.

Figure 101f. The spotlight ellipse after dragging the radius inward to make the light beam rounder.

Figure 101g. *The spotlight ellipse with the Exposure Property set to Over.*

Figure 101h. *The spotlight ellipse with the Exposure Property set to Under.*

Figure 101i. *The spotlight ellipse with a Positive Ambience Property.*

Figure 101j. *The spotlight ellipse with a Negative Ambience Property.*

Figure 101k. *The default Omni light is round. The effect is like shining a flashlight perpendicular to the picture.*

Figure 101l. *Drag a new light source onto the preview box. A new ellipse will appear where the mouse is released.*

✔ Tips

■ To create a pin spot, choose Spotlight from the Light Type pop-up menu, move the Intensity slider to about 80, move the Focus slider to about 30, and drag the side points of the ellipse inward. Move the whole ellipse by dragging its center point to cast light on a particular area of the picture.

■ If the background of a picture has been darkened too much from a previous application of the Lighting Effects filter, apply the filter again to add another light to shine into the dark area and recover some detail. Move the Exposure Properties and Ambience Properties sliders a little to the right.

■ To see the picture in the Preview box without the ellipses, drag the light bulb icon just inside the bottom edge of the Preview box. Delete the extra light when you're finished.

■ To delete a light source ellipse, drag its center point over the Trash icon.

■ Check the Light Type/On box to pre-view the lighting effects in the Preview box.

■ To duplicate a light source ellipse, hold down Option and drag its center point.

■ The last used settings of the Lighting Effects filter will remain in the dialog box until you change the settings or quit Photoshop. To restore the Default settings, choose a different style from the Style pop-up menu, then choose Default from the same menu.

■ To add your own Lighting Effects settings to the Style pop-up menu, click Save before clicking OK.

■ Click Delete to remove the currently selected style from the pop-up menu.

■ Press Tab to select various light sources.

Lighting Effects Filter

235

Our custom lighting effect

To produce Figure 104, we chose RGB Color mode, chose a target layer (the figures), and chose Lighting Effects from the Render submenu under the Filter menu.

In the Lighting Effects dialog box, we:

- Chose Spotlight from the Light Type pop-up menu.

- Set the Intensity halfway toward Full.

- Set the Focus toward Wide.

- Dragged the side points of the ellipse inward to make it narrower.

- Dragged the centerpoint of the ellipse to cast the light over the face on the left in the picture.

- Set the Exposure Property slightly toward Over to brighten the light source.

- Moved the Ambience Property slider to 2 to darken the background of the picture.

- Dragged the endpoint of the Radius slightly inward to focus the beam of light more intensely on the face.

- When we were satisfied with the light source on one face, we Option-dragged the centerpoint of the ellipse to duplicate the light, and move the duplicate light over the face on the right.

- To create a subtle backlight, we dragged the light bulb icon into the Preview area to create another light source, rotated the ellipse sideways, and set the Intensity to be less Full than the other lights. We left the Focus setting between Narrow and Wide and left the Properties setting alone.

✔ **Tip**

- Apply Lighting Effects to the Background layer first, then to successive layers above it.

Figure 102. *The original RGB picture.*

Figure 103. *The three ellipses used to produce Figure 104.*

Figure 104. *The picture after applying the Lighting Effects filter with our own settings.*

Note: If you convert a multi-layer document to Indexed Color mode, the layers will be flattened. To preserve layers when converting a picture to Indexed Color mode, use our technique for saving a copy of a layer in a separate document *(see page 153).*

*Figure 1. Choose **Indexed Color** from the **Mode** menu.*

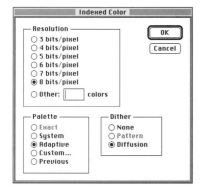

*Figure 2. Click **Resolution**, **Palette**, and **Dither** options in the **Indexed Color** dialog box.*

SOME MULTIMEDIA and video programs and some computer systems will not import a Photoshop picture containing more than 256 colors (8-bit color). By converting a picture to Indexed Color mode, the number of colors in its color table can be reduced. This chapter covers conversion to Indexed Color mode as well as some "arty" effects that can be produced by editing the color table of an Indexed Color picture.

To convert a picture to Indexed Color mode:

1. If the picture is not in RGB Color mode, choose RGB Color from the Mode menu.

2. Choose Indexed Color from the Mode menu (**Figure 1**).

3. Click a Resolution to specify the number of colors in the table (**Figure 2**). If you click 4 bits/pixel, the table will contain 16 colors. If you click 8 bits/pixel, the table will contain 256 colors. The fewer bits/pixel, the more dithered the picture will be.

4. Click a Palette. If the RGB Color picture contains 256 or fewer colors, you can click Exact.
or
Click Adaptive for the best color substitution.
or
Click System if you are going to export the file to an application that only accepts the Macintosh default palette.

5. Click None, Pattern, or Diffusion Dither. Diffusion may produce the closest color substitution.

6. Click OK or press Return.

Convert a Picture to Indexed Color Mode

To edit an Indexed Color table:

1. Choose Color Table from the Mode menu (**Figure 3**). The Color Table will display all the picture's colors.

2. Click on a color to be replaced (**Figure 4**).
or
Drag across a series of colors.

3. Move the slider up or down on the vertical bar to choose a hue, then click a variation of that hue in the large rectangle (**Figure 5**).

4. Click OK to exit the Color Picker.

5. Click OK or press Return.

✔ Tip

■ In Indexed color mode, the Pencil, Airbrush, and Paintbrush tools produce only opaque strokes. For those tools, leave the Opacity slider on the Options palette at 100%. Dissolve is the only tool mode that will produce a different stroke.

Figure 3. Choose Color Table from the Mode menu.

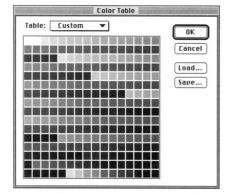

Figure 4. Click a color in the Color Table dialog box, or drag across a series of colors.

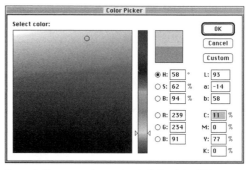

Figure 5. Choose a replacement color in the Color Picker.

Edit an Indexed Color Table

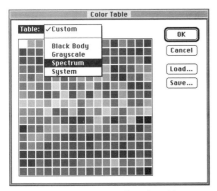

*Figure 6a. Choose **Spectrum** from the **Table** pop-up menu in the **Color Table**.*

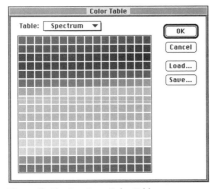

*Figure 6b. The **Spectrum Color Table**.*

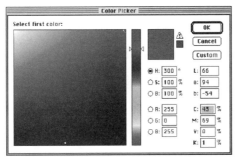

*Figure 7. Choose a first and last color from the **Color Picker**.*

We've gotten beautiful effects and atrocious effects using the Spectrum Color Table.

To choose the Spectrum table:

1. Choose Color Table from the Mode menu (**Figure 3**).

2. Choose Spectrum from the Table pop-up menu (**Figures 6a-b** and **Gallery 6a-b**).

3. Click OK or press Return.

✔ Tip

■ You can convert a Grayscale picture directly to Indexed Color mode, and then modify its Color Table.

For the best results, choose a warm "first color" and a cool "last color," or vice versa, for steps 3 and 5 below.

To reduce an Indexed Color table to two colors and the shades between them:

1. Choose Color Table from the Mode menu (**Figure 3**).

2. Drag across the Color Table from the first swatch in the upper left corner to the last swatch in the lower right corner.

3. Choose a "first color" from the Color Picker: move the slider up or down on the vertical bar to choose a hue, then click a variation of that hue in the large rectangle (**Figure 7**).

4. Click OK.

5. Choose a "last color" from the Color Picker.

6. Click OK to exit the Color Picker.

7. Click OK or press Return.

You can create a painterly effect by generating an Indexed Color picture from an RGB Color picture, then pasting the Index Color picture back into the RGB Color picture.

To recolor an RGB picture:

1. If the picture is not in RGB mode, choose RGB Color from the Mode menu.

2. Follow the steps on page 237 to convert the picture to Indexed Color mode.

3. Choose Color Table from the Mode menu (**Figure 3**).

4. In the Color Table dialog box, choose Spectrum from the Table pop-up menu (**Figure 8**).

5. Click OK or press Return.

6. Choose All from the Select menu.

7. Choose Copy from the Edit menu.

8. Choose Revert from the File menu.

9. Click Revert to restore the picture to RGB Color mode (**Figure 9**).

10. Choose Paste Layer from the Edit menu, then click OK, to paste the Indexed color picture onto a new layer.

11. Double-click the new layer name (**Figure 10**).

12. Choose from the Mode pop-up menu (**Figure 11**). Dissolve, Soft Light, Difference and Color produce interesting results.

Steps 13 and 14 are optional.

13. Change the Opacity percentage.

14. Move the black Underlying slider to the right to restore shadows from the underlying layer.
and/or
Move the white Underlying slider to the left to restore highlights from the underlying layer.

15. Click OK or press Return (**Gallery 6c-d**).

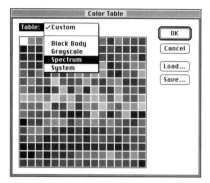

*Figure 8. Choose **Spectrum** from the **Table** pop-up menu in the **Color Table** dialog box.*

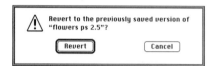

*Figure 9. Click **Revert** to revert to RGB Color mode.*

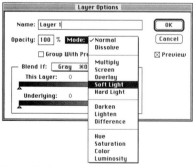

*Figure 10. Double-click the new layer name on the **Layers** palette.*

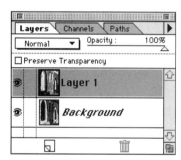

*Figure 11. Choose a **Mode** in the **Layers Options** dialog box and/or move the **Underlying** sliders. To restore midtones, Option-drag to split the triangle slider.*

RESOLUTION OF OUTPUT DEVICES

Hewlett Packard LaserJet	300 *or* 600 dpi
Apple LaserWriter	300 *or* 600 dpi
IRIS SmartJet	300 dpi
3M Rainbow	300 dpi
QMS Colorscript	300 dpi
Canon Color Laser/Fiery	400 dpi
Linotronic imagesetter	1,200–3,386 dpi

A PICTURE CAN BE printed from Photoshop to a laser printer, to a color printer (thermal wax, dye sublimation, etc.), or to an imagesetter. A Photoshop picture can also be imported into and printed from another application, such as QuarkXPress.

Printer settings are chosen in the Print dialog box and Page Setup dialog box, opened from the File menu. The following pages contain output tips, information about file compression, instructions for outputting to various types of printers, and instructions for creating duotones. Figure 14 on page 248 identifies Page Setup dialog box options.

Press and hold on the Sizes bar in the lower left corner of the document window to display a thumbnail preview of the image in relationship to the paper size and other specifications chosen in the Page Setup dialog box (**Figure 1**).

Note: Many of the terms used in this chapter are defined in *Appendix A: Glossary,* including *CMYK, Color separation, DCS, DPI, Dye sublimation, EPS, Film negative, Halftone screen, Imagesetter, Ink jet, JPEG compression, Lab, LPI, Moirés, PostScript, Process color, Registration marks, Resolution, Screen angles, Screen frequency, Thermal wax,* and *TIFF.*

*Press and hold on the **Sizes** bar to display the **print preview**.*

```
451K    ⬦
```

```
Width:      432 pixels (6 inches)
Height:     288 pixels (4 inches)
Channels:     3 (RGB Color)
Resolution:  72 pixels/inch
```

Figure 1. *Hold down **Option** and press and hold on the **Sizes** bar to display **file information**.*

Output tips

Before outputting your file at a service bureau, ask your print shop or publisher if they have any specifications for the paper or film output you give them. Make sure the picture is saved at the appropriate resolution for the output device. Also ask what halftone screen frequency (lpi) the print shop will use and output your file at that frequency.

You might also ask your service bureau if you should save your file with special settings for a particular printer, such as in a particular picture mode or resolution. Let the service bureau calculate the halftone screen angle settings. *(See also "Potential Gray Levels at various output resolutions and screen frequencies" on page 37)*

File Compression

To reduce the storage size of a picture, use a compression program, such as Disk-Doubler or StuffIt. Compression using this kind of software is non-lossy, which means no information is lost during the compression process.

If you do not have compression software, choose Save As from the File menu, choose TIFF from the File Format pop-up menu, and check the LZW Compression box in the TIFF Options dialog box. If you want to save any alpha channels as part of the file, check the Save Alpha Channels box. LZW compression is also non-lossy. Some applications will not import an LZW TIFF; other applications will import an LZW TIFF only if it doesn't contain an alpha channel.

We don't recommend saving pictures in the JPEG file format or using the Compress EPS/JPEG command for pictures that will be printed. JPEG compression is lossy — more information is lost each time the Compress EPS/JPEG command is applied. The loss of data may not be noticeable on screen, but it will be very noticeable on high resolution output.

QUESTIONS TO ASK YOUR PRINT SHOP ABOUT COLOR SEPARATIONS

Yes, you can get good color separations out of Photoshop, but color separating is an art. As a starting point, ask your print shop these questions so you'll be able to choose the correct scan resolution and settings in the Printer Inks Setup and Separation Setup dialog boxes:

What lines per inch setting is going to be used on the press for my job? This will help you choose the appropriate scanning resolution.

What is the dot gain for my paper stock choice on that press? Allowances for dot gain can be made using the Printer Inks Setup dialog box.

Which printing method will be used on press — UCR or GCR? GCR produces better color printing and is the default choice in the Separations Setup box. (GCR stands for Gray Component Replacement, UCR stands for Undercover Removal.)

What is the total ink limit and the Black ink limit for the press? These values can also be adjusted in the Separations Setup box.

Note: Change the dot gain, GCR or UCR method, and ink limits **before** you convert your picture from RGB Color mode to CMYK Color mode. If you modify any of these values after conversion, you must convert the picture back to RGB Color mode, adjust the values, then reconvert to CMYK Color mode.

To print to a black-and-white laserwriter:

1. Choose Print from the File menu.
or
Hold down Command (⌘) and press "P".

2. Click Color/Grayscale (**Figures 2-4**).

3. Click Printer.

4. If the picture is in CMYK Color mode, make sure the Print Separations box is unchecked to print a composite image.

5. Click Binary.

6. Click Print or press Return.

✔ Tips

■ If your picture does not print and you have a print spooler, try printing with ASCII Encoding selected. ASCII printing takes longer.

■ To print only a portion of a picture, select the area with the Marquee tool and check the Print Selected Area box in the Print dialog box.

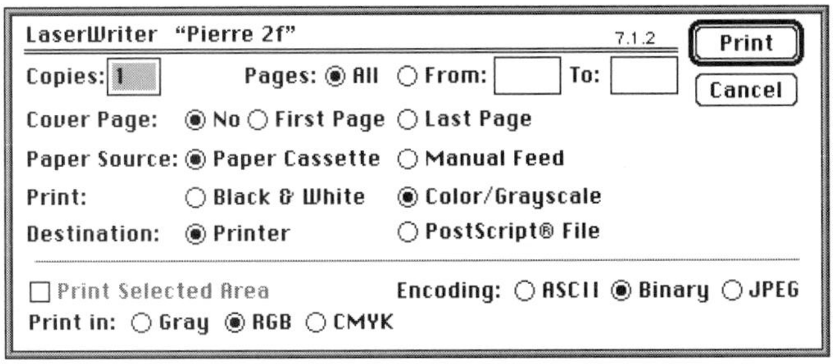

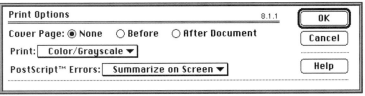

*Figure 2. In the **Print** dialog box, click **Color/Grayscale**, and click **Binary**. This illustration shows the Print dialog box for a picture in RGB Color mode. For a picture in CMYK Color mode, leave the **Print Separations** box unchecked to print the composite picture.*

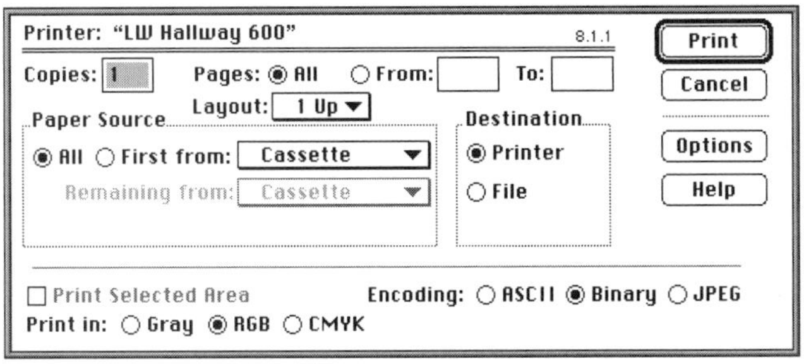

*Figure 3. The **Print** dialog box when using the **LaserWriter 8** driver. Leave the **Print In** buttons as is to print a composite picture, click **Binary**, then click **Options**. This illustration shows the Print dialog box for a picture in RGB mode.*

*Figure 4. In the **LaserWriter 8 Print Options** dialog box, choose **Color/Grayscale** from the **Print** pop-up menu, then click OK.*

To print to an Apple LaserWriter with Photograde:

1. Choose Page Setup from the File menu (**Figure 5**).

2. Click Screen (**Figures 6-7**).

3. Click Use Printer's Default Screens, then click OK.

4. Click OK or press Return.

5. Choose Print from the File menu (**Figure 5**).
or
Hold down Command (⌘) and press "P".

6. Click Color/Grayscale.

7. Click Printer.

8. Make sure the Print Separations box is unchecked.

9. Click Print or press Return.

File	
New...	⌘N
Open...	⌘O
Place...	
Close	⌘W
Save	⌘S
Save As...	
Save a Copy...	
Revert	
Acquire	▶
Export	▶
File Info...	
Page Setup...	
Print...	⌘P
Preferences	▶
Quit	⌘Q

Figure 5. *Choose* **Page Setup** *from the* **File** *menu.*

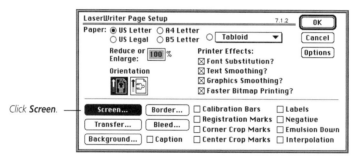

Click **Screen.**

Figure 6. *Click* **Screen** *in the* **Page Setup** *dialog box.*

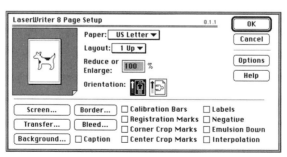

Figure 7. *The* **LaserWriter 8 Page Setup** *dialog box. Don't change the default Paper, Layout, Reduce and Orientation settings. Read about other Page Setup options on page 248.*

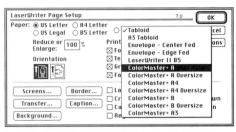

*Figure 8. Choose the correct color printer option from the pop-up menu in the **Page Setup** dialog box.*

*Figure 9. In the **Print** dialog box, click **Color/Grayscale** and click **Binary**. This illustrations shows the Print dialog box for a CMYK file.*

*For each ink color you can enter **Frequency** and **Angle** values and choose a **Shape**.*

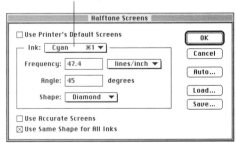

*Figure 10. The **Halftone Screens** dialog box.*

To print to a PostScript color printer:

1. To print to a PostScript Level 1 printer, choose CMYK Color from the Mode menu. CMYK color will be simulated on the screen (**Figure 11**).

or

To print to a PostScript Level 2 printer, choose Lab Color from the Mode menu.

2. Choose Page Setup from the File menu.

3. Choose the correct color printer option from the pop-up menu (**Figure 8**).

4. Click OK or press Return.

5. Choose Print from the File menu (or hold down Command (⌘) and press "P").

6. Click Color/Grayscale (**Figure 9**).

7. Click Binary.

8. Click Print or press Return.

✔ Tips

■ For a PostScript Level 1 printer, check the Use Same Shape for All Inks box. For a PostScript Level 2 printer, check the Use Accurate Screens box, and don't change the ink angles (**Figure 10**).

■ If the printout is too dark, lighten the picture using the Levels dialog box, opened from the Adjust pop-up menu under the Image menu. Move the gray Input slider a little to the left and the black Output slider a little to the right.

Print to a Color Printer

To prepare a file for an IRIS printer, a dye sublimation printer or an imagesetter:

1. To print on a PostScript Level 1 printer, choose CMYK Color from the Mode menu (**Figure 11**).

   or

   To print on a PostScript Level 2 printer, choose Page Setup from the File menu (**Figure 12**), click Screen, and check the Use Accurate Screens box. Ask your service bureau whether the file should be in CMYK Color or Lab Color mode.

2. Choose Save As from the File menu.

3. Choose EPS from the File Format pop-up menu.

4. Choose Preview: Macintosh (8–bits/pixel) (**Figure 13**).

5. Choose Encoding: Binary.

6. Click OK or press Return.

✔ Tips

- Ask your service bureau to recommend a picture resolution for the color printer or imagesetter you plan to use. *(See also "Resolution" on page 35)*

- To superimpose type over a picture, import the Photoshop picture into a document in an illustration or page layout program, add the type, and output the file from that program. Your service bureau will need the original Photoshop file to output the file.

- If your picture is wider than it is tall, ask your service bureau if it will print more quickly if you rotate it first using Photoshop's Rotate command.

Figure 11. Choose **CMYK Color** from the **Mode** menu.

Figure 12. Choose **Page Setup** from the **File** menu.

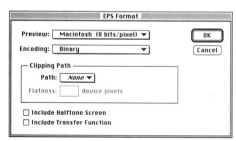

Figure 13. In the **EPS Format** dialog box, choose **Preview: Macintosh (8-bits/pixel)** and **Binary Encoding**.

Prepare a File for a High-end Printer

TO PRINT VIA QUARKXPRESS

To color separate a Photoshop picture from QuarkXPress, first convert it to CMYK Color mode. Ask your prepress service bureau whether to save it in the TIFF or EPS file format. For example, to color separate a picture on a Scitex–Dolev imagesetter, save it as an EPS with the Desktop Color Separation (DCS) option Off. Instructions for saving a file as an EPS are on page 52. Instructions for saving a file as a TIFF are on page 53.

Leave the Include Halftone Screens and Include Transfer Functions boxes unchecked. Your prepress service bureau will choose the proper settings.

Printing technology is developing rapidly. Your service bureau is in the best position to recommend appropriate file formats for color separation on its printers.

TO OUTPUT VIA A FILM RECORDER

Color transparencies, also called chromes, are widely used as a source for pictures in the publishing industry. A Photoshop file can be output to a film recorder to produce a chrome. Though the output settings for each film recorder may vary, to output to any film recorder, the height and width dimensions of the picture file must conform to the pixel count the film recorder requires for each line it images. If the picture originates as a scan, the pixel count should be taken into consideration when setting the scan's resolution, dimensions, and file storage size.

For example, let's say you need to produce a 4 x 5-inch chrome on a Solitaire film recorder. Your service bureau advises you that to output on the Solitaire, the 5-inch side of your picture should measure 2000 pixels and the file storage size should be at least 10 megabytes. (Other film recorders may require higher resolutions.) Choose New from the File menu, enter 2000 for the Width (in pixels) and 4 inches for the Height, enter a Resolution value to produce an Image Size of at least 10MB, and choose RGB Color Mode. Click OK to produce the picture entirely within Photoshop, or note the resolution and dimensions, and ask your service bureau to match those values when it scans your picture.

If the picture is smaller than 4 x 5 inches and you would like a colored background around it, click Background in the Page Setup dialog box, then choose the color your service bureau recommends.

Print via QuarkXPress, Film Recorder

Page Setup Options

*A picture will print faster with **Portrait Orientation** (left) than with **Landscape Orientation** (right). If your picture is wider than it is tall, choose Rotate 90° CW from the Image menu. Then you can print it with the **Portrait** Orientation.*

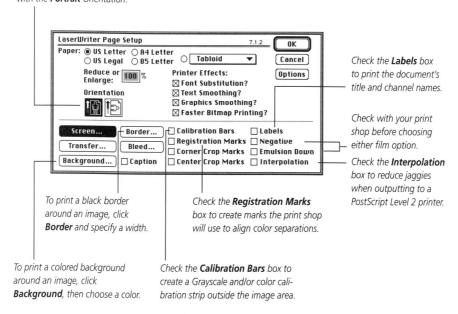

*Check the **Labels** box to print the document's title and channel names.*

Check with your print shop before choosing either film option.

*Check the **Interpolation** box to reduce jaggies when outputting to a PostScript Level 2 printer.*

*To print a black border around an image, click **Border** and specify a width.*

*Check the **Registration Marks** box to create marks the print shop will use to align color separations.*

*To print a colored background around an image, click **Background**, then choose a color.*

*Check the **Calibration Bars** box to create a Grayscale and/or color calibration strip outside the image area.*

Figure 14. *The **Page Setup** dialog box.*

Arizona.gray —— *Label*

Corner Crop Mark

Registration Mark

Calibration Bars ——

Caption —— picture w/ print options

Figure 15. *A printout showing* **Page Setup** *options.*

About 50 shades of an ink color can be printed from one plate. Printers sometimes print a grayscale picture using two or more plates instead of one to extend the tonal range. The additional plate can be gray or a color tint. You can convert a picture to Duotone mode in Photoshop to create a duotone (two plates), tritone (three plates), or quadtone (four plates).

Note: Printing a duotone is complex. The proper order of inks must be selected in the Duotone options dialog box and then on the press. Ask your print shop for advice. A duotone effect cannot be "proofed" on a PostScript color printer.

To create a duotone:

1. Choose Grayscale from the Mode menu.

2. Choose Duotone from the Mode menu (**Figure 16**).

3. Choose Duotone from the Type pop-up menu (**Figure 17**).

4. Click the Ink 2 color square.

5. If necessary, click Custom. Choose from the Book pop-up menu, then type a color number or click a swatch.
   or
   If necessary, click Picker, then enter C,M,Y, and K percentages.

6. Click OK or press Return.

7. For a process color, enter a name next to the color square.

8. Click the Ink 2 curve.

9. Drag the curve in the Duotone Curve dialog box (**Figure 18**).

10. Click OK or press Return.

11. Click the Ink 1 curve, then repeat steps 9 and 10.

✔ Tip

■ The Photoshop Tutorial folder contains dutone, tritone, and quadtone curves that you can use. (Click Load in the Duotone Options box).

Figure 16. Choose **Duotone** from the **Mode** menu.

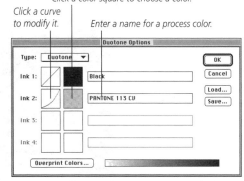

Click a color square to choose a color.
Click a curve to modify it.
Enter a name for a process color.

Figure 17. In the **Duotone Options** dialog box, choose **Duotone** from the **Type** pop-up menu, then click the **Ink 2** color square.

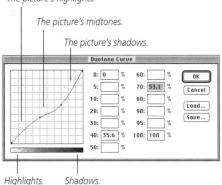

The picture's highlights.
The picture's midtones.
The picture's shadows.

Highlights.   Shadows.

Figure 18. With this curve shape in the **Duotone Curve** dialog box, Ink 2 will tint the picture's midtones. **Make the Ink 1 curve different from the Ink 2 curve.**

Duotones

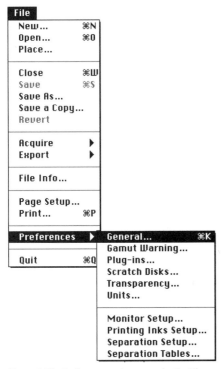

*Figure 1. The **Preferences** submenu under the **File** menu.*

DEFAULTS ARE settings that are chosen to apply generally, such as which ruler units are used, or if channels display in color. Default dialog boxes are opened from the Preferences submenu under the File menu (**Figure 1**).

Choose basic defaults in the **General Preferences** and **More Preferences** dialog boxes, such as whether file icons will contain a thumbnail preview of the picture, or which Color Picker will be used.

Choose a color and an opacity of that color for displaying out-of-gamut colors in the **Gamut Warning** dialog box.

Choose a hard disk to be used as Photoshop's extra work area in the **Scratch Disks** dialog box.

Choose the grid size and color of the checkerboard used to represent transparent areas on a layer, or if no grid will be used, in the **Transparency Options** dialog box.

Choose ruler units in the **Units** dialog box.

Choose your monitor type and ambient lighting conditions in the **Monitor Setup** dialog box to optimize display and RGB-to-CMYK conversion.

Adjust your monitor in the **Gamma** dialog box, opened from the Control Panels folder.

Note: Don't move the program's internal **Plug-Ins** module out of the Photoshop folder unless you have a specific reason for doing so. Moving it could inhibit access to the Acquire, Export and File Format commands. Don't confuse the Plug-ins module with third-party plug-ins.

Defaults

Key to the General Preferences dialog box.

1 Choose the Photoshop **Color Picker** to access the program's own Color Picker.

2 Choose an **Interpolation** option for reinterpretation of a picture as a result of resampling, scaling, etc. Bicubic is slowest, but the highest quality. Nearest Neighbor is the fastest, but the poorest quality.

3 Choose whether **CMYK Composites** for the RGB screen version of a CMYK file will be rendered Faster, but simpler, or Smoother and more refined.

4 Check **Color Channels in Color** to display individual RGB or CMYK channels in color. Otherwise, they will display grayscale.

5 Check **Use System Palette** to have the Apple System Palette be used rather than the document's own

color palette. Turn this option on to correct the display of erratic colors on an 8–bit monitor.

6 Check **Use Diffusion Dither** to smooth colors on an 8-bit monitor.

7 Uncheck **Video LUT Animation** to disable the interactive screen preview if you are using a video card that is causing conflicts between Photoshop and your monitor.

8 For Painting **Tool Cursors** (Gradient, Line, Eraser, Pencil, Airbrush, Paintbrush, Rubber Stamp, Smudge, Blur/Sharpen and Dodge/Burn/Sponge tools) choose **Standard** to see the icon of the tool being used, or choose **Precise** to see a crosshair icon, or choose **Brush Size** to see a round icon the exact size and shape of the brush tip (up to 300 pixels). For other tools, choose Standard or Precise cursor icons.

General Preferences

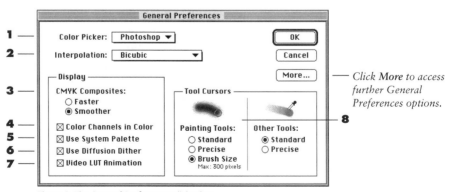

*Figure 2. The **General Preferences** dialog box.*

Key to the More Preferences dialog box.

1 Check **Image Previews/Always Save: Icon** to display a thumbnail of a picture in its file icon on the desktop. Click **Thumbnail** to display a thumbnail of a picture when its name is highlighted in the Open dialog box. Click Full Size to include a 72 dpi PICT preview for applications which require this option when importing non-EPS files. Click Ask When Saving to choose to save previews on a file-by-file basis.

2 Check **Anti-alias Postscript** to optimize the rendering of EPS graphics in Photoshop.

3 Check **Export Clipboard** to have the current Clipboard contents stay on the Clipboard when you quit Photoshop.

4 Check **Short PANTONE Names** if your picture contains Pantone colors and you are exporting it to another application.

5 Check **Save Metric Color Tags** if you are exporting your file to Quark-XPress and are using EFIColor.

6 Check **Beep When Tasks Finish** for a beep to sound after any command, for which a progress bar displays, is completed.

7 Check **Dynamic Sliders in Picker** to have the color bars over the Picker sliders update when the sliders are moved.

8 Check **2.5 Format Compatibility** to automatically save a flattened, Photoshop version 2.5 copy in every 3.0 document. This option increases the file storage size.

9 With **Restore Palette & Dialog Positions** checked, palettes and windows that are open when you quit Photoshop will appear in their same location the next time you launch Photoshop. Uncheck Restore Palette & Dialog Positions to restore the palettes' default groupings.

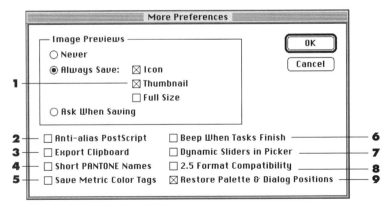

*Figure 3. The **More Preferences** dialog box.*

The Primary and Secondary scratch disks are used when available RAM is insufficient for processing or storage.

To choose scratch disks:

1. Choose Scratch Disks from the Preferences submenu under the File menu (**Figure 4**).

2. Choose an available hard drive from the Primary pop-up menu. Startup is the default (**Figure 5**). If you only have one hard drive, you will only be able to choose a Primary Scratch Disk.

3. *Optional:* Choose an alternate hard drive from the Secondary pop-up menu to be used as extra work space when necessary.

4. Click OK or press Return.

5. For the changes take effect, choose Quit from the File menu, then launch Photoshop again.

✔ Tip

■ If you choose a removable cartridge as a Scratch Disk, don't remove the cartridge while Photoshop is running or the program may crash.

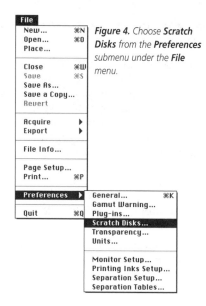

Figure 4. Choose **Scratch Disks** from the **Preferences** submenu under the **File** menu.

Choose Show Rulers from the Window menu to display rulers on the top and left sides of the document window. The position of the pointer will be indicated by a mark on each ruler.

To choose ruler units:

1. Choose Units from the Preferences submenu under the File menu (**Figure 4**).

2. Choose a unit of measure from the Ruler Units pop-up menu (**Figure 6**).

3. Click OK or press Return.

✔ Tip

■ If you change the ruler units, the Info palette units will also change, and vice versa.

Figure 5. Choose a **Primary** and **Secondary** scratch disk in the **Scratch Disk Preferences** dialog box.

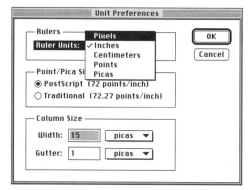

Figure 6. Choose a unit of measure from the **Ruler Units** pop-up menu in the **Unit Preferences** dialog box.

Scratch Disks, Ruler Units

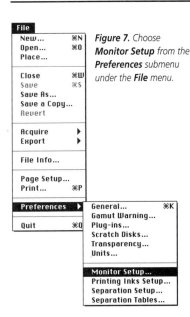

Figure 7. Choose *Monitor Setup* from the *Preferences* submenu under the *File* menu.

Follow the instructions on this page and the next page to adjust your monitor for Photoshop. These are the first steps in monitor-to-output calibration. See the Photoshop User Guide for information about calibrating your system.

Note: After choosing monitor specs and making your desktop gray (instructions on the next page), adjust the brightness and contrast knobs on your monitor and do not change them (put tape on them, if necessary). Then follow instructions on the next page to adjust the Gamma.

To choose Monitor Setup options:

1. Choose Monitor Setup from the Preferences submenu under the File menu (**Figure 7**).

2. Choose your monitor name from the Monitor pop-up menu. If it's not listed, consult the documentation supplied with your monitor to find the closest equivalent (**Figure 8**).

3. Choose the manufacturer of your CRT from the Phosphors pop-up menu. This information should also be supplied with your monitor.

4. Choose Low, Medium, or High from the Ambient Light pop-up menu.

5. Click OK or press Return.

✔ Tips

■ Leave the Gamma at 1.80 and the White Point at 6500°K, unless you have a specific reason to change it.

■ The Monitor Setup affects color substitution when a picture is converted from RGB Color mode to CMYK Color mode.

■ Try to keep the light in your computer room consistent while you're working.

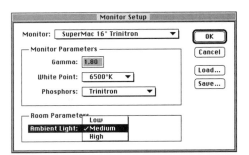

Figure 8. In the *Monitor Setup* dialog box, choose your monitor type from the *Monitor* pop-up menu, and choose *Low*, *Medium*, or *High* from the *Ambient Light* pop-up menu.

Monitor Setup

Use the Gamma Control Panel to make your monitor grays more neutral and monitor color a little more accurate. If your desktop is already gray, proceed directly to "To adjust the Gamma."

To make the Desktop gray:

1. Choose Control Panels from the Apple menu.

2. Double-click General Controls in the Control Panels folder.

3. Click the left or right triangle to locate the gray Desktop pattern, then click the gray pattern in the same window (**Figure 9**).

4. Click the General Controls close box. *(Adjust the brightness and contrast knobs on your monitor. See the "Note" on the previous page)*

To adjust the Gamma:

1. Choose Control Panels from the Apple menu.

2. Double-click Gamma.

3. Click Target Gamma: 1.8 if you plan to print your pictures (**Figure 10**).

4. Hold up a white piece of paper next to the monitor. The warm or cool cast of the paper will affect the Gamma settings you choose.

5. Click the White Pt button, then move the White Point sliders until the rightmost square on the calibration bar matches the paper.

6. Click the Black Pt button, then move the Black Pt sliders until the dark calibration squares look neutral.

7. Click the Balance button, then move the Balance sliders until the gray calibration squares look neutral.

8. Move the Gamma Adjustment slider to blend the light and dark bars.

9. Readjust any of the sliders, if needed.

10. *Optional:* Click Save Settings, then rename and save the Gamma settings.

11. Click the Gamma close box.

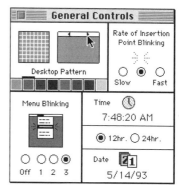

Figure 9. *Choose a gray* **Desktop Pattern** *in the* **General Controls** *dialog box.*

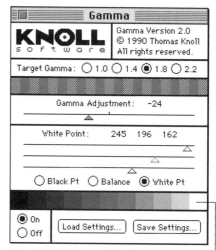

Figure 10. *The* **Gamma** *dialog box.*

Calibration squares

Adjust the Gamma

Alpha channel

A special 8-bit grayscale channel used for saving a selection.

Anti-alias

The blending of pixel colors along the perimeters of hard-edged shapes, such as type, to smoooth undesirable stair-stepped edges, or "jaggies."

ASCII

(American Standard Code for Information Interchange) A standard editable format for encoding data.

Background color

The color applied when the Eraser tool is used or when selected (non-floating) pixels are moved or deleted.

Bezier curve

A curved line segment drawn using the Pen tool. It consists of anchor points with direction lines with which the curve can be reshaped. Bezier curves can also be created using illustration software.

Binary

In Photoshop, a method for encoding data. Binary encoding is more compact than ASCII encoding.

Bit

(Binary digit) The smallest unit of information on a computer. Eight bits equal one byte. (see *Byte*)

Bit depth

The number of bits used to store a pixel's color information on a computer screen.

Bitmap

The display of a picture on a computer screen via the geometric mapping of a single layer of pixels on a rectangular grid. In Photoshop, Bitmap is also a one-channel mode consisting of black and white pixels.

Blend (see *Gradient*)

Brightness (see *Lightness*)

Burn

To darken an area of a picture.

Byte

The basic unit of storage memory. One byte is equal to eight bits.

Canvas size

The size of a picture, including a border, if any, around the image.

CD-ROM drive

A special digital drive for reading CD-ROM disks. One CD disk can store at least 650 megabytes of information. At this writing, most CD-ROM drives are read-only, and are used as a source for stock photographs, fonts, software, games, clip art, etc.

Channel

A color "overlay" which contains the pixel information for that color. A grayscale picture has one channel, an RGB picture has three channels, and a CMYK picture has four channels.

Clipboard

An area of memory used to temporarily store a selection. The Clipboard is accessed via the Cut, Copy, and Paste commands.

Clipping

In Photoshop, the automatic desaturation of colors that are too pure to print properly.

Clone

To duplicate all or part of a picture using the Rubber Stamp tool.

CMYK

(Cyan, Magenta, Yellow, and Black) The four colors of ink used in process printing. Cyan, Magenta, and Yellow are the three subtractive primaries. When combined in their purest forms, they theoretically produce black. Actually, they produce a dark muddy color. CMYK colors are simulated on a computer screen using additive colors. To color separate a picture from Photoshop, it must be in CMYK Color mode.

Color correction

The adjustment of color in a picture to match original artwork or a photograph. Color correction is usually done in CMYK Color mode to prepare for process printing.

Color separation

The production of a separate sheet of film for each color of ink that will be used to print a document. Four plates are used in process color separation, one

each for Cyan, Magenta, Yellow, and Black.

Color table

The color palette of up to 256 colors of a picture in Indexed Color mode. Sometimes referred to as a color palette.

Continuous-tone image

A picture, such as a photograph, in which there are smooth transitions between gray shades or colors.

Contrast

The degree of difference between lights and darks in a picture. A high contrast picture is comprised of only the lightest and darkest pixels.

Crop

To cut away part of a picture.

Crop marks

Short, fine lines placed around the edges of a page to designate where the paper is to be trimmed by a print shop.

DCS

(Desktop Color Separation) A file format in which a color picture is broken down into five PostScript files: Cyan, Magenta, Yellow and Black for high resolution printing, and an optional low resolution PICT file for previewing and laser printing.

Defloat

To replace underlying pixels with the contents of a floating selection. A selection remains active when it is defloated.

Defringe

A technique used for softening the edge of a selection inward from the marquee a specified number of pixels.

Digitize

To translate flat art or a transparency into computer-readable numbers using a scanning device and scanning software.

Dimensions

The width and height of a picture.

Disk

A carrying medium for processing, reading, and storing electronic files, such as a hard drive, floppy disk, or CD-ROM disk.

Dither

The mixing of adjacent pixels to simulate additional colors when available colors are limited, such as on an 8-bit monitor.

Dodge

To bleach (lighten) an area of a picture. Also, a so-so car model.

Dot gain

The undesirable spreading and enlarging of ink dots on paper.

DPI

(Dots Per Inch) A unit used to measure the resolution of a printer. DPI is sometimes used to describe the input resolution of a scanner, but ppi, or "sampling rate" is a more accurate term.

Duotone

A grayscale picture printed using two plates for added tonal depth. A tritone is printed using three plates. A quadtone is printed using four plates.

Dye sublimation

A continuous-tone printing process in which a solid printing medium is converted into a gas before it reaches the paper. Each printing color can vary in intensity.

8-bit monitor

A monitor in which each pixel stores eight bits of information and represents one of only 256 available colors. Dithering is used to create the illusion of additional colors.

EPS

(Encapsulated PostScript) A picture file format containing PostScript code and, in the case of Photoshop, an optional PICT image for screen display. EPS is a commonly used format for moving files from one application to another and for imagesetting and color separating.

Equalize

To balance a picture's lights and darks.

Feather

To fade the edge of a selection a specified number of pixels (the Feather Radius).

Fill

To fill a selection with a shade, color, pattern, or blend.

Film negative

A film rendition of a picture in which dark and light areas are reversed.

Floating selection

An area of a picture that is surrounded by a marquee and can be moved or modified without affecting underlying pixels. The Paste and Float commands create floating selections. Newly created type also appears as a floating selection.

Font

A typeface in a distinctive style, such as Futura Bold Italic.

Foreground color

The color applied when a painting tool is used, type is created, or a Fill command is executed.

Gigabyte

(G, Gb) A unit of memory equal to 1,024 megabytes. (see *Megabyte*)

Gradient fill

In Photoshop, a graduated blend between the Foreground and Background colors produced by the Gradient tool.

Grayscale

A picture containing black, white, and up to 256 shades of gray, but no color. In Photoshop, Grayscale is a one-channel mode.

Halftone screen

A pattern of tiny dots used for printing a picture to simulate smooth tones. (see *Screen frequency*)

Highlights

The lightest areas of a picture.

Histogram

A graph showing the distribution of a picture's color and/or luminosity values.

HSB

See *Hue*, *Saturation*, and *Brightness*.

Hue

The wavelength of light of a pure color that gives a color its name, such as red or blue, independent of its saturation or brightness.

Imagesetter

A high-resolution printer (usually 1,270 or 2,540 dpi) used to generate paper or film output from computer files.

Indexed color

In Photoshop, a color mode in which there is only one channel and a color table containing up to 256 colors. All the colors of an Indexed color picture are displayed in its Colors palette.

Ink jet

A color printer in which four colors of ink are forced through small holes to produce dots.

Interpolation

The recoloring of pixels as a result of changing a picture's dimensions or resolution. Interpolation may cause a picture to look blurry when printed. You can choose an interpolation method in Photoshop.

Inverse

To switch the selected and non-selected areas of a picture.

Invert

To reverse a picture's light and dark values and/or colors.

Jaggies

Undesirable stair-stepped edges of computer rendered images. (see *Anti-alias*)

JPEG compression

(Joint Photographic Experts Group) A compression feature in Photoshop that can be used to reduce the storage size of a file. Some information is lost during JPEG Compression.

Kern
To adjust the horizontal spacing between a pair of characters.

Kilobyte
(K, Kb) A unit of memory equal to 1,024 bytes. (see *Byte*)

Lab
A mode in which colors are related to the CIE color reference system. In Photoshop, a picture in Lab Color mode is composed of three channels, one for lightness, one for green-to-magenta colors, and one blue-to-yellow colors.

Leading
The space between lines of type, measured from baseline to baseline. In Photoshop, leading can be measured in points or pixels.

Lightness
(Brightness) The lightness of a color independent of its hue and saturation.

Linear fill
A straight gradation from edge to edge. (see *Radial fill*)

LPI
(Lines Per Inch, halftone frequency, screen frequency) The unit used to measure the frequency of rows of dots on a halftone screen.

Luminosity
The distribution of a picture's light and dark values.

Marquee
The moving border that defines a selection.

Mask
A device used to protect an area of a picture from modification.

Megabyte
(M, MB) A unit of memory equal to 1,024 kilobytes. (see *Kilobyte*)

Midtones
The shades in a picture midway between the highlights and shadows.

Mode
A method for specifying how color information is to be interpreted. A picture can be converted to a different mode using the Mode menu; a mode can be chosen for a painting or editing tool via palette pop-up menus. Grayscale, RGB Color, CMYK Color, and Lab Color are commonly used picture modes.

Moirés
Undesirable patterns caused by the use of improper halftone screen angles or when the pattern in an image conflicts with proper halftone patterns.

Noise
In Photoshop, filters that randomly recolor pixels to create a texture or make an image look grainy.

Object-oriented
(also known as vector) A software method used for describing and processing computer files. Object-oriented graphics and PostScript type are defined by mathematics and geometry. Bitmapped graphics are defined by pixels on a rectangular grid. Photoshop pictures are bitmapped, not objected-oriented.

Glossary

Opacity

The density of a color or shade, ranging from transparent to opaque. In Photoshop, the opacity for a painting or editing tool is specified by using the Brushes palette.

Palette

A floating window used to specify options for a tool or feature. Also, a collection of color swatches displayed on the Colors palette.

Path

A shape composed of straight and/or curved segments joined by anchor points. Paths are created with the Pen tool and modified via the Paths palette.

PICT

A Macintosh file format used to display and save pictures. Save a Photoshop picture as a PICT file to open it in a video or animation program. PICT files should not be color separated.

Pixels

(Picture elements) The individual dots used to display a picture on a computer screen.

PPI

(Pixels per inch) A unit used to measure of the resolution of a scan or a picture in Photoshop.

Plug-in module

Third-party software placed in the Photoshop Plug-ins folder so it is accessible from a Photoshop menu. Or, a plug-in module that comes with Photoshop that is used to facilitate the Acquire, Export, and file format conversion operations. There is no icon for the plug-in module in the Finder.

Point

A unit of measure used to describe type size (measured from ascender to descender), leading (measured from baseline to baseline), and line width.

Polygon

A closed shape composed of three or more straight sides.

Posterize

Produce a special effect in a picture by reducing the number of shades of gray or color to the darkest shade, the lightest shade, and a few shades in between.

PostScript

The page description language created and licensed by Adobe Systems Incorporated for displaying and printing fonts and pictures.

Process color

Ink printed from four separate plates, one each for Cyan (C), Magenta (M), Yellow (Y), and Black (K), which in combination produce a wide range of colors.

Quick Mask

In Photoshop, a screen mode in which a translucent colored mask covers selected or unselected areas of a picture. Painting tools can be used to modify a Quick Mask.

Radial fill

A gradation radiating from the center of the blend area outward.

RAM

(Random Access Memory) The system memory of a computer used for running an application, processing information, and temporary storage.

Rasterize

The conversion of an object-oriented picture into a bitmapped picture, such as when an Adobe Illustrator graphic is placed into Photoshop. All computer files are rasterized when printed.

Registration marks

Crosshair marks placed around the edge of a page that are used to align printing plates.

Resample

Modify a picture's resolution. Lowering a picture's resolution is called resampling down. Increasing a picture's resolution is called resampling up. Both cause interpolation. (see *Interpolation*)

Resolution

The fineness of detail of a digitized image (measured in pixels per inch), a monitor (measured in pixels per inch — usually 72 ppi), a printer (measured in dots per inch), or halftone screen (measured in lines per inch).

RGB

Color produced by transmitted light. When pure Red, Green, and Blue light (the additive primaries) are combined, as on a computer monitor, white is produced. In Photoshop, RGB Color is a three-channel picture mode.

Saturation

The purity of a color. The more gray a color contains, the lower its saturation.

Scan

To digitize a slide, photograph or other artwork using a scanner and scanning software so it can be displayed, edited, and output from a computer.

Scratch disk

(also known as virtual memory) Hard drive storage space designated as work space for processing operations and for temporarily storing part of an image and a backup version of the image when there is insufficient RAM for these functions.

Screen angles

Angles used for positioning halftone screens when producing film to minimize undesirable dot patterns (moirés).

Screen frequency

(also known as screen ruling) The resolution (density of dots) on a halftone screen, measured in lines per inch. (see *lpi*)

Selection

An area of a picture that is isolated so it can be modified while rest of the picture is protected. A moving marquee denotes the boundary of a selection, and can be moved independently of its contents. A selection can contain underlying pixels or temporarily float above underlying pixels.

Shadows

The darkest areas of a picture.

Sharpness

The degree of fineness of detail of an image, of a computer monitor, and of printer output.

Size

The number of storage units a file occupies, measured in kilobytes, megabytes, or gigabytes.

Spacing

The space between brush marks created with painting and editing tools. Also, the horizontal space between letters, specified in the Type Tool dialog box.

Spot color

A mixed ink color used in printing. A separate plate is used to print each spot color. Pantone is a commonly used spot color matching system.
(see Process color)

Thermal wax

A color printing process in which a sequence of three or four ink sheets are used to place colored dots on special paper.

TIFF

(Tagged Image File Format) A file format used for saving bitmapped images, such as scans. TIFF pictures can be color separated.

Tolerance

The range of pixels within which a tool operates. For example, the range of shades or colors the Magic Wand tool selects and the Paint Bucket tool fills.

Trap

The overlapping of adjacent colors to prevent undesirable gaps from occuring as a result of the misalignment of printing plates or paper.

24-bit monitor

A monitor with a video card in which each pixel can store up to 24 bits of information. The card contains three color tables for displaying an RGB picture, one each for Red, Green, and Blue, and each contains 256 colors. Together they can produce 16.7 million colors. On a 24-bit monitor, smooth blends can be displayed, so dithering is not necessary.

Underlying pixels

The pixels comprising the unmodified picture, on top of which a selection or placed image can float.

Virtual memory (see *Scratch disk*)

Zoom

To enlarge or reduce a picture's display size.

KEY: ↖ Click   ↖↖ Double-click   ⋯↖ Press and drag

File menu

New...	⌘ N
Open...	⌘ O
Close...	⌘ W
Save	⌘ S
Print...	⌘ P
Quit	⌘ Q

Edit menu

Undo	⌘ Z, or F1 *

The Clipboard

Cut	⌘ X, or F2
Copy	⌘ C, or F3
Paste	⌘ V, or F4
Fill dialog box	Shift delete

Image menu

Map commands

Invert	⌘ I
Equalize...	⌘ E
Threshold...	⌘ T

Adjust commands

Levels...	⌘ L
Curves...	⌘ M
Brightness/Contrast...	⌘ B
Color Balance...	⌘ Y
Hue/Saturation...	⌘ U

Filter menu

Reapply last filter chosen	⌘ F
Last Filter dialog box	⌘ Option F
Cancel a filter while a Progress dialog box is displayed	⌘ . (period)

* The Function key shortcuts listed in this appendix (F1, F2, etc.) are the default **Commands palette** shortcuts. Follow the instructions on pages 22-23 to assign your own Commands palette shortcuts.

Keyboard Shortcuts

Select menu

All	⌘ A
None	⌘ D
Float/Defloat	⌘ J
Grow	⌘ G
Show/Hide Edges	⌘ H

Window menu

Zoom In	⌘ +
Zoom Out	⌘ –
Show/Hide Rulers	⌘ R
Hide/Show Brushes	F5
Show/Hide Picker	F6
Show/Hide Layers	F7
Show/Hide Info	F8
Show/Hide Commands	F9

Display sizes

Enlarge display size	⌘ Space bar ⭡ *(works with some dialog boxes open)*
Reduce display size	Option Space bar ⭡ *(works with some dialog boxes open)*
Magnify selected area	⭡ with Zoom tool
1:1 view	⭡⭡ Zoom tool on Toolbox
Fit picture in document window	⭡⭡ Hand tool on Toolbox

Palettes

Shrink palette to a bar	⭡⭡ a palette tab *or* Option-click palette zoom box
Show/Hide Toolbox and palettes	Tab
Open/activate tool's Options palette	Return *or* ⭡⭡ any tool other than Hand or Zoom

Tools

With any painting or editing tool selected:

Temporary arrow cursor	⌘
Opacity percentage (Options palette)	Keypad key 0=100%, 1=10%, 2=20%, etc.
Change to next larger brush size	[
Change to next smaller brush size	]

Channels palette

RGB Channels

RGB	⌘ 0
Red	⌘ 1
Green	⌘ 2
Blue	⌘ 3

CMYK Channels

CMYK	⌘ 0
Cyan	⌘ 1
Magenta	⌘ 2
Yellow	⌘ 3
Black	⌘ 4

Hand tool

Temporary Hand tool with any other tool selected	Space bar

Eyedropper tool

Select color for the non-highlighted color square	Option ⌐ color
Temporary Eyedropper tool with Paint Bucket, Gradient, Line, Pencil, Airbrush, or Paintbrush tool selected	Option

Eraser tool

Magic eraser, restores last saved version	Option ⌐
Constrain eraser to 90° angle	Shift ⌐

Line tool

Constrain to 45° or 90° angle	Shift ⌐

Pencil, Airbrush, Rubber Stamp, Smudge tool

Constrain to 90° angle	Shift ⌐

Pen Tool

Add anchor point with Path Select tool highlighted	⌘ Option ⌐ line segment
Delete anchor point with Path Select tool highlighted	⌘ Option ⌐ anchor point
Constrain straight line segment or anchor point to 45° angle	Shift ⌐
Delete last created anchor point	Delete
Erase path being drawn	Delete Delete
Temporary Path Select tool with any Pen tool selected	⌘
Temporary Convert-direction point tool with the Path Select tool or any Pen tool selected	⌘ Control

Sharpen/Blur tool

Switch between Sharpen and Blur	Option ⌐ picture or Option ⌐ Sharpen/Blur tool on Toolbox

Smudge tool

Temporary Finger Painting tool .... Option ⌁➤

Selections

Add to a selection .... Shift ⌁➤
Subtract from a selection .... ⌘ ⌁➤
Float a selection .... Option ⌁➤ selection
Move selection marquee .... ⌘ Option ⌁➤ selection
Move selection marquee, Move tool
 selected .... Option ⌁➤ selection
Move selection in 1-pixel increments .... Arrow keys
Move selection in 10-pixel increments .... Shift and Arrow keys
Maintain proportions of Scale
 command marquee .... Shift ⌁➤ corner box
Fill selection with Foreground color .... Option Delete
Switch Masked Areas/Selected Areas .... Option ➤ Quick Mask icon
on Toolbox

Rectangular Marquee and Elliptical Marquee tools

Draw selection from center .... Option ⌁➤
Square or circlular selection .... Shift ⌁➤

Magic Wand tool

Add to a selection .... Shift ➤
Subtract from a selection .... ⌘ ➤
Temporarily select wand tool with
 Marquee or Lasso tool selected .... Control

Lasso tool

Create straight side in a selection .... Option ➤
Create curved side in a straight-sided
 selection .... ⌁➤ or Option ⌁➤

Dialog boxes

Restore original settings .... Hold down Option, click Reset
Delete to the right of the cursor .... del
Highlight next field .... Tab
Highlight previous field .... Shift Tab
Increase/decrease number in
 highlighted field by 1 unit .... Up or down arrow
Increase/decrease number in
 highlighted field by 10 units .... Shift and Up or down arrow
Cancel out of dialog box .... ⌘ . (period)

Swatches palette

Delete a color .... ⌘ ➤
Replace swatch with new color
 swatch .... Shift ➤ color to be replaced
Insert new color between two colors .... Option Shift ➤

Layers palette

Select all pixels on layer	⌘ Option T
Choose layer directly below target layer	⌘ [
Choose layer directly above target layer	⌘]
Choose topmost layer	⌘ Option]
Choose bottommost layer	⌘ Option [
Add a new layer to the Layers palette	Option ⬉ new layer icon
Turn on/off Preserve Transparency option on Layers palette	/
View layer mask channel	Option ⬉ layer mask thumbnail
Temporarily hide layer mask effects	⌘ ⬉ layer mask thumbnail
Choose a layer from the document window with Move tool selected	⌘ ⬉ object in picture

Print preview box

Picture information	Option hold down on Sizes bar

Keyboard Shortcuts

Send us your comments, compliments, corrections...

NEW YORK, NY 102
PM
7 OCT
1390

Elaine Weinmann & Peter Lourekas
c/o Peachpit Press
2414 Sixth Street
Berkeley, CA 94710

More from Peachpit Press

Director 5 for Macintosh: Visual QuickStart Guide

Andre Persidsky

Learn how to create animations, movies, and multimedia presentations in Macromedia Director 5 through this generously illustrated *Visual QuickStart Guide*. You'll learn how to use the basic tools and windows such as the Cast window, the Paint window, the Control Panel and the Stage. In addition, you'll learn how to work with sound and tempo, and all the steps you'll need to create your first presentation. *$18.95 (256 pages)*

HTML for the World Wide Web: Visual QuickStart Guide

Elizabeth Castro

This best-selling book is all you need to start building web pages. It's a primer in basic Hypertext Markup Language, with guidelines on how to format your text, work with images, create links and navigational buttons, and add goodies like tables, forms and sounds to your web site. *$17.95 (192 pages)*

Illustrator 6 for Macintosh: Visual QuickStart Guide

Elaine Weinmann and Peter Lourekas

Like our other *QuickStart* guides, this book guides you through the basics of Illustrator with lots of pictures, including a gallery of color illustrations. Learn the basics of how to use the palette tools, create objects, reshape paths, play with type, create gradients, work with layers and masks, and much more. From the authors of our popular *QuarkXPress* and *Photoshop Visual QuickStart* books. *$19.95 (288 pages)*

The Non-Designer's Design Book

Robin Williams

Robin Williams wrote this one "for all the people who now need to design pages, but who have no background or formal training in design." Follow the basic principles clearly explained in this book and your work is guaranteed to look more professional, organized, unified, and interesting. You'll never again look at a page in the same way. Full of practical design exercises and quizzes. Runner-up for Best Introductory Systems How-to Book in the 10th Annual Computer Press Awards. *$14.95 (144 pages)*

The Photoshop 3 Wow! Book

Linnea Dayton and Jack Davis

This book is really two books in one: an easy-to-follow, step-by-step tutorial of Photoshop fundamentals and over 150 pages of tips and techniques for getting the most out of Photoshop version 3. Full color throughout, *The Photoshop 3 Wow! Book* shows how professional artists make the best use of Photoshop. Includes a CD-ROM containing Photoshop filters and utilities. *$39.95 (288 pages, includes CD-ROM)*

QuarkXPress 3.3 for Macintosh: Visual QuickStart Guide

Elaine Weinmann

Teachers all across the country have used this guide to help their students become proficient Quark users. This book covers how to create and format a document, use style sheets, set up master pages, import and stylize graphics, use spot color, and much more. Its numerous illustrations make it an intuitive learning tool. *$15.95 (248 pages)*

Order Form

USA 800-283-9444 • 510-548-4393 • FAX 510-548-5991
CANADA 800-387-8028 • 416-447-1779 • FAX 800-456-0536 OR 416-443-0948
http://www.peachpit.com

Qty	Title	Price	Total

		SUBTOTAL	
		ADD APPLICABLE SALES TAX*	
Shipping is by UPS ground: $4 for first item, $1 each add'l.		SHIPPING	

*We are required to pay sales tax in all states with the exceptions of AK, DE, MT, NH, and OR. Please include appropriate sales tax if you live in any state not mentioned above.

TOTAL

Customer Information

NAME

COMPANY

STREET ADDRESS

CITY   STATE   ZIP

PHONE (   )   FAX (   )
[REQUIRED FOR CREDIT CARD ORDERS]

Payment Method

❏ CHECK ENCLOSED   ❏ VISA   ❏ MASTERCARD   ❏ AMEX

CREDIT CARD #   EXP. DATE

COMPANY PURCHASE ORDER #

Tell Us What You Think

PLEASE TELL US WHAT YOU THOUGHT OF THIS BOOK: TITLE:_____

WHAT OTHER BOOKS WOULD YOU LIKE US TO PUBLISH?

MAC   **PEACHPIT PRESS • 2414 Sixth Street • Berkeley, CA 94710**

Ten Questions and Answers About Copyright
By Tad Crawford, Esq.

1 Why is copyright important?

If you are a creator of images (whether Photoshop user, photographer, designer, or fine artist), copyright protects you from having your images stolen by someone else. As the copyright owner, you may either allow or prevent anyone else from making copies of your work, making derivations from your work (such as a poster made from a photograph), or displaying your work publicly. Your copyrights last for your lifetime plus another fifty years, so a successful work may benefit not only you but your heirs as well. If you are a user of images, it is important that you understand the rights and obligations connected with their use so you don't infringe on the copyright of someone else and expose yourself to legal or financial liabilities.

2 What is an infringement?

Infringement is unauthorized use of someone else's work. The test for infringement is whether an ordinary observer would believe one work was copied from another.

3 Is it an infringement if I scan an old image into Photoshop and change it?

If the image was created in the United States and is more than 75 years old, it is in the public domain and can be freely copied by you or anyone else. You will have copyright in the new elements of the image that you create.

4 Is it an infringement if I scan a recent photograph into Photoshop and change it?

The scanning itself is making a copy and so is an infringement. As a practical matter, however, it is unlikely you will be sued for infringement if you change the photograph to the point where an ordinary observer would no longer believe your work was copied from the original photograph.

5 What does "fair use" mean in terms of copyright?

A fair use is a use of someone else's work that is allowed under the copyright law. For example, newsworthy or educational uses are likely to be fair uses. The factors for whether a use is a fair use or an infringement are: (1) the purpose and character of the use, including whether or not it is for profit (2) the character of the copyrighted work (3) how much of the total work is used and (4) what effect the use will have on the market for or value of the work being copied.

6 · Can I use a recognizable part of a photograph if the entire source photograph is not recognizable?

You would have to apply the fair use factors. Obviously, factor (3) in the previous answer relating to how much of the total work is used would be in your favor, but if the use is to make a profit and will damage the market for the source photograph it might be considered an infringement.

7 · What are the damages for infringement?

The damages are the actual losses of the person infringed plus any profits of the infringer. In some cases (especially if the work was registered before the infringement), the court can simply award between $500 and $20,000 for each work infringed. If the infringement is willful, the court can award as much as $100,000.

8 · Do I have to register my images to obtain my copyright?

No, you have the copyright from the moment you create a work. However, registration with the Copyright Office costs $20 and will help you in the event your work is infringed. To obtain *Copyright Application Form VA* (for Visual Arts), write to the Copyright Office, Library of Congress, Washington, D.C. 20559 or call (202) 707-9100. Ask for the free Copyright Information Kit for the visual arts and you will receive many helpful circulars developed by the Copyright Office.

9 · Do I need to use copyright notice to obtain or protect my copyright?

It is always wise to place copyright notice on your work, because it is a visible symbol of your rights as copyright owner. Prior to 1989 the absence of copyright notice when the images were published or publicly distributed could, in certain circumstances, cause the loss of the copyright. Since March 1, 1989, the absence of copyright notice cannot cause the loss of the copyright but may give infringers a loophole to try and lessen their damages. Copyright notice has three elements: (1) "Copyright" or "Copr" or "©" (2) your name and (3) the year of first publication.

10 · How do I get permission to reproduce an image?

A simple permission form will suffice. It should set forth what kind of project you are doing, what materials you want to use, what rights you need in the material, what credit line and copyright notice will be given, and what payment, if any, will be made. The person giving permission should sign the permission form. If you are using an image of a person for purposes of advertising or trade, you should have them sign a model release. If the person's image is to be altered or placed in a situation that didn't occur, you would want the release to cover this. Otherwise you may face a libel or invasion of privacy lawsuit.

Tad Crawford, Esq. is the author of *Legal Guide for the Visual Artist, Business and Legal Forms for Fine Artists, Business and Legal Forms for Photographers,* and other books published by Allworth Press, 10 East 23rd Street, New York, NY 10010.